# The Gaze of the Gazelle

# The Gaze of the Gazelle

## THE STORY OF A GENERATION

ARASH HEJAZI

LONDON NEW YORK CALCUTTA

**Seagull Books 2011**

Copyright © Arash Hejazi, 2011

ISBN 978 1 9064 9 790 3

**British Library Cataloguing-in-Publication Data**
A catalogue record for this book is available
from the British Library

Typeset by Seagull Books
Printed and bound by Hyam Enterprises, Calcutta, India

To Neda,

whom I knew for only 47 seconds

To Emad, a friend whose courage made all this possible

And to

Hussein Tahmasbi (27), Bahman Jenabi (20), Mehdi Karami (25), Nasser Amirnejad (26), Mohammad Hussein Barzegar (25), Reza Tabatabaii (30), Iman Hashemi (27), Parisa Keli (25), Mohsen Haddadi (24), Mohammad Nikzadi (26), Ali Shahedi (24), Abolfazl Abdollahi (21), Salar Tahmasbi (27), Fahimeh Salahshour (25), Reza Tabatabaii (29), Ashkan Sohrabi (18), Kaveh Alipour (19), Saiid Abbasi (24), Alireza Eftekhari (24), Salar Ghorbani (22), Maryam MehrAzadeh (24), Hamed Besha-rati (26), Mohammad Hussein Feizi (26), Ramin Ramezani (22), Sohrab Arabi (19), and the hundreds of other innocents slain, detained or tortured during the post-election protests, most of whom belonged to a generation that was not even born when its destiny was sealed during the Islamic Revolution of Iran in 1979.

All the events in this book are real. I have changed the names of a few characters and their relationships with me in order to protect them, both from being prosecuted for being part of my life and from the invasion of their privacy.

*Contents*

Oh yes, yes, life is a grace
Life is a truly, long living fireplace,
It is up to us, to kindle the fire
and see everywhere
dancing flames of desire.
Or else it dies out,
darkness is our fault.

Siyavash Kasraii, from the poem 'Arash the Archer'

*Foreword*

On 20 June 2009, a video clip was circulated all over the world. It showed the death of a unarmed young woman called Neda, shot in the chest while taking part in a protest in Tehran and bleeding to death on the street. Few images in the contemporary world have had such an instant and powerful impact. This footage was so intense that it forced the world's attention on what was happening in Iran and prompted world leaders to condemn the way in which the Iranian government was treating its citizens.

For me, however, it was more personal. There was a young man in the video trying to save Neda. He was my friend, Arash.

When I met him for the very first time, I could never have imagined that this slim young man would get caught in the crossroad of history 10 years later. Even if I had the power to look into the future and see that this passionate doctor-publisher-author was destined to be present in one of the most important documents of contemporary history, I couldn't have imagined the way he would react to it. I couldn't have imagined that he would have the courage to testify against an unspeakable crime and be prepared to forsake everything to expose the truth.

I met Arash in Tehran in 2000. Arash was the Iranian publisher who, despite the fact that Iran has not signed any of the international copyright agreements, had made the decision to
publish my work with my authorization.

I was in a state of confusion when I met him. Finally I was
in Iran. While I had been looking forward to visiting Iran for
some time, I had no idea what to expect. I didn't know what the
implications of my visit would be, or if Christina and I were in
any kind of danger. However, I had made the decision to venture this visit; I already knew that I had thousands of readers
waiting for me and I was ecstatic at the thought of seeing the
land of Rumi, Saadi, Hafiz and Omar Khayyam.

A constant traveller, there is little to surprise me when I
step into a new land. But every country has its own spirit; and
until you understand that spirit, you remain a stranger. Be-
friending this spirit, trying to understand it, trying to make it
understand me and trying to find the inevitable bonds between
this spirit and the universal soul has been my main objective
whenever I visit a new place. The older the culture the stronger
the bond; and the more difficult for it to open up to a new
traveller passing through. Just like Sinbad, who travelled the
seven seas and was forced, each time, to undertake impossible
challenges before the island would open up and reveal to him
that this small, simple mound was actually a whale of unspeakable power. It was only then that he could return home, trusting
he knew the island's secret.

Christina and I became friends with Arash and his family.
While the officials were trying to control what I saw and where
I went, Arash tried hard to show me the true Iranian spirit. We
had long conversations about what Iran was about. He took me
to the secret Sufi ceremonies, to passion plays, and he enabled
my Iranian readers to approach me and share their thoughts with
me. His love for his country and his high hopes for a better

future appearing on the horizon made me realize that I had made the right decision. The true spirit of Iran was the passion for literature, love, sharing and a real mastery of the universal language.

Since 2000, Arash has been a very close friend. I invited him and his wife to visit Europe with me, and the companionship of these travels helped me understand him better. We were in Madrid in December 2000 when he, with tears in his eyes, told me the legend of Arash the Archer and how he hoped to live up to his name. Arash the Archer was an Iranian mythical hero who, in order to end the war between Iran and its invaders, put his life into his single arrow so that it could fly far enough to land on the original border between the two countries and restore peace.

Three years later in Berlin, he told me over dinner that he thought Berlin was the 'city of hope'. During the Cold War, Berlin was at the crossroads between West and East. If anything happened, Berlin, rebuilt from the ashes of the Second World War, would be the first city to be destroyed. That was why the spirit of the city had realized that every day could be its last. And instead of living in constant fear, the Berliners discovered the true value of joy. They seized every moment while it lasted. Fortunately, the city lived long enough to witness the fall of the Wall and the birth of a new hope. Berlin gave Arash hope that one day happiness would be possible for the people of Iran and he believed that until then, they would need to seize every moment.

There is always a moment in your life when you have to make a decision. I have always said that God is the Lord of the valiant and real courage lies in making difficult decisions based on what you should do, not on what prudence recommends.

Did Arash live up to his name? I don't know. But he did put his life into his single arrow, the arrow that has unified the aspirations of the Iranians under the image of a dying Neda.

But Arash's story is not summed up in that moment: he has a story of a generation to tell. It came as no surprise when he produced an important and life-affirming memoir. In the *Gaze of the Gazelle*, Arash reveals the true spirit of Iran. He looks un-flinchingly into the mirror and reflects on the recent past of his family and of Iran itself. More than many a historical textbook, this memoir illuminates the sense of nationhood and pride that keeps a society together despite the hardships that are thrown at it. A nation that can be stopped by nothing in its pursuit of happiness across thousands of years has learned that there is no tomorrow, there is no yesterday. There is only what you choose to do today, now, in this moment.

*Paulo Coelho*

*Prologue*

On the evening of 20 June 2009, at approximately 7 p.m. GMT, a brief video-clip was posted on YouTube and Facebook. Within minutes it had been picked up and broadcast globally by virtually every news channel. A mere 47 seconds of film shook the world.

It shows a young woman, shot in the chest and bleeding. As she falls to the ground, dying, she gazes unknowing into the lens of a camera-phone. It is this accidentally shot clip that is circulated and watched by millions around the world.

'Stay, Neda! STAY WITH ME!' a voice cries out in the background.

Her name is Neda. In Persian, Neda means 'the call', 'the voice'.

In a few days, Neda became the symbol of Iran's Green Movement. On the day of her death, millions of Iranians had rallied in the streets of Tehran to protest against the widespread rigging of the recent presidential election. People called these protests 'rallies of silence' in the belief that the sound of silence would echo their frustrations better than any shouts or slogans.

Then, Neda, 'the call', 'the voice', who was killed alongside hundreds of other silent protesters, became their symbol.

Neda continued to haunt the world's media and politicians: U2 and Bon Jovi sang in homage to her and in solidarity with the Iranians; in London, the *Times* pronounced her its '2009 Person of the Year'; US President Barack Obama called her death 'unjust' and 'heartbreaking'; the 'unnamed people' who captured her death on camera and made it public were chosen as winners of a George Polk Award, the first time the journalism prize had honoured an anonymous work. UK Prime Minister Gordon Brown, showing the photo of her lying on the street, said: 'What we see unlocks what we cannot see. What we see unlocks the invisible ties and bonds of sympathy that bring us together to become a human community . . .'

There is someone else in that video: a man in a white shirt and jeans who exerts pressure on the wound in a fruitless attempt to stop the bleeding.

I am that person. I was there when she died. I tried to save her but failed. It was a friend who captured the tragedy on his camera-phone; it was I who sent it out anonymously. I saw her gaze before she passed, the gaze of the gazelle that has been running from the hunter for many hours and now lies on the ground, exhausted and with an arrow deep in her side. She sinks in her own still-warm blood. Sprawled on the ground, she watches the hunter approach with a knife in his hand. Her gaze reflects neither hope nor despair. She has no desire. A vague perception of life creeps into her veins, runs into her soul and spreads through her mind.

How can I name her feeling in that last moment anything but the Gaze of the Gazelle?

The government of Iran first claimed that the video was a fake and that Neda was alive; then they claimed she had been shot by the BBC's correspondent in Iran. Later, they accused the CIA of shooting her 'in the head'.

I left Iran a few days after this incident and when I realized how far the government was ready to go to cover its crimes, I decided to speak up. In two interviews—with the BBC on 25 June and with the *Times* on 26 June—I told the story of her death to the world. My interviews travelled across the world's media as fast as the original video. Since then, video and interviews have joined together in exposing the hidden face of one of the most violent and treacherous governments in the world.

But the story is not over. I look back even as I struggle to recover from the effects of that bloody scene and the mesmerizing gaze of that innocent girl, as the shouting continues to echo in my ears and the teargas stings my eyes. It is hard to believe that this is Iran. Its culture is as old as human civilization itself, it is the land of Scheherazade of *One Thousand and One Nights* and was once the fountain of poetry and science whose poets and scientists set the scene for the global blossoming of mathematics, medicine, astronomy and literature.

Iran has always been at the centre of world attention and played an important role in international affairs: first as the greatest empire in the world, then in opposing the Arab invasion in the seventh century and today as the home of one of the most hated governments in the world, one that propagates hatred above all else.

Iran is the world's fourth-largest exporter of oil and contains possibly the world's biggest natural gas deposits. With its high mountains and vast deserts, green fields and endless seas and its strategic communications highway, Iran has been declared one of the 13 'enemies of the Internet'. In a land where its most revered sage, Zarathustra, once preached that redemption is only achievable through Good Thought, Good Deed and Good Word, the police and the militia are massacring their own people, the government has been accused of sponsoring global terrorism, hundreds of reporters, writers, intellectuals and scholars are being tortured in prison and young people under the legal age are being executed daily. This is a country that practises one of the most sophisticated censorship systems, where millions of people suffer from absolute poverty and drug addiction and prostitution are common in the cities. Those with the courage to stand up for lost dreams are falling to the ground like the last remaining leaves of a dying tree.

*How did it come to this?*

There were no camera-phones back then when everything began but Neda's gaze is working as one now, opening old scars, these gaping wounds that have worked as my own camcorders. It's playback time now.

I have already shown and told your story to the world, Neda; millions of people know how you were murdered, just because you wanted to have a voice. You are the martyr. People are chanting your name all over the world like a mantra, crystallizing the accumulated hopes and dreams of the Iranian nation.

I have lost everything because I told your story; my career, my country, my family, my security . . . and the worst part is that I cannot be healed: not until I tell my own story, the story of a generation that was there to see everything, bear everything and lose everything. I need simply to be able to bear witness to an era full of dark hate and bright hopes. I am tired of seeing everything and saying nothing. Your death has become my business. I had to be there at that time and at that place. I was the only one present who had access to the technology and contacts that could take your story out to the world and I was the only one who could leave Iran to bear witness to your unjust death. It is as if all my life's achievements, failures, horrors, advantages and trivial experiences were destined to lead me to that time and to that place. I didn't believe in destiny and I am still trying not to. But it's hard, given everything I've been through. You are the sum of my life Neda; the sum of the life of my entire generation.

We were part of a generation that was later called the Burnt Generation—the generation known in the US as 'Generation X'. We were between seven and 15 at the time of the Islamic Revolution. We were the generation that witnessed the murder of its uncles during the Revolution and the execution and imprisonment of its parents afterwards. A generation doomed to spend the best years of its life amid the horrors of the Iran–Iraq war, either on the front, running on landmines to open up a path for the troops, or at home, dreading the return of a friend from the front in a coffin and then walking in the funeral procession that set out from the schoolyard. A generation that entered puberty while being trained how to use AK-47 assault rifles, a generation not permitted to have any contact with the opposite sex and not allowed to dance or make merry. A generation that was taught not to trust anyone. A generation that dreaded its own shadow and saw too much, far more than anyone should be forced to witness in a lifetime.

But we were also a generation that, for lack of anything else to do, spent its time learning. We were the true witnesses of our nation. We were the hunted but, in the course of the parallel evolution of the hunter and the hunted, we evolved faster. We survived to bear witness to what we had endured for the next generation: Neda's generation.

## PART I

*Since your love became my calling*

(Autumn 1978–Summer 1980)

'Who is this Ayatollah Khomeini?' I asked Madar, my paternal grandmother. I had heard his name over and over but I didn't know who he was. Every night people went to the rooftops to see his face etched upon the full moon and I really wanted to know what he was doing there.

'He is the vicar of the Hidden Imam,' Madar explained, trying to fit her cigarette into its holder. 'While the Hidden Imam is in Occultation, the vicar is in charge of the Muslims' faith,' she continued, then lit her cigarette. 'He is our saviour.'

'And why is his face on the moon?'

'God has etched his face on the full moon as a sign,' she said with a smile that heightened her mystic aura as she sat cross-legged on the floor, 'so that people will know he is the Chosen One.'

The more I looked at the moon, the better I could identify a shape. But it wasn't the face of a man; clearly not of a holy man. It seemed, rather, very much like a *rabbit*—very much like Bugs Bunny, in fact.

Madar believed I wasn't ready yet.

According to Twelver Shia Islam, the official religion of Iran, the Hidden Imam or Mahdi is the Twelfth Imam, an offspring of Prophet Muhammad who went into Occultation in AD 874 when he was only five years old. He is still alive—but in hiding—and will emerge at the end of time as our saviour; he will bring peace and justice to the world and re-establish Islam as the only righteous path. I still couldn't figure out why he needed a vicar, though. The argument seemed to me illogical. If he were supposed to wait in hiding until the right time to save the world, why would he send someone else to save the world earlier? And if it were time to save the world, why didn't he show up himself?

'Don't be silly,' Madar said. 'We're not supposed to question God's plans.'

It wasn't the first time I'd asked that question. Ever since I had heard Khomeini's name whispered by my parents and their friends, by my classmates (with the utmost respect) and sometimes on the BBC Persian Service that my parents listened to secretly every night, I had been asking the same question, hoping to receive two answers that matched up. Madar's answer was not the one I'd had from Dad.

'He's a cleric, son, a mullah. He was exiled from Iran 15 years ago because of his protests against the Shah's tyranny. He has now become politically active again and gained a huge following among the people.'

This long speech may seem a little too sophisticated for an eight-year-old but, luckily, it was the kind of language with which I was familiar. Sadly, I was not quite the genius that my father assumed. I learnt to read at four, could write by the time I was five—both in Persian and English—and read my first 'serious' book at six, a 200-page novel on the life of Thomas Edison. Dad had given it to me hoping I'd choose Edison as my role model. I did—only until I discovered Peter Pan and Superman.

I was born on 17 February 1971 in Tehran, the same year that Apollo 14 landed on the moon, Pablo Neruda won the Nobel Prize for Literature and Nikita Khrushchev and Jim Morrison died. When I was a year old, we moved to England so that Dad could study for his PhD at the University of Birmingham. My most prominent memory of the four years we spent there, apart from the ordinary ones of an ordinary child living in the UK—of friends, school, games and constant complaints about the weather—has been carved upon my mind with the help of a photograph: Dad, in his gown and mortarboard in front of the main building of the University on his graduation day. Thirty-four then, he's holding his degree certificate, his eyes shining with joy and hope and his serious expression not quite concealing his smile of infinite happiness.

Having known him for many years now, I can imagine what he is thinking about in that photograph: his imminent return to Iran; teaching; executing his plans for reforming Iran's higher education system; and, being an authentic genius unlike me, beginning his research in the field of material sciences.

Exactly 34 years later, in August 2009, when Mum and he had come to England to visit me after Neda's death, we rented a car and went to the University of Birmingham again. I asked him to stand in front of the main building on the precise spot on which he had been photographed on his graduation day. But when I held the camera in front of my eyes, I had to wait for a few seconds before pressing the button, until the tears that blurred my vision had cleared. We had been on such a long journey since then. So many things had been turned upside down: his hair had gone completely white and he was no longer possessed of the vitality of a 34-year-old but the main change lay in his face. He was smiling this time, too, but the smile was trying in vain to conceal the deep sorrow that stemmed from the shattered hopes of a man still in love with a dream that no longer exists.

We returned to Iran in 1975 and my sister Golnar was born. Dad began teaching as a senior lecturer in metallurgical engineering. Mum decided to study and get her diploma and then take the National University entrance exam for a nursing course. And I went to nursery school. We rented a small flat in central Tehran and Dad managed to buy a colour TV. This introduced me to the world of Charlie Chaplin and, of course, the superheroes: Superman, Batman, Aquaman, the Fantastic Four and Spiderman. It was through these characters that I realized that a name should *mean* something and I decided to ask Dad why I had been named Arash.

'Arash means "bright" in Avestan, one of the ancient Iranian languages,' Dad explained, 'but that isn't why I chose this name for you,' and he went on to tell me the legend of Arash the Archer.

'Four thousand years ago, when the wars began between Iran and the neighbouring country of Turan, Arash was an ordinary archer in the Iranian army. The Turanians defeated the Iranians and laid siege to the capital. Then, to humiliate the defeated Iranians, they forced the Iranian king to an agreement. An Iranian archer would shoot an arrow from Iran. Wherever the arrow landed would determine the new border between Iran and Turan.

'No archer dared volunteer for this task. Even the best of them could not shoot an arrow farther than a league. This agreement meant losing most of the Iranian territories to the enemy and no one wanted to be responsible for that.

'But Arash stepped forward and declared he was ready to shoot the arrow. As there were no other candidates, the king had to accept his offer. Arash climbed the Alborz Mountains and shot his only arrow. But before releasing the string, he put his life in that arrow.

'The arrow flew for three days. The horsemen who followed it found it on the third day embedded in a walnut tree at the original border between Iran and Turan. Peace was restored and the war was over. The Turanians were forced to retreat to their own lands and happiness and prosperity returned to Iran.

'But Arash had disappeared. He had put his life into his arrow and died instantly. However, the legend says he is still there, on Mount Damavand in the Sierra Alborz—more commonly known as the Alborz Mountains—helping those who have lost their way along the misty mountain paths if they call his name.'

Dad believed that Arash's sacrifice was more important than any American superhero's stunts. Arash shot an arrow that brought an end to the war without killing anyone. And he gave up his life for that.

This story, mingling with the superhero adventures, inflamed my love of tales and legends, and it was then that Madar stepped in and quenched my thirst. She knew hundreds of tales. Mum told me fairy tales by the Brothers Grimm, while Dad recounted the lives of historical figures and famous Iranian scientists such as Khayyam and al-Khwārizmī. But it was Madar, with her tales full of mysteries, magical gems and hidden treasures, as well as her accounts of the lives of Islamic saints and Imams, who created my passion for storytelling and the supernatural.

And that is why I had to ask her the question about Ayatollah Khomeini—the one I had already asked Dad. For her answer was important. The only thing she had in common with Dad—apart from their familial bond—was a keen intelligence. Once I had both their answers to a question, I could shape my own perception of the truth, inevitably a mix of Dad's realism and Madar's fantastic world.

Dad, a strong advocate of logic, would give me answers based on the facts and, in their absence, rational deduction. The more difficult my questions, the more excited he would become in his quest for the best possible answer. He would hold his chin with a grip that covered his mouth, leaving only his handlebar moustache visible while he talked me through the deductive process. Sometimes, when finding the right logical answer turned out to be harder than he had imagined, he would put his hand on his already balding pate and remain silent for a while. But explanations there always were, even for miracles such as Moses' splitting of the sea or Prophet Muhammad's splitting of the moon. Once, when I asked him how Jesus could have resurrected Lazarus, he simply answered, 'Who knows, maybe he wasn't dead in the first place.'

Madar, on the other hand, would react in a completely different way. She did her best to come up with answers but using her own particular form of rational deduction. Staring into the emptiness in front of her she, too, would answer my questions but with very complicated responses which were not always in harmony with the laws of nature.

She and Dad, despite their different approaches, had something else in common: both believed that there was *always* an answer. Dad would justify the unanswered question with 'Science will find out soon' whereas Madar said. 'God will reveal the answer in due course'.

Madar was a strange old woman and the love of my life. Born to a baker, she was forced to marry my grandfather when she was only 13 and he a widower with two daughters, one aged five and the other seven. Madar had to be their mother when she might more easily have been their sister. However, when my grandfather Agha-djoon chose to have two more wives and filled the house with 12 children in whom he took very little interest, Madar left him without ever looking back or even filing for divorce. Now she lived in the religious city of Qom, near the shrine of Holy Masoumah. She sustained herself by weaving fine high-quality lace for the dowry of brides-to-be and visited the holy shrine at least once a day.

Once I asked her why she had left Agha-djoon.

'It was about time someone showed men that they didn't own their wives. We're human too.' I liked to believe she was in her own way one of the first authentic feminists in Iran.

After analyzing both their answers to my Ayatollah Khomeini question, my personal interpretation turned out to be: 'Khomeini is a very important person who is soon going to be even more important.'

There was one bit of prophecy missing from my conclusion which no one could have imagined at the time, neither my over-religious grandmother nor my secular father nor his leftist, rightist, moderate, reformist, nationalist, fundamentalist, Islamist, atheist friends who all hated the Shah. It took us a few years to discover what we had all overlooked: it was not so much that the Shah was corrupt but that absolute power corrupts absolutely, no matter who holds it.

I felt the tension for the first time at the beginning of September 1978 when we reached the Turko-Iranian border on our way home from our summer trip to the UK. We were travelling in Dad's brand-new dark-red Ford Taunus, the same car that had brought Mum, Aunt Marjaneh, my two-year-old sister Golnar and me all the way from the UK to Iran via France, Italy, Yugoslavia, Bulgaria and Turkey. My parents planned to go to the UK every summer so that I could keep practising my English and they could visit their friends. But this was not to be. Our first summer holiday in Europe was to be our last for many years to come. That summer was going to change many plans. The Islamic Revolution was on its way.

My parents had no way of knowing what was going on in Iran. The Internet, mobile phones and satellite TV were yet to be invented and there was no radio in our car. It was there, at the border, that we realized something was up. Dad returned to the car after talking to a young man in Customs, flushed with anxiety and rage. He bent to whisper to Mum: a cinema had burnt down in Abadan while screening the Iranian film *The Deer* and 300 people had burnt to death.

The journey from the border to my grandfather's house in Tehran took two days through the mountains, fields and deserts of Iran. I hadn't travelled much in Iran before and it was my first glimpse of the complete range of landscapes, from the high, cold mountain roads and the eternally green fields of the north to the burning desert sun of Qazvin. Dad drove all the way without stopping for a night's sleep. We slept in the car while he drove and Mum and Aunt Marjaneh took turns during the night to keep Dad company and make sure he didn't fall asleep at the wheel. Mum insisted a few times that we pull over and sleep for a few hours in a hotel but Dad refused. He was very concerned about the situation and wanted to get to Tehran as fast as possible. After weeks of living in the car, fed up with sleeping and eating in it, I wanted to get home too. Dad thought it would be a good experience for us to drive through all those countries but I didn't find it interesting any more; all I wanted was my own bed to sleep in. Eventually, Dad stopped the car in front of Hadj-Agha's house. He was my maternal grandfather and we were going to stay with him for a few days before moving into the new flat that Dad had rented from friends.

No sooner had we arrived than we heard that Khomeini, in exile in Iraq, had issued a statement blaming the Shah for the tragedy in the cinema. I don't remember how he related this incident to the Shah but people believed him; they always believed what a mullah said and, since the film was critical of the regime and advocated armed resistance against its tyranny, it seemed plausible enough. This incident was the trigger that ignited the rage of the nation against the regime, a rage that would accumulate over the next few months and explode with the sudden overthrow of 2,500 years of Iranian monarchy.

That was the first time I heard the name Ruhollah Khomeini. Twenty days later, something else happened. The police had opened fire against a demonstration in Tehran's Jaleh Square and killed a great many people: some said 4,000, others 90,000. Everyone was enraged. Unfamiliar with the notion of death, I couldn't understand why. But that state of innocence was soon to be lost. Only a few days later Mum took me to school to enrol me in the second grade and someone mentioned that Charlie Chaplin was dead. This was someone I knew, someone who made me laugh—and I understood death for the first time.

The next two months are a blur. My clearest memory is of the tension: the tension in the air, rank with a mixture of fear and bravado. And the red slogans on the walls: 'Death to the Shah!' 'Hail to Khomeini!' And the twisted faces of the people who were afraid to speak to one another and who wondered how this drama was going to end.

Then, all of a sudden, the silence broke and the vibrations in the air turned into a storm . . . The main Bazaar, the heart of the Iranian economy, along with all the schools, universities and hundreds of shops and other businesses, went on a national strike. I didn't fully appreciate what was going on except for the joy of not having to go to school any more. It was a second summer holiday, although it also meant that I was not going to see my very best friend, Azadeh. We sat beside one another, we studied together and we chatted between classes. I still remember her dark curly hair and her brilliant mathematical mind: she could do the most complicated sums in her head, without putting pen to paper. When the schools shut down I didn't get a chance to say goodbye nor did I have her phone number. We took our time together for granted; when you are a child, everything seems eternal. I would discover all too soon just how wrong we were.

My father and his friends got together every night, endlessly discussing the changes over vodka and cigarettes. Sometimes, they listened to Khomeini's fiery speeches, recorded on audiocassettes and smuggled into the country through Kuwait or Iraq. They were excited and happy, eager to be a part of what was happening. I remember some of them: Reza Company, an electrical engineer, and Hormoz, a lecturer in electronics, both members of the Tudeh (People) Communist Party; and Bahram, a nationalist like Dad.

I found it hard to understand why everyone hated the Shah. At school we'd been taught that the Shah was our nation's loving father; he cared about all his children and shed tears whenever he heard of a citizen in distress. We also sang the National Anthem every morning: 'Long live our king of kings, for whose grace the country stands forever . . .' But Dad disagreed and finally expressed his contempt when he heard me humming the Anthem one day. I felt his hand on my shoulder and when I turned back I saw 'the look' in his eyes. He was very angry.

'Arash, the Shah is bad!' he said. 'We don't want him to live long! He has killed many young people, he doesn't let people talk, he has sold our homeland to America, he has ruined the country. I don't want my son to sing this cursed anthem.'

'Then what *should* I sing, Dad?'

It was then that he taught me 'Oh, Iran', a song by the poet Gol-e Golab, written during the Second World War when Iran was occupied by British and Russian forces. Although it never was, nor would ever become, the official anthem of Iran, it has always been considered so by the people.

*Oh Iran, oh bejewelled land*
*Oh, your soil is the wellspring of the arts*
*Far from you may the thoughts of evil be*
*May you remain lasting and eternal*

. . .

*Since your love became my calling*
*My thoughts are never far from you*

When I returned to England after Neda's death in June 2009, to testify to her death and to finish the course in publishing I had begun in Oxford the previous year, my Italian friend Nina told me, 'I can't believe it! These Iranians on the streets are being killed, beaten, detained, tortured, but they're not giving up!'

'Yes, I know,' I answered briefly, and left. Late for an appointment with my professor, I didn't have time to explain that this was part of the package of being Iranian. I couldn't tell her that Iran is not a mere country to Iranians but a concept that unites them regardless of ethnicity, dialect or religion. As an identity it is both a blessing and a curse; it is also a dream that has helped the nation endure a history full of struggles, the only dream worth dying for. Iran is a proud and stubborn nation. I couldn't tell Nina that the Iranians were already 'Irani' when the Aryans began their long migration south from the frozen lands of Siberia 4,000 years ago. Some left for the Indian peninsula, some settled in the green lands of Central Asia and some others entered the plateau that is today called Iran, 'the land of the Aryans'. This land has been invaded and destroyed several times over the past 2,500 years, yet throughout a succession of occupations by Assyrians, Greeks, Romans, Arabs, Mongols, Turks, British and Russians, the people have remained Iranians. Four hundred years after the Arab occupation they revived their language. When they realized that they could not resist the might of the Arabs and that they must either accept Islam or die, they transformed it into Shiism, a religion more compatible with their own Zoroastrian and Manichaean beliefs. Unlike many other ancient civilizations conquered by the Arabs, the Iranians never 'became' Arabs nor did they accept Arabic as their native language. Today, they speak the same language in which their beloved poets Roudaki, Firdowsi and Khayyam wrote their poems more than a millennium ago.

'Iranian' is not a nationality but a way of life. It would stretch Nina's credibility if I told her that the Iranians, in keeping with Zarathustra's 3,000-year-old teachings—that their only choice lay between being a Soldier of Darkness or a Warrior of Light— still believed in the eternal battle between Good and Evil. They had to choose and their decisions would determine the outcome of the war. Dying on this battlefield is the highest honour for an Iranian. That is why, over the past century, Iran has witnessed at least four major uprisings and a war: the Constitutional Revolution of 1905–11; the uprising in defence of Prime Minister Mosadeq in 1953; the Islamic Revolution of 1979; the war with Iraq from 1980 to 1988 and the 2009 uprising against the fraudulent presidential election.

But let's go back to 1978.

The Shah, deciding in desperation to suppress the riots, appointed one of his generals as the new prime minister and initiated a curfew after dark. Khomeini, who had moved from Iraq to Paris, directed the people to shout '*Allah-o Akbar*' (God is Great) from the rooftops every night at 9 in protest against the curfew. People obeyed, including my father and his friends, none of whom were even remotely religious. Khomeini also asked the soldiers to either defect or join the civilians. It was then that Uncle Reza, Mum's brother doing his military service, defected and went into hiding so that he would not be forced to take up arms against the people.

It was a joy to go up to the rooftops every night; we knew all our neighbours would be there, shouting '*Allah-o Akbar*' and sharing the latest jokes about the Shah or his prime minister. We children were allowed to stay up past our bedtimes and join our parents on the roof. We lived in a flat in a two-storey building that my father had rented from an old friend and university colleague; he lived on the first floor with his family and his son Kami and his daughter Nazi were my friends. We played on the roof while our parents laughed and shouted; every once in a while we joined in the '*Allah-o Akbar*', too.

'Why are you shouting "*Allah-o Akbar*"?' I once asked Dad. 'You're not religious!'

'We have to show this tyrant king that his commands are no longer valid in this country,' he responded. 'We have to show him that we are many and that we are united.'

Thirty years later, Mir-Hussein Mousavi invited the people of Iran to do the same thing every night, to show their outrage at the 2009 election fraud and to protest against the tyranny of the regime. Ironically, shouting '*Allah-o Akbar*' from the rooftops was banned in 2009 by the same regime that was born from these shouts 30 years earlier. Even more ironic was that while the Shah merely ignored the shouts, the police of the Islamic Republic attacked our homes and arrested our people.

A few days later, General Azhari, the new prime minister, was questioned by the press about the nocturnal shouting. 'I have been investigating the case,' he answered. 'I was even out last night. Those are not real people shouting: they are only a few playing "*Allah-o Akbar*" tapes.' The idiocy of his comments further inflamed the people. Invited by Khomeini to rally in the streets on the day of Ashura, to prove to Azhari that, in fact, the people against the Shah were not so few, they responded in force.

Ashura is the most important day in the Shia lunar calendar and one of the most significant annual events in Iran. It is the anniversary of Imam Hussein's martyrdom about 1,300 years ago. Imam Hussein was the son of Imam Ali and the grandson of the Prophet Muhammad. When he defied the tyranny of Caliph Yazid, he and 71 of his friends and family were massacred in an unequal battle near Karbala, south of Baghdad in today's Iraq. Since then, every year, Shia Muslims honour this day by mourning for Imam Hussein. For the Iranians, he is the ultimate symbol of the battle between Good and Evil, of resistance and bravery and of the fight to the death for an ideal.

17

Dad took me to the enormous Ashura demonstrations of 1978. Though practically no one stayed indoors, Hadj-Agha was one of the few who did. A zealous believer and a self-taught Muslim scholar with a deep knowledge of Islam, he was not happy with the Islamic movement led by the clerics. He was also a fierce critic of Khomeini. He owned a prestigious Islamic bookshop near the main Bazaar, which was also a meeting place for religious scholars and clerics. Almost everyone in the book industry and in religious circles believed him to be the absolute authority in the field of Islamic books. He was the one who cautioned Mum and my aunt each time they left the house to join the demonstrations.

'You don't know these mullahs as I do. You shouldn't trust them.'

Once he told me a story about his encounter with Khomeini. They had met in the late 1950s when they were both middle-aged and Khomeini was only one mullah among many. Khomeini had gone to Hadj-Agha's bookshop and asked for a particular book. Hadj-Agha brought it out and criticized the author's point of view. Khomeini frowned and told Hadj-Agha that he was not supposed to talk about such delicate matters; that he had better take care of his bookshop instead of meddling with specialist fields. Hadj-Agha remained silent for a second, and then said: 'I know as much as you about these matters. The only difference is that I am working hard to earn a decent living. You've never done a day's work in your life! You prefer to exploit people's religion for your livelihood.' Khomeini threw the book on the counter and stormed out. I like to imagine that it was then that Khomeini decided to be more than a mullah; to be, rather, a political leader.

Nonetheless, Hadj-Agha was also a fundamentalist. He forced my mother to leave school when she was 16 despite all her tearful pleas to be allowed to study for a few more years. He believed that girls weren't supposed to study beyond a certain level; although when it came to Aunt Marjaneh, four years younger than Mum, he changed his mind in the light of the current feminist movements and decided to let her go to university. He even paid for her stay in Cambridge while she studied English.

But Mum was forced to marry when she was 17. She had to choose between several suitors and she chose Dad only because he promised to allow and help her study for as long as she wished. But Mum soon became pregnant; I was born and then they had to move to the UK. She attended an art college in Birmingham for a while but she had to wait a few more years for her high-school diploma.

Hadj-Agha was furious with Dad for naming me after Arash instead of after an Islamic hero such as Ali or Muhammad; he believed these pagan names would propagate heresy in Iran. He always teased me by saying that Arash wasn't a hero at all: a proper hero wouldn't die after simply shooting an arrow. According to him, Imam Ali was the real hero: he could decapitate 700 heretics and traitors in only a day!

Anyway, there we were in the crowd on the day of Ashura 1978. I had never seen so many people in the same place asking for the same thing—neither had the rest of the world. It was said to be the biggest protest meeting in history. Millions of people marched from 24 Esfand Square to Shahyad Square. Given the multitude of people, the police were advised not to interfere. Men and women walked in separate clusters. The most important thing I noticed was the dramatic change of fashion among women. Those young girls who had appeared in tight jeans or miniskirts and fashionable hairstyles just the day before were now completely covered in Islamic hijabs, chadors or headscarves, even those who, like my mother, didn't usually observe the hijab. Khomeini was now the official leader of the anti-Shah movement and people strongly believed that Islam was their last resort and only saviour.

There was more diversity among the men: they wore fashionable bell-bottoms, long, pointed shirt collars and sported the layered hair and sideburns popular in the 1970s. I could also see men with short hair and beards that marked them as zealous Islamists; they were in their mid-30s and mid-40s and wore long-sleeved shirts with or without a jacket—short sleeves were far too immodest for the likes of them. I could also see unshaven older men who wore the brimless, rounded Kufi hat and who were immediately identifiable as the true followers of Khomeini. It was a sea of diversity among the men and a wave of uniformity among the women.

When I could no longer walk, Dad carried me on his shoulders and we continued towards our destination. He believed it was something I had to witness because he thought it unlikely that such a thing would ever happen again. The Shah was doomed and victory was close.

But he was wrong. Thirty years later, on 15 June 2009, I saw and was part of an even larger demonstration at the same place. There were differences, of course. For one thing, the names had changed: 24 Esfand was now Enghelab (Revolution) Square and Shahyad was Azadi (Freedom) Square. But the changes in the people were more drastic: this time men and women walked together, and the diversity was more evident among the women despite the fact that they were all forced to wear the hijab, the legacy of their mothers. In 1978, women chose to abandon their freedom to dress as they pleased; in 2009, women were struggling to regain this very freedom.

I remember most of the chants and slogans at the Ashura rally. The most popular was also the most amusing: in response to Azhari's stupid remark about the nightly '*Allah-o Akbar*', people shouted: 'Azhari, you idiot, tell us if we are tapes now! Tapes don't walk in the streets, you four-starred ass!' Other slogans were simpler and more to the point: 'Down with the Shah!' 'Hail to Khomeini!' 'Independence, Liberty, Islamic Revolution'.

But there were significant differences between the many chants and slogans. The communist guerrillas sang the Persian version of 'El pueblo, unido, jamas sera vencido' (The People, united, shall never be defeated); the Mujahideen-e Khalgh or the People's Mujahideen, a group that followed an ideology based on an incompatible mixture of Islam and Marxism, sang: 'I swear by the name of freedom, I swear by the name of your last moments, that your path will be our path, oh martyrs'; the Islamists chanted '*Allah Allah Allah, Allah-o Akbar, La Ilaha Illallah*'. Some people simply walked quietly, and there were others, including Dad, who cherry-picked the slogans. He would shout 'Down with the Shah!' but remained silent when others hailed Khomeini or asked for the Islamic Revolution. When I asked him why, he simply answered that he didn't believe in Khomeini.

'So why are you here with all these people who love him?' I asked.

'After the Shah is gone, we will be free and people can choose whoever and whatever they want. That is the meaning of democracy. No one man will have all the power: the power belongs to the people, even the minority.'

He was wrong, *again*.

I couldn't care less about the freedom of our nation at the moment as I was furiously trying to regain my individual freedom from Dad. *Star Wars: A New Hope* was on at the cinema and all my friends had been to watch it. Mum and Dad, fearing a repeat of the Cinema Rex tragedy in Abadan, refused to let me go. I begged them, with tears in my eyes but they were un-relenting. I listened enviously to friends who chatted about the film, about Darth Vader's outfit and all the strange creatures and robots. This to me was the cruellest thing parents could do to their children—deny them what their peers had the right to know—and for that I couldn't forgive them.

Confronted with the huge uprising, the Shah sacked General Azhari and appointed a new prime minister. Shapour Bakhtiar was a moderate member of the Nationalist Front and one of the followers of Dr Mosadeq, the popular prime minister of the 1950s. After nationalizing Iranian oil and winning his case against the UK at the International Court of Justice, he organized a semi-coup and forced the Shah to leave the country only to be counter-attacked by US forces who overthrew him and returned the Shah to his throne. This incident was the main source of anti-US feeling among Iranians. If the people wanted a change of regime, insisted Bakhtiar, it should happen through a referendum. But Khomeini declared that it was too late and demanded Bakhtiar's immediate resignation if he wanted to be accepted by the Revolution. Bakhtiar attempted to encourage the people to accept a democratic process but in vain. It was all over for the Shah—he now had to reap what he had sown for the past 30 years: the suppression of the media, the torture and execution of any man or woman who opposed him and his iron-fisted rule of the country. Weary, the people no longer wanted the reinstatement of a constitutional monarchy.

On 16 January 1979, I was at my aunt's. I was playing in the alley with my cousins Kazem, Soussan, Soheila and their neighbour Ahmadreza, a few years older than I, who was encouraging us to write slogans—'Death to the Shah' and 'Hail to Khomeini'—on the walls with our crayons. Suddenly, Dad's dark-blue Peugeot 304 turned into the narrow alley and screeched to a halt. He jumped out of the car, flushed with excitement and smiling from ear to ear. Crushing me in a bear hug, he shouted: 'Arash, the Shah is gone!'

It was a simple piece of news that had seized the city: 'The Shah is gone.' '*Shah Raft*' was the headline in every newspaper in the country, printed in the biggest, boldest typeface and celebrated by a veritable tsunami of people in the streets dancing and shouting 'The Shah is gone!'

Dad took me home to pick up the rest of the family. Aunt Marjaneh was staying with us but suffering from a bad back ever since the long trip from the UK. Hence no one expected her to join us on our celebratory trip. But she began to cry; she had always dreamt of this day and now she couldn't be part of it. So Dad helped her down the stairs and adjusted the car seat to let her lean back in a comfortable position. And we set off to celebrate the Shah's flight into exile.

People wore hats made of newspapers with the headline 'The Shah is gone' and danced and chanted as they wiped the city clean of every symbol that reminded them of the reign of the Pahlavi dynasty. Pictures of the Shah were pulled down and burnt and statues of the Shah and his father, Reza Shah, were smashed to pieces. With the rest of the country that night, I witnessed one of the greatest collective festivals of our nation.

Unfortunately, it was also going to be the last time that the people of Iran would partake of such unanimous and unadulterated joy.

The Shah left the country on 16 January 1979. Khomeini returned from exile two weeks later, on 1 February, and went to the holy city of Qom to choose his government.

On 9 February, all my father's friends gathered at our home. The Revolution had almost succeeded. The Army had joined the people on Khomeini's order. People had taken control of the infantry and were now armed. The only barrier between the people and the final victory was the Immortal Guard, or Javidan, the main unit of the Imperial Guard named after the ancient Persian royal guard or Persian Immortals, and National Television, which had been totally under the regime's control. My friend Kami and I were in the living room, in front of the TV, waiting for the weekly *Rangarang* show that broadcast clips of the latest Iranian pop music. But the TV was only broadcasting classical music: no news, no shows, not even a presenter. Kami decided to call the TV channel; after many attempts, someone finally answered.

'Excuse me, sir, why isn't the *Rangarang* show on air?'

After listening for a few seconds, he hung up in silence.

'What did they say?' I asked, excited.

'He said what a stupid boy I was to call at this point asking for a stupid show. He said that they were "in a bloodbath". What's a bloodbath?'

The final battle took place on 10 February. Armed civilians had already confronted the Immortal Guard and the streets were red with blood. Mum, Golnar and I were not allowed to leave the house but Dad left early in the morning. Later, I realized that he had been driving the university ambulance all day, taking wounded people to hospitals; he had nearly been shot, too.

But there was more terrible news on the way. Dad did not come home until late. When the phone began to ring violently— in those days it was hard to interpret any movement, sound or image as non-violent—I answered it. It was Agha-djoon asking for Dad in a strange tone of voice that I couldn't quite understand. Later that night, when Dad finally came home soaked in the blood of God knows how many murdered civilians, his eyes red from the teargas, I finally understood. Uncle Habib, Dad's 70-year-old uncle, had been shot by the Immortal Guard in front of his bakery while trying to save a wounded protester. He had died on the spot. A photo of Uncle Habib's body in the morgue, lying alongside two other 'martyrs' of the Revolution killed on the same day, was published in the press the following morning. That sight of his pale, naked and lifeless body introduced me to the gruesome face of death, a face I was destined to live with. This was the first of many deaths I would face in my life.

The people finally took over the TV and the next day the first thing we heard was the excited voice of a guerrilla declaring, 'From now on you will hear the real voice of the people and the Revolution.' Khomeini called that day, 11 February, 'The Day of Allah' and declared the end of 2,500 years of monarchy in Iran and the beginning of the reign of Islam, a new era in which the people would control their own destinies. Kami and

I, on the other hand, had no idea that we would never see *Rangarang* or any other kind of pop music on TV for many years to come.

I began to look for Azadeh as soon as I arrived in the school yard on that cold morning in February 1979. I had just turned nine. I was happy to be back after the long strike, to be able to see my classmates again, especially Azadeh, and to be able to play in the yard. I was also happy because my parents were happy. Although I still couldn't realize the full extent of the change, I clearly felt that the tension in the air had been lifted, a good enough reason to be happy.

I wanted to share this happiness with Azadeh. No one knew why she wasn't there since none of us had been in touch during the strike. I thought that perhaps her family was away and had not managed to return in time for school and I tried to cling to this theory in order to deal with the disappointment of not seeing her. Then the bell rang and we were called to stand in line. We wondered what was going to happen; in the past, this was when we had to chant 'Long live our king of kings' but there were no kings left to pray for.

I was asking my friend who stood behind me in the line about Azadeh, when the sound of a strange song in a different language interrupted me. A fifth grader on the balcony beside the headmaster was reciting some verses from the Quran. We were supposed to stand in silence and listen to those Arabic words whose meaning completely eluded us.

When it was over, the headmaster, a middle-aged, bald man, took the microphone, thanked the boy and invited him to leave the balcony. Then he began to talk about the changes. He welcomed us back to school and then went on to tell us how important this Revolution and our new-found freedom were. He said that, henceforth, instead of chanting that evil anthem of the previous regime, we would listen to a few uplifting verses of the Holy

Quran every day and . . . I lost track of his words. He talked for half an hour while we stood there, shivering in the cold. We soon began to yawn and shuffle our feet. I began to tease the girl in front of me; others shared jokes or planned games for the break after the first class. And then, suddenly, we realized that the headmaster was silent. We looked up at him again and saw lines of deep sorrow marking his face. My heart began to pound. The students fell silent, as if they had realized that the most important part of the speech was yet to come.

'This freedom has not been achieved without the sacrifices of thousands of martyrs, whose blood has washed this land free of the Devil's footprint,' the headmaster shouted, trying to hide his emotions. 'Our school, too, has lost an angel in this battle for Freedom and Justice.'

I felt I could no longer breathe.

'Azadeh, your classmate, was shot last week while she was with her father in the street. She is one of the martyrs to whom we owe . . .'

I seemed to have frozen at the words. The headmaster's voice translating a verse from the Quran echoed in my ears, a verse we were destined to hear hundreds of times over the next decade, 'Think not of those who are slain in Allah's way as dead. Nay, they live, finding their sustenance in the presence of their Lord.'

How can I describe the feelings of a child who realizes that he has lost his beloved friend? I was filled with a deep and overwhelming hatred. The Shah disgusted me—he had killed my Azadeh, he had killed Uncle Habib. It was then that I knew why the people hated him so and why they demanded his death in their angry shouts. The coward who claimed to be the Father of the Nation had killed my Azadeh to keep his throne. I couldn't cry because of the immense void that opened up within me. I felt as if someone had ripped out my heart.

I couldn't go back to school the next day or the day after; a high fever burnt me up from within. I couldn't believe that Azadeh was no more. So this then was death: when there is no chance left to see a loved one again. No, it wasn't death. Perhaps death would be easier. This was grief. I never really understood how she died. A stray bullet on the street had hit her and that was all I ever knew. Despite my parents' care and the visits to the doctor, it was Madar who saved me from going mad. She was there for me through it all, telling me stories about Heaven and how wonderful it was: no one had to go to school or wash their hands or brush their teeth; children were turned into little angels with wings. I could talk to Azadeh in my prayers; and each time I prayed her wings would grow a little more until, one day, she could fly back to our world and see if I were all right.

And I believed her. That's how I survived. After a few months I could no longer remember Azadeh's face, no matter how hard I tried, but I continued to pray for her. Every night at first, then every other night, then every week, then every once in a while, until I grew up and realized that no wings were large enough to help her fly back to me. And after a few years it was too late anyway; I had lost my faith in angels.

This was how our generation entered childhood, baptized in death and hatred. We learnt about death even before we had a chance to learn about life. We were told that when the Hidden Imam emerged, accompanied by his 313 supporters and riding on his horse, he would slay all the infidels in the world and he wouldn't stop shedding blood until the waves of blood lapped against his saddle. It was imprinted on our flesh and written into our bones that today might be our last day on earth and that we must make the most of it.

Islam had taken over. The revolutionaries broke the prison gates and released the political prisoners while thousands of convicted criminals seized this opportunity to flee. Khomeini appointed Mehdi Bazargan, a religious liberal nationalist, as provisional prime minister while a new constitution was being written. Then, in the blink of an eye, he founded the 'Committees'—a parallel police force controlled by the revolutionaries who did not trust the official police—and the Revolutionary Court which was made responsible for trying the officials of the Shah's regime or the 'traitors to the nation' as they were called.

Then the arrests began. Former ministers and prime ministers, generals, heads and agents of SAVAK—Sazeman-e Ette-la'at va Amniyat-e Keshvar, the National Intelligence and Security Organization—and other officials who had not managed to flee the country in time were arrested within a few days and taken to the Revolutionary Court. The trials were fast and ruthless. Almost all the detained officials were accused of being 'corruptors on earth', the ultimate accusation in Islam and one that demanded the death penalty, a fate that befell most of the new political prisoners.

People lingered over every photograph showing the bullet-riddled bodies of the 'traitors' lying in the morgue. No one appeared to be critical of these arbitrary executions; everyone was convinced that they had been served their due. I certainly agreed: these were the people responsible for Azadeh's death. We children cut out pictures of the executed pro-Shah traitors and collected them without comprehending the meaning of execution. We were taught to celebrate these deaths: the disciples of Lucifer slain by the Angel of Justice. We had no idea that this dreadful death would soon come knocking at our own doors.

No one knew exactly what was meant by an Islamic Republic but more than 98 per cent of the people voted for it on 1 April 1979, in the so-called Spring of Freedom, merely because Imam Khomeini had said, in reply to discussions on the nature of the future regime, 'I say *Islamic Republic*: not a word more, not a word less.'

This wasn't the only concept invented by the new leader; he also came up with the Velayat-e Faqih (Rule of the Islamic Jurisprudent; a *faqih* is an Islamic jurist). No one knew what this meant either but the people voted for it all the same when they opted for a constitution based on this concept. By the time they understood what it really meant—that an Islamic government should be ruled by a Shiite *faqih* acting as a vicar for the Hidden Imam during his Occultation—it was too late. This *faqih*, whose power is said to come directly from God and whom the people may only identify or recognize rather than elect, is the omnipotent ruler of the country. The Vali-e Faqih or Supreme Leader is identified by a council of *faqihs* whose members are elected by the people. However, the candidates have to be first approved by the Guardian Council, another council of *faqihs* whose members are, unsurprisingly, chosen by none other than the Leader himself. This closed circuit offers no options for disqualifying the Supreme Leader. He—it could never be a she—has the authority to make legal decisions within the confines of Islamic law. He also has absolute control over every political, judicial, legislative, economic, social and cultural decision in the country. He has the power to suspend the Constitution and some of the Islamic Laws (Sharia) if he sees fit. The Supreme Leader is endowed with the same authority that the Hidden Imam would have after emerging from his centuries of Occultation.

People were so intoxicated with joy at the abolition of the monarchy and the fall of the Shah, and so hypnotized by the charisma of Khomeini, that they did not realize what they were doing: they were replacing a constitutional monarchy (with limited power) by an absolute monarchy. They were giving their ruler free reign over their lives, they who had fought so hard to win their freedom.

The last two months of school were over before we knew it. We were ordered by our teachers to tear out the first pages of our schoolbooks, the ones containing portraits of the Shah and the Royal Family, and to burn them in the school yard. Other pages relating stories of the Shah and his kindness were to be dealt with in the same way. Two of the three TV channels had been shut down. Since most of the station's staff had been sacked and there had been as yet no time for restructuring, the one remaining channel broadcast for only three hours a day and its repertoire consisted almost entirely of news bulletins, recitations from the Quran and revolutionary songs.

At the beginning of the summer, when Mum finally got her high-school diploma and was admitted to an undergraduate course in nursing, we moved to a larger house with a swimming pool in North Tehran. The only reason Dad could afford the rent was that the owner of the house had fled Iran for fear of being arrested as a collaborator with the Shah's regime and he had been looking for a decent family to take care of the belongings he was leaving behind in the cellar. That house, with its swimming pool and large garden full of fruit trees, marked a new period in my life: for a while, at least, I was happy. It was also during this summer that I met Imam Khomeini.

Madar, who wanted to help me forget the tragedy of Azadeh, believed I should stay with her in the city of Qom for a while. But Dad disagreed. While Madar believed religion would help me endure the pain better, Dad believed that family rather than religion should be my source of strength. Then Madar played her trump card: if I went with her to Qom, she would take me to meet Imam Khomeini. This was an offer I could not resist; it would silence my classmates forever. And I had a most important request for the Imam.

Dad finally agreed to let me go with Madar. We set off very early in the morning to avoid the intolerable summer heat. We changed buses twice before we reached Tehran's South Bus Terminal where we bought two tickets for Qom. Madar bought a sandwich and a drink for me, and we were on our way.

Between Tehran and Qom lies a desert, a yellow sandscape that extends in every direction until it meets the cloudless blue sky. Buses then did not have air-conditioning; as soon as the sun came up, everyone began to perspire and had to fan themselves. It was the day before Ramadan and everyone was in a state of high excitement at the thought of beginning the month of fasting in the Holy City of Qom. Every so often, someone would shout: '*Salawat* for the health of Imam Khomeini!' or '*Salawat* for the health of the driver!' or '*Salawat* for your own health!' *Salawat* may be loosely translated as 'blessings' but it actually refers to a specific kind of prayer that is very important to the Shiites. Whenever someone shouted '*Salawat*', all the passengers followed it with 'Oh God, let your blessings be upon Muhammad and his family.' The Sunnis only use the first part; they do not mention Muhammad's family for they do not believe in the transmission of sanctity from father to son. This is the source of a major conflict between the Shiites and the Sunnis.

When the Prophet Muhammad died in AD 632, a dispute broke out over his successor. Those who were to become the

Shiites—the followers of Ali—believed that, shortly before his death, Muhammad had publicly named Ali, his son-in-law and cousin, as his successor and the first Muslim Caliph. Those who went on to become the Sunnis claimed that Muhammad had never nominated a successor. As Ali was arranging the Prophet's funeral, another group met to choose Abu-Bakr, the Prophet's father-in-law and one of his closest companions, as Caliph. Since then, the followers of the Prophet have been divided into the Shiites, who believe Ali was the successor chosen by God, and the Sunnis, who believe the Caliph should be chosen by the elite. The Shiites, especially the Twelver Shiites, believe that Ali and the 11 descendants of Muhammad (the Imams) through his daughter Fatima Zahra and Ali carried the true legacy of the Prophet; that they were immaculate like the Prophet and that they remain the true governors of the Muslim world. According to the Shiites, the direct descendants of the Prophet should be venerated and be paid the highest respect. A male descendant is known as *sayyed* ('Master' or 'Lord') and a female is known as *sayyedeh*, and they represent a form of Islamic aristocracy.

Our family is part of this group and my father is designated 'Sayyed Jalal' rather than merely 'Jalal' on any of his ID. But, being a sceptic, he refused to use the title when registering my name. It wasn't even an Iranian title, he was quick to point out, but an Arab one.

Khomeini was a *sayyed* and this lineage nourished the prophecy-stricken minds of the public who had been waiting for more than a thousand years for a son of the Prophet to come forth and shake the pillars of earthly tyranny. Not surprisingly, and unlike Dad, being a *sayyedeh* meant a lot to Madar. The title confers a certain authority and people would, by and large, trust those who bore it. She believed that as true carriers of the Prophet's blood as well as Ali's, we had a responsibility to be there for our people, to care for them and to help them when they were in need.

Many years later, after the extraordinary success of Dan Brown's *The Da Vinci Code*, my wife Maryam asked me to tell her the story; she didn't have time to read it herself. I explained that the author claimed that Jesus Christ had not been celibate; that he had fathered a child, whose bloodline still existed and that the mythical Holy Grail represented this bloodline. Maryam laughed and said, 'Really? That's what it's all about? He's simply introducing the concept of *sayyed* into Christianity! That too at the beginning of the twenty-first century when even we have begun to rid ourselves of these superstitions!'

The *sayyeds* were granted the right to use a green shawl or hat as a mark of their unique lineage, green being the colour of the Prophet's family. It was the colour Mir-Hussein Mousavi, also a *sayyed* and one of the supposedly 'unsuccessful' candidates at the 2009 presidential election, chose for his campaign. Rapidly taken up by his followers, it turned into a symbol of the protest that rose up against the electoral fraud and which was later transformed into a general call for democracy. According to Shiite believers, green reflects the true nature of Islam—peace and prosperity—and thus was chosen as the symbol of this concept 1,400 years before the foundation of Greenpeace, dedicated to environmental activism.

The only exception to this 'wearing of the green' was among the mullahs: mullahs who were *sayyeds* used a black turban to distinguish themselves from the others who wore white.

This was how Madar began my initiation into the Shiite faith through the stifling heat of that long journey across the endless desert. But it helped to take my mind off the mirage of a distant sea on the horizon that constantly appeared and disappeared. We passed a large whiteness in the desert which Madar told me was the Salt Lake, a small lake surrounded by a thick layer of salt left from Tethys, the ocean that had covered Iran around 90 million years ago. This white field and the frequent '*Salawats*' of the passengers were to be our only distractions on the road; hence my attentiveness to Madar's stories on the way.

After two hours of that brutal journey, a change in the scenery was greeted by joyous shouts and incessant '*Salawats*': the Golden Dome had appeared on the horizon, a tangible replacement for the recurrent illusion of the sea. This, I realized, was the highlight of the pilgrimage: the travellers had endured the heat, the boredom, the bumpy road and the alarming noises of the coach's engine just for this glimpse of the Golden Dome of Holy Masoumah. We had arrived!

A few years later, when the motorway between Tehran and Qom was opened, the journey became much shorter and easier, especially as the coaches and cars were now air-conditioned and there were more service stops on the way. But this modernization seemed to take away the magic of that first glimpse of the Golden Dome long before one actually arrived at Qom. Today, Qom has become a large city; even when you stand in the heart of town, you have to search for signs of the holy shrine and its golden dome.

Madar lived in a room rented from an old lady who had a house with a small garden. The old lady lived alone and each evening one of her many children would pay her a visit. She had let out the room to Madar for a very low rent in return for her company. The house was only five minutes from the Haram or shrine of Holy Masoumah; so after lunch and an afternoon nap the first thing we did was set off on a visit.

Holy Masoumah was the sister of the eighth Shia Imam, Imam Reza, one of the most respected Imams who is now buried in Mashad in eastern Iran. She began her long journey from

Medina in the Arabian peninsula to her brother in Mashhad but fell ill on the way and died in Qom in AD 816 when she was only 18 and still a virgin. Her tomb became one of the most venerated pilgrimage sites for the Shiites and one of the most prestigious religious schools was founded in Qom in her honour, turning it into one of the most important religious centres in the Shia world alongside Najaf and Karbala in Iraq.

It was a long time before I fully understood her importance; it seemed to me that she had done nothing special to deserve such veneration. But many years later, during my studies of Iranian mythology, I finally understood. 'Masoumah' in Arabic can be translated as 'the Immaculate One', just like the name of the ancient Iranian goddess Anahita, an idea that may have lent itself to the concept of the Immaculate Conception. Anahita was the goddess of water—springs, rivers and seas—and associated with fertility, healing and wisdom. The peoples of the deserts and wastelands, who were particularly devoted to her, built shrines to encourage her to bless their lands with water. Legend has it that Qom once held a shrine to Anahita; it was rededicated to and renamed in honour of Masoumah to prevent the Arab conquerors from destroying the shrine or banning worship there. This was only one of the many Islamic masks that the Iranians put on their ancient traditions and holy places to prevent their destruction by the Arabs who sought to demolish every remnant of the pre-Islamic civilization of Iran. In South Tehran, for example, an Anahita temple atop a mountain was renamed 'Mount of Bibi Shahrbanoo', Imam Hussein's wife, and the tomb of the Iranian Emperor Cyrus the Great in Pasargad was renamed 'Tomb of Prophet Solomon's Mother'.

None of this was of the slightest interest or concern to those zealous believers who went every evening to visit the shrine and to pay their respects to Holy Masoumah, including Madar.

There were hundreds of people there, perhaps even more than a thousand, preparing for the month of fasting by asking the saint to purify their souls and intercede on their behalf with God so that He would accept them in the month of his feasts, which was what Ramadan was usually called: the Feast of God. I, however, could never understand why people were not allowed to eat or drink anything during God's feast.

Almost half the crowd comprised clerics or students at the religious school of Qom on their way to becoming mullahs. I was hoping to see Imam Khomeini there but Madar disappointed me by saying that he had more important things to do at the moment. However, another Grand Ayatollah was present and people were waiting in queues for a chance to kiss his hand. (It was Ayatollah Shariatmadari, whose rank among the Shiite clergy was by no means lower than Khomeini's.) I, too, joined the queue for the privilege of kissing his hand, for privilege it seemed to me then. He was one of the clergy who, in 1963, declared Khomeini a Grand Ayatollah to prevent the Shah from executing him: the judiciary did not have the authority to execute, or even imprison, a Grand Ayatollah.

When it was my turn to kiss the old man's hand, I felt just a little disappointed. I had expected a personality with eyes as piercing as those of Imam Khomeini. But this was just an old man, sitting there with his hand extended, indifferent to the kisses bestowed upon it by the people. I bent and kissed his hand and walked away towards Madar who was waiting for me, both excited and envious for women were not allowed this show of affection. How could I have known that Ayatollah Shariatmadari was now one of the most prominent critics of Khomeini? That he claimed Khomeini's idea on the Rule of the Jurisprudent to be completely against Shiite ideology? In three years' time, he would be arrested, beaten and dismissed from his rank of Grand

Ayatollah on the orders of the very man to whom he had given the title 15 years earlier. He died while still under house arrest in 1986.

Madar took me inside the shrine. It was a huge building with three gigantic prayer halls, in the centre of which stood the burial chamber, confined in a golden cage. An opening above the cage allowed people to throw in money, offerings to ensure an answer to their prayers. It was almost sunset and everyone was waiting for the sound of the azan, the call to prayer.

Although I am not a religious person, the sound of the azan has always fascinated me. There I was, standing in the middle of the huge courtyard, watching people doing the wuzu—the Islamic pre-prayer ablutions—when thousands of white doves landed on the golden dome of the shrine and turned it white. The sun had disappeared; the sky had turned crimson and flung red and yellow shadows on the scattered clouds when the first words of the azan suddenly echoed in the air, inviting people to collective prayer: '*Allah-o Akbar, La Ilah a Illallah.*'

Madar stood among the women and said her prayers. I didn't know how to pray, so I stood a little way off, near the pool, watching the birds.

Praying was another thing I was going to learn during my stay in Qom.

Meeting Imam Khomeini had been my only reason for coming to Qom with Madar and I kept asking her about it. 'We have to wait for Mustafa, the landlady's son, to show up first,' she said. He was a volunteer who had joined the newly founded Revolutionary Guard and had many friends in Khomeini's household. While we waited for his visit, Madar and the old lady took on the task of my Islamic training, of which praying and fasting were the most difficult aspects. Praying involved my memorizing a lot of Arabic words that meant nothing to me despite Madar's efforts at explaining. I wondered why we had to pray in Arabic and not in Persian; if God knew everything, surely he must know all the languages. But Madar explained that Islam was not an individual religion; it was a religion that united mankind, and prayers, especially collective prayers, were a symbol of this unity in which no race or colour enjoyed any advantage. Muslims have to pray to God in a common language and, as Allah had spoken to his Prophet in Arabic, Muslims offered their prayers in that language. So in Mecca, when millions of people from around the world join in prayer, they all pray in the same language: a remarkable demonstration of unity. Years later, I realized that Muslims, despite their common language of prayer, are far from being unified. Exactly a year after this trip to Qom, Iraq attacked Iran and the two Muslim nations slaughtered one another for eight years, both in the name of Islam.

The fasting aspect was more challenging, although the rules were simpler: don't eat or drink anything; don't tell any lies; don't swear; and don't hurt anyone between sunrise and sunset. Not swearing and not lying were easy but not eating or drinking for 15 hours for a nine-year-old stuck in the summer heat of that desert city was an entirely different matter. I was therefore allowed to practice 'Sparrow-head Fasting'. I would fast from sunrise till noon; then I would have lunch and fast again till the evening. A gentler version of the adult fast, this is designed to encourage children to participate in the fasting month. For me, even this was a serious challenge.

We were not supposed to tell lies or swear during the month of fasting; were we then allowed, I asked Madar, to do so during the rest of the year? She smiled and replied that human beings are creatures led by the twin drives of anger and self-protection. Swearing is a natural way of releasing anger, and lying is an instinctive attempt at self-defence. However, these instincts belong to the lower regions of the human soul and we have to learn to overcome them through this month of spiritual discipline.

As I had nothing else to do, I learnt how to pray and began to practise my fasting skills.

The big day finally arrived. After talking to one of the guards at Khomeini's residence, Mustafa took me there on his motorcycle. Every afternoon, the Imam opened the door of his house to visitors even though not all of them could be admitted for the house was small. The guard took me in through the back door and before I knew what was happening I found myself in a corridor, standing in front of a tall old man in a white gown and a black turban.

'Where are you running to, young man?' he asked, putting his hand on my shoulder.

'I want to see . . .' I held my breath as soon as I looked up and saw those two black eyes under the two thick eyebrows and that white beard, so much like Santa Claus. I was silent for a few seconds, and it was only his encouraging smile that helped me continue.

'I . . . I wanted to see you, Imam.'

He chuckled and patted my cheek.

'So you have, son. What important matter brings you to me?'

I had none. All I could come up with was, 'I want sugar cubes . . . for Dad.'

Everyone laughed at my answer, while the Imam nodded to the young man beside him who went off somewhere. The sugar was Madar's idea. According to her, Dad did not observe his duties as a Muslim: he did not pray nor did he fast; hence, the only thing that could absolve him would be eating something blessed by the vicar of the Hidden Imam.

'What is your name, son?'

'Arash, sir.'

'And your father's name?'

'His name is Jalal, sir.'

'Master Jalal, you are not supposed to disrespect your father's name.'

The young man returned with a handful of sugar cubes. Imam took them in his hands, put his hands in front of his mouth and uttered a prayer and a blessing. Then he put the cubes in my hand and asked, 'Is that all, Master Arash?'

I bent to kiss his hand but he responded in a manner quite different from Ayatollah Shariatmadari: he withdrew his hand, bent over me and kissed my forehead.

'You never bow to anyone other than Allah, of whom I am only a humble servant,' he whispered in my ear. His gaze was overwhelming. A blazing intelligence mixed with a kindness and a seriousness that made it impossible for anyone to hold his gaze for more than a few seconds. Caressing my face, he moved towards the crowds waiting in the courtyard for a glimpse. 'Send my greetings to your father, Master Arash,' he said as he left.

And that was it. I never got the chance to tell him that I had lost my friend to the Revolution. I wanted him to pray for her, I wanted to make sure that she became an angel. That was my main reason for wanting to see him. Despite not a word on the matter, something in his eyes assured me that Azadeh was happy.

Summer was over sooner than I thought. At the school enrolment we were told that girls and boys were no longer allowed to go to the same schools; since my school had been chosen as a school for girls, my parents had to find a boys' school for my third grade. Mum began her undergraduate nursing course and was very excited about the dawn of a new phase in her life. Dad had become Dean, Faculty of Metallurgy, University of Science and Technology, and Uncle Mohammed, my mother's brother, back from Paris after completing his PhD in Sociology, was employed at the Sociology Research Centre at National TV. Despite being forced to change my school, everything still seemed all right. I didn't really care about having no female classmates; I would have more fun with the boys. The girls would only remind me of Azadeh.

However, after a while, not having any female classmates felt strange. We no longer competed for the girls' attention and the rate of cursing, swearing and bad language steadily increased. It was then that I learnt about sex and I couldn't believe my ears until I asked Dad what 'fuck' meant and why anyone would want to fuck his friend's mum. Dad was forced to give me 'the talk' much earlier than he had planned.

We were given new schoolbooks with the picture of Imam Khomeini on the first page. Every morning we stood in line in the yard while someone recited a few verses from the Quran and then we had to listen to the new National Anthem:

*The Islamic Republic has been established,*
*To give us both religion and this world.*
*Because of the Iranian Revolution,*
*The palace of oppression has been destroyed.*
*The image of our future is the picture of our Imam*
*Our everlasting force is our faith and unity*
*God's hand is helping us,*
*And in this battle He is our guide.*
*In the shadow of the Quran,*
*Let Iran stand forever.*

It would be many years before it was replaced by something a little more meaningful.

Nothing had really changed in our lives other than what we were taught each day at school: to love Khomeini, which I didn't mind since I loved him anyway; the atrocities of the Shah's regime, which I already knew about; and training in Islam, which I was already receiving in good measure from both Madar and Hadj-Agha. But Dad was already beginning to worry. Other than classical music and revolutionary songs, music was banned under the Sharia. Films, when they were shown again at the cinemas and on TV, were censored. Most of what we saw on TV was either revolutionary films such as *Z* and *State of Siege*, or from the Second-World-War era about Yugoslavian partisans fighting the Nazis, or Russian black-and-white films such as *How the Steel Was Tempered*. More and more women began to wear headscarves or chadors—although it wasn't compulsory yet—and more and more men displayed short beards, thus conforming to the Islamic prohibition on shaving facial hair.

Aunt Marjaneh, a graduate in political science, had been employed by the Ministry of Education and appointed the headmistress of a small elementary school in an extremely poor district in South Tehran. She was very happy with her post because it gave her an opportunity to educate and help some of the city's poorest children. She had always dreamt of following in the footsteps of her role model, Samad Behrangi, a teacher and children's writer who had drowned in the river Aras 10 years ago. It was a mysterious death that most of the opposition groups attributed to the Shah's secret service.

It was Aunt Marjaneh who took charge of educating me in the concepts of justice and equality. She wasn't a communist but she had considerable respect for its ideas, especially the need to provide equal opportunity. She was always encouraging me to read Samad's stories, the most important of which was *The Little Black Fish*. A little fish lived with his family in a small stream but wanted to know about the world beyond. He decided to leave the dirty stream in search of the sea, about which he had heard from a travelling fish. When he finally reached the sea, he fought the dreaded Pelican and ultimately sacrificed his life to free the other fish from the terror of that predator. I remember crying for nights when I first read it; Mum had to ask Aunt Marjaneh not to recommend any more stories to me. But neither Marjaneh nor I cared and she continued to initiate me in the world of stories without happy endings—the life of Che Guevara, of Martin Luther King and of the Iranians who had been assassinated by the Shah's regime. She believed I needed to grow up strong in order to survive in a cruel world. I believe she was right— although I still preferred the fairy tales with their happy endings.

Her position as headmistress would give her the power to put some of her ideas into practice; at least, that was what she thought at the beginning. Every once in a while she took me to her school where I made friends with the boys even though we were from completely different worlds. They were from poor and uneducated families, the sort of people I couldn't and wouldn't have known if it weren't for Aunt Marjaneh. She tried hard in the local department of the Ministry of Education to raise enough funds to buy new clothes for her pupils before New Year's Eve, and added extra classes for them dedicated to reading and discussing books. On one occasion, accompanied by the 'Tutor of Islamic Manners', a new post in the school created after the Revolution to ensure that children received proper instruction on Islamic good manners, she took me to the homes of a few of her students to hand out the new clothes she had succeeded in buying for them. Seeing the smiles on the faces of those children and their families in those modest little flats gave me enormous pleasure. Aunt Marjaneh was doing her best to teach me that I didn't need to be rich to be happy. Whenever I craved something, the memory of the sparkle in their eyes brought me down to earth.

But Aunt Marjaneh didn't really succeed in her efforts. A year later, the parents of one of her pupils complained about her to the Ministry of Education, claiming that she was trying to corrupt their child's mind with communist ideas while teaching them things that they didn't need to know. She was soon demoted to teaching Arabic and, two years later, was relegated to administrative work with no direct contact with the children. She became seriously depressed and some time later, on the spur of the moment, she resigned from all her responsibilities and left Iran for Germany with her husband and young son. Other than very short visits to the family, she never returned to Iran.

The combination of her teachings and my Islamic training turned me into a fanatic. I began to pray three times a day, trying to hide it from Dad who I believed was opposed to my new and consuming interest in Islam. I refused to sleep in my comfortable bed and preferred the bare floor without a pillow or a mattress on the grounds that there were millions of people who couldn't afford a comfortable bed and I wanted to show my solidarity with them. I ate only as much as I needed and refused to eat anything delicious lest I be led astray by the pleasures of this world . . . I was only nine years old.

But it wasn't easy to deceive Dad. Once, while I was praying, he opened the door to my room. I couldn't interrupt my prayer; it is a cardinal sin to do so unless it is a matter of life and death. Dad said nothing and quietly closed the door. When I finished praying, I didn't dare walk out of my room; I didn't want to face Dad who, I believed, would receive me with 'the look'. After a while, however, he knocked on the door and entered my room with a smile.

'I'm sorry I entered your room without knocking. If you want to pray Arash, pray,' he chuckled. 'It's your decision. Don't be afraid. I've always taught you to be a free man. You are free to choose what you want to believe in.' He knew that my fervour wouldn't last long but he did begin to pay me more attention. It was then that we set off on our book-hunting quests.

If you go to Enghelab Street in front of the University of Tehran, you will be overwhelmed by the smell of books. About 200 bookshops stand side by side, a heaven for book-lovers. There are all kinds of bookshops: specialist, academic, trade or children's. But, quite literally, all you see as you leave the university are books. It's hard to walk in Enghelab Street and not buy a book; or, at least, to not spend a good deal of time browsing.

This was where Dad took me once every month. I was given a certain budget to buy whichever books I liked, provided that I read them before our next visit. Of course, 'whichever books' is a little exaggerated, for Dad had a huge influence on my choices. I was introduced to the classics of world literature: Leo Tolstoy, John Steinbeck, Anton Chekhov, Alexandre Dumas, Jules Verne, Mark Twain, Robert Louis Stevenson and more. We also bought books by Iranian authors such as Sadeq Chouback and Bahram Sadeqi, although, because of the bitterness of their content, Dad preferred that I begin by reading the world classics.

I was fascinated by Enghelab Street. This was the wellspring of democracy. Thousands of people walked on the pavements and discussed current affairs as they browsed. On the other side of the pavement, facing the row of bookshops, stood the stalls of the second-hand book dealers who also sold alternative 'white-cover' books, books by communist authors and not published by mainstream publishing houses. In-between the stalls stood the newspaper sellers, each with their particular titles. Hundreds of papers and news-sheets were published at that time, each with a specific political affiliation: Islamic, nationalist, liberal and a wide range of leftists, and each with slightly different approaches—Marxist Islamist, Leninist, Trotskyite, Maoist, etc. And everyone stood around passionately debating the latest issues, defending their ideologies and propounding their views on the best ways of governing the country.

I looked forward to our monthly visits to Enghelab Street and, in-between them, fervently read everything I could. My introduction to world literature was Dad's way of preventing me from becoming a dogmatist, which was what happened to most of the children who received only the Islamic training that dominated school curricula. On the other hand, Madar and Hadj-Agha bombarded me with religious books containing the stories of Adam and Eve, Noah, Abraham, Moses, Jesus, Muhammad and the 12 Imams. It was as if there were an unspoken competition between Dad and Aunt Marjaneh on one side and Madar and Hadj-Agha on the other for my attention. However, I didn't think about these things at the time. I just enjoyed reading and became addicted to books.

The scenes I saw in Enghelab Street in 1979 were actually the dying breaths of a newborn democracy that was soon to be suffocated by the smoke of a fiery tyranny whose flames had just appeared on the horizon. There was nothing tangible to support these anxieties. Khomeini in Qom acted as the spiritual Father of the Nation and pretended he wasn't interfering directly in politics. Bazargan, the liberal-nationalist prime minister was trying to prevent the fundamentalists from taking over the government and to open the doors to negotiation with the US and other Western countries. Various political groups and parties were jostling for seats in the first Islamic Consultative Assembly, or Parliament, and a fundamentalist Islamic terrorist group which had assassinated a few prominent political and religious figures after the Revolution was quelled and its leaders tried and executed. Nevertheless, everything seemed to promise a golden age of democracy and liberty.

Nothing could be farther from the truth.

Every child in every corner of the world knows about limits. Parents would be at a loss without limits. The moment children begin to talk, sometimes even before that, parents make sure they know what they must *not* do: must not swear, must not speak with your mouth full, must not pee in your pants, must not hurt other children or animals, must not be rude to your parents, must not watch TV if you have homework, must not stay up after bedtime, etc. And children must, by their very nature, keep pushing at these limits. This constant tussle over boundaries between parents and children is part of what psychologists call 'growing up'.

Like any other child, I knew there were things that I wasn't supposed to do but in the autumn of 1979 I faced a whole new pedagogic phenomenon: what we couldn't do didn't bother me any more; it was what we *could* do that I was desperately eager to find out. And it wasn't only us, the children, who had to worry about pushing the limits. For the first time, our parents and teachers were all in the same boat.

The Revolution had revealed a whole new aspect of prohibition. Regardless of people's age, as 1979 drew to its close, almost everything was prohibited: contact between the sexes; dancing; laughing loudly; eating pork or drinking alcohol; keeping dogs; wearing short-sleeved shirts, T-shirts or shorts; listening to music; enjoying American films; watching superhero cartoons; Walt Disney; singing; partying; listening to foreign radio stations; going to the beach with the family; playing cards or chess or backgammon; wearing a tie; shaving your beard; showing any part of the body other than your hands and face, wearing make-up or smoking (for women); criticizing government figures; following any religion other than Islam, Judaism, Christianity and Zoroastrianism; converting from Islam; saying that America was not the Great Satan; not hating Israel; not cursing the royal family; not shouting three '*Salawats*' whenever we heard the name of Khomeini . . .

And it wasn't a matter of choice. People could be punished for what they did or did not do. The vigilante committees formed after the Revolution were now responsible, instead of the old official police force, for making sure that people acted in accordance with 'good Islamic manners'. They took over the streets after 9 p.m. and checked cars at crossroads and squares. They searched the boot to make sure it carried nothing suspicious, be it weapons or alcohol. Sometimes, especially if the driver wore a tie, he was asked to exhale directly into their faces—to check whether or not he had been drinking. Before the Revolution, before the prohibition on alcohol, no one indulged in drinking and driving. But in an ironic turn of events, ever since the Revolution, Iran has been one of the few countries where people continue to drink and drive. Alcohol is illegal anyway and using public transport when you smell of drink is even more dangerous than driving a car in that condition. You may just get away with the latter but certainly not with the former.

People began to fight back, of course, and combated the terrors of the night guards with a unique and unbeatable weapon: the cucumber. Cucumbers became the most important evening accessory for those who had been drinking. As soon as a driver saw the beams from the guards' torches waving down his car, he and his friends would wolf down a cucumber in an attempt to hide the telltale smell. Another popular weapon was garlic. Iran must be the only place, outside of vampire legends, where garlic has been used as a weapon against evil. Well, peppermint sprays were not yet available in the Iranian market—and nor was the breathalyser.

Wearing ties was not as strictly prohibited but it was seriously frowned upon. Imam Khomeini, assuming that the tie was something Western, had dismissed it as a 'collar and chain', 'the symbol of our enslavement to imperialist cultures'.

Painting human figures and sculpting were also frowned upon. These forms of artistic expression were considered attempts at imitating God the Creator as well as an unwanted reminder of the pagan tradition of idol worship. Music was considered sacriligeous because the pleasure it provided its listeners was capable of making them forget the real ecstasy achieved through prayer. But it soon got rather complicated. Every revolution relies firmly on its symbols and most of these are the result of some form of artistic expression; hence, the authorities needed to draw a line between what art was good and what was evil: what was allowed and what was not. All music other than revolutionary songs and traditional Iranian music was banned; solo female voices were absolutely taboo. Every form of painting was considered evil unless it portrayed Imam Khomeini or a revolutionary or religious scene.

We were in school until midday, after which I went home, had a nap and then began my homework, which, even at the elementary school level, seemed overwhelming. The children's programmes on TV would begin at 5 p.m. and I had to struggle to finish my homework in time.

Feature programmes were broadcast only between 4 and 10 p.m. There would be a recitation from the Quran between 4 and 4.30, after which would begin *Missing Persons*. I couldn't go out. I was alone at home and had usually finished my homework. I had even found time to read a few more pages of my book. By the time *Missing Persons* began, I was bored to death, impatiently waiting for the children's shows. *Missing Persons* had the simplest structure in the world: a photo of a missing person appeared on the screen and the narrator gave a brief description about him or her: the date of disappearance; the age of the person; and whom to call if anyone knew their whereabouts. Initially indifferent to it, in time I devised an entertainment out of the show. Looking at the missing persons' photos while listening to their details, I would try to imagine what might have happened to them. In my mind they had all run away from home to see the world. They were wandering aimlessly, bent under the weight of their rucksacks, or were tracing the path along some mysterious map at one end of which lay treasure. A series of extraordinary events and fantastic creatures. That was how I killed time, and most of the novels and stories I wrote years later grew out of those imaginings.

At last the children's shows would begin. They were meant to last for an hour but two-thirds of that hour was devoted to instructions in good Islamic manners or to the greatness of the Revolution and Imam Khomeini. These were interspersed with some short animated films, the most memorable being a Polish one about a dog looking for its bone, and another about two brothers quarrelling all the time until they were taught to share their belongings.

When the children's show came to an end, there was nothing left to watch on TV: a mullah would appear and speak for hours on religious matters. In any case, my parents would have come by then and we could play a board game while they waited for *News Hour* to begin, the signal for us children to go to bed.

It was the most boring life imaginable, and it seemed as if the days would never end. But events outside our home were not so boring. Things were changing. Despite Bazargan's efforts to rebuild the bridge between Iran and the US, Khomeini's anti-US remarks were continually fuelling the tension. On 4 November 1979, around 500 students who called themselves the 'Muslim Student Followers of the Imam's Line', attacked the US Embassy and took 53 US diplomats hostage. Despite Bazargan's efforts at persuading Khomeini to release them, Khomeini issued a statement supporting the takeover of the US Embassy: he called it 'the second revolution' and claimed that the Embassy was 'a den of spies'. Bazargan resigned and sanctions were imposed against Iran for the first time.

Most of these students later became prominent political figures in Iran. They became the main supporters of Muhammad Khatami's call for reform in 1999, and most of them are now in prison or in exile.

The grown-ups talked about nothing but the first presidential election of 1980. We children, too, had finally found something to be excited about: something new was happening in a society rendered dead and silent after the occupation of the US Embassy. There were 10 candidates from different political groups. Masoud Rajavi was the only person whose candidacy was not approved. Leader of the People's Mujahideen Organization, an extremely popular group especially among the young, he was disapproved of because he hadn't voted for the Constitution of the Islamic Republic. That was interpreted as possible disloyalty to the regime.

Looking back at those days I see them filled with a sense of unreality. Of the candidates on the first presidential list, seven suffered gruesome fates only a few years later: Bani-Sadr, Madani and Mokri fled Iran and chose exile; Forouhar, Sami and Ayat were assassinated; Ghotbzadeh was executed.

Everyone was aware that Khomeini supported Abolhasan Bani-Sadr against the will of the Islamic Republic Party led by Muhammad Beheshti, Hashemi Rafsanjani, Ali Khamenei and Mir-Hussein Mousavi. Bani-Sadr was a nationalist Islamist and a close friend of Khomeini in Paris. Khomeini never supported him publicly but his support was undeniable. That was why, although no one really knew him, Bani-Sadr won the election with 76 per cent of the votes. He made it his job to attempt to reconcile different groups and parties and he tried to prevent the regime from becoming a religious fundamentalist one. He tried to control the Revolutionary Guard, the Committees and the Revolutionary Court, and to restore the professional army, police force and the judiciary. But his efforts only succeeded in precipitating what he most feared.

It was the beginning of a new era in Iran, one in which Iran was to make more enemies than friends, and any hopes for a real democracy were to vanish into a distant future. The sequence of events put an end to all hopes of reconciliation between Iran and the US. It also put an end to Khomeini's alleged detachment from politics. Shortly after the presidential election, on the pretext of a heart attack, Khomeini returned from Qom to Tehran because of 'the proximity of better medical facilities' but, as events proved over the next few months, it was to take over the country and get rid of any opposition standing in the way of his vision of an ideal Islamic society. And the first step in this direction was the war he launched against one of Iran's most important national traditions: the highly un-Islamic Norouz or Iranian New Year celebrations.

The Gregorian calendar used in the West and in many other parts of the world means nothing to the Iranians other than a convenient method of communication with the rest of world. The Iranians have their own solar calendar in which the New Year begins not on1 January but on 21 March, the date of the vernal equinox. The origin of the tradition, which is at least 3,000 years old, is attributed to Iran's mythical King Jamshid. Paradoxically, the inception of the Iranian calendar is determined to be AD 622, the time of Prophet Muhammad's Hegira or Migration from Mecca to Medina, thus making it a blend of Iranian and Arab traditions. Accordingly, 1980 corresponds to the year 1359 in the Iranian solar calendar. The Iranians also recognize the Islamic lunar calendar, which is the point of reference for important religious dates and ceremonies but no one can deny that the most important day in an Iranian's year is Norouz.

There are special traditions for celebrating this day of which the Wednesday Feast or Fireworks Wednesday (Chaharshanbe Suri) is the most important. The Wednesday Feast, a prelude to Norouz, is held on the last Tuesday night of the solar year. People are supposed to cleanse their souls by leaping over a fire, chanting, 'Let your fiery redness be mine and my yellow paleness be yours.' This passage through fire, the only element that cannot be polluted, is believed to burn away all the evil in them so that they may enter the New Year with their souls purified.

Another part of the ritual involves people, especially children, knocking on their neighbours' doors with white blankets draped over their heads. Those who open the doors are supposed to hand out a special mixture of nuts traditionally known as 'problem-solver nuts'. It is believed that eating these nuts will help overcome problems. This tradition is rooted in the Zoroastrian belief that in the last days of the old year, the *farvahars* or guardian spirits return to earth to visit their families. The children draped in blankets symbolize these spirits and the giving of the nuts is a sign of both respect and hospitality. Since time immemorial, Iranians have celebrated the Wednesday Feast by lighting fires in the alleys and in the fields and setting off fireworks. For children and young people it is the most joyful day in the year after Norouz itself.

Norouz begins precisely at the time of the vernal equinox, when the sun enters Aries—the beginning of spring in the Northern Hemisphere. Unlike the fixed date of the Christian New Year, the beginning of the Iranian year varies with the date of the equinox. And there are things that must be taken care of before the turn of the year.

All the members of the family sit round a *haft-sin* table, a crucial part of the Eve. On the table must be seven items, all of which begin with the letter '*s*' in their original Persian form: *sabzeh*, sprouting wheat or lentils symbolizing rebirth and greenery; *samanu*, a traditional sweet pudding symbolizing affluence; *senjed*, the dried fruit of the oleaster tree symbolizing love; *sîr* or garlic symbolizing medicine and healing; *sîb*, an apple symbolizing beauty and health; *somaq*, berries from the sumac tree symbolizing the redness of sunrise; *sonbol* or hyacinth symbolizing youth; and *serkeh*, vinegar, symbolizing age and patience. The other items on the table are candles; a goldfish—a recent addition to the table inspired by the Chinese tradition of releasing a goldfish in water on New Year's Eve; the Quran—in pre-Islamic times this would be the *Avesta*, the sacred book of the Zoroastrians; and the collected poems of Hafiz, Iran's national poet.

After the turn of the year, officially announced by the firing of canons, people greet one another with kisses and the children receive gifts or money. Then everyone sets out to visit friends and family. This visiting ceremony continues for 13 days; and on the thirteenth day of the first month of the year, Farvardin, the New Year ceremonies end in Sizdah Be-dar, the day of Getting Rid of Thirteen'. Since 13 is considered unlucky, on the thirteenth day of Farvardin, which often corresponds to 1 April or April Fools' Day in the Western calendar, the day is spent outdoors, picnicking, telling jokes and playing pranks. Many believe that April Fools' Day springs from this more ancient custom.

At the end of the day, people leave the green sprouts in running water, release the goldfish into a lake and return home. Norouz is over and they are now ready to begin the year.

I describe these things in such detail because Norouz is the Iranians' last shred of hope at a time when their own particular identity is under threat of disappearing into a global, undifferentiated homogenized Islamic dogma. Keeping that identity alive is a matter of life and death for them. When the Arabs invaded and occupied Iran, the Muslim Caliphs tried hard to abolish Norouz and replace it with the Islamic Eids or other celebrations. The Iranians absorbed these Eids into their calendar but not at the expense of Norouz; it was never lost and retained its primacy in the calendar as the most important day of the year. This single day symbolizes the coexistence of diverse tendencies embedded at the heart of Iranian society: 3,000 years of a proud history alongside deep-rooted Islamic beliefs. These two elements do not always work well together.

Iran's new Islamic regime, believing in a certain Islamic internationalism, was against any national tradition that could jeopardize the unity of Muslims worldwide and hence did not support Norouz. One of the first things that happened before the first Norouz after the establishment of the Islamic Republic was a series of long speeches by several mullahs and close friends of Khomeini condemning Norouz as 'pagan superstition'; the Wednesday fireworks were also banned a little later. When we heard from our teachers that there would be no fireworks that year, we were furious for the first time since the Revolution. The Wednesday meant a lot to us; it was a night when we got together, had fun, pursued our own little adventures, enjoyed the fireworks, jumped over the fire and celebrated all night. Our decision to ignore this order was almost unanimous and, surprisingly, also backed by our parents' support.

On the last Tuesday of the year, people ignored the ban and went out into the streets to carry on with their ceremonies as usual. However, everyone felt the renewed tension in the air, a tension we had thought was over with the Revolution. Revolutionary Committee vehicles moved through the streets trying to extinguish the fires but as soon as they had moved on we set off new ones. There was no violence but Committee members tried to convince people that this was a pagan tradition and that good Muslims should not follow the ceremonies of the 'fire-worshippers', a name commonly given to the Zoroastrians. These were semi-independent bodies established in the chaotic early months of the Revolution. They were not answerable to the central government and they were armed and dangerous.

No one wanted trouble.

Everyone knew that Chaharshanbe-Suri could never be abandoned. What no one realized was that, for many years to come, this last Tuesday of the year would mark a symbolic opportunity for the Iranians to prove to the fundamentalist regime that they would never forsake their Iranian identity and traditions. They would venerate Chaharshanbe-Suri and Norouz as much as they did Ashura and Ramadan—they had to coexist. Each year, police brutality against the Chaharshanbe-Suri ceremonies increased. The following year the police attacked the boys and girls who were celebrating, thereby inciting the crowds to react violently. Soon the ban on fireworks was flouted through the use of home-made ones that often exploded with disastrous results. Chaharshanbe-Suri, the day of soul-cleansing and joy and charity, turned into a violent and dangerous day when young people were beaten and persecuted by the police on the one hand and endangered by their home-made fireworks on the other. But Chaharshanbe-Suri was never abandoned. In the suffocating fundamentalist atmosphere that was soon to be established, it became the one day in the year when people could shout out how much they missed their joyful celebrations.

The climax of this confrontation occurred in March 2010, when Supreme Leader Ayatollah Khamenei declared that Fireworks Wednesday was against the Sharia; it amounted to 'fire-worship' and he forbade people from going out and celebrating on the streets. Furious with the way he had authorized the use of violence against the Green Movement after the presidential election of 2009, millions of people around the country challenged his authority by lighting fires in the streets.

The government attack on Norouz itself was milder because it had succeeded in locating a quote from Imam Jafar Sadeq in praise of Norouz. But Khomeini tried to downplay its importance in his speech on the first day of the New Year by declaring,

'As long as there is oppression in the world, we have no celebrations.' He failed to make a similar pronouncement on Islamic celebrations, though. They tried to cancel the holiday on the Thirteenth of Farvardin but the people simply ignored their efforts and refused to show up for work. Instead, they went out to the countryside and celebrated their 'Getting Rid of Thirteen', thus forcing the regime to recognize this day; it did so but changed its name to 'Day of Nature' in an attempt to deny its pre-Islamic origins.

The 13 days of Norouz was my only opportunity to meet almost every member of our large family. In the first week, it is the duty of the younger generation to visit its elders; the following week the elders reciprocate. In the spring of 1980 we did everything that the traditions demanded in order to guarantee a fabulous year ahead: we cleansed our souls by fire, we summoned the support of our guardian spirits, we did charitable deeds, we showed our respect to our elders, we sat beside the *haft-sin* table, we killed the Unholy Thirteenth and we released the goldfish and put the green sprouts in water. Nothing could go wrong in the year that had just begun.

We could not have been more wrong.

'Have you not seen what your Lord did to the friends of the elephant?'

We recited the 'Surah Elephant' from the Quran all day at school and heard it repeatedly on the radio and on TV. For those unfamiliar with Quranic lore, it may seem odd that God should really care about punishing the friends of an elephant; those who advocate animal rights might well be offended. But for us it was very significant: the story of the 'friends of the elephant' is to Muslims what the story of David and Goliath is to Jews.

But why was it relevant to that day, 25 April 1980? After all attempts and negotiations to release the 53 American hostages had met with failure, the US military launched a rescue operation. But three out of the eight helicopters in Operation Eagle Claw were caught in a sandstorm in Iran's Tabas Desert and three more were destroyed or left behind because of a refuelling accident, thus leading to the death of eight Americans. Operation Eagle Claw ended with an embarrassing statement by Jimmy Carter which, later, became instrumental in his defeat in the US presidential election.

But, on our side, we were reliving a myth. According to Islamic lore, Abraha, ruler of Yemen, decided to destroy the pilgrimage site of Kaaba in Mecca, the most important city in Arabia—and now in the entire Muslim world—in order to draw the pilgrims to his own magnificent church. Leading an army of 40,000 men on a white elephant, he attacked Mecca and none of the nomadic Arabs could stop him. But just before he entered the city, a cloud of birds called Ababil—more familiar in Iran today as the name of one of the unmanned aerial vehicles—appeared in the sky and began to throw stones at the army of Abraha. It was destroyed within minutes and he was forced to retreat.

The regime announced that the failure of the US Air Force was a repeat of the Mecca incident: Allah had again destroyed the forces of evil attempting to invade the Holy Land. This proved that God was protecting the new Islamic Republic and that Khomeini was, indeed, God's Chosen One. In his speech, he said:

> This stupid operation failed according to God's command. O warrior nation of Iran, you heard about the American military intervention and you also heard Carter's excuses. I have said several times that Carter is ready to do anything to be re-elected; he is prepared to burn the world . . . Carter has not realized what sort of nation he is facing and what doctrine he is challenging.

Khomeini insisted that the sandstorm was a sign of God's support and the nation believed him. I, of course, wondered how the Americans reacted to being called 'friends of the elephant'. However, when the diplomats were finally released seven months later as a result of increasing international pressure and the threats of newly elected US President Ronald Reagan, no one asked if they were to be released without any gains for the regime of Iran. No one wondered what the point of the Ababil was, anyway.

From then on the US became the Great Satan and the Islamic Republic of Iran became the rightful capital of God's sovereignty on earth. It was time to move forward and destroy the last remnants of the empire of evil in Iran and Khomeini launched his campaign with the hijab. Now that it had been demonstrated that he was indeed God's Chosen One, no one dared defy his orders.

It was officially announced that, henceforth, women had to wear a hijab in public workplaces and regulations were designed to define exactly what was meant by correct hijab: hair should be covered; a long, loose coat should be worn to conceal the prominent parts of the female body; and no make-up was to be used. Amazingly, men, even non-religious ones, were the strongest advocates of the hijab movement and many forced their wives to submit to this new law. President Bani-Sadr claimed in a press conference that a certain ray emanating from a woman's hair could prompt lustful thoughts in a man. And the hijab was designed to prevent the pernicious and evil effects of this very ray. It took a year before the law on the hijab was passed; from then on, women were compelled to wear it everywhere.

I was finishing my third grade and I had already made new friends. However, because the sanctions against Iran had caused massive inflation, I couldn't keep up with my friends financially. Inflation didn't have a significant effect on their lives—their parents were entrepreneurs who could simply increase the price of their goods in response to the rate of inflation. My father, on the other hand, was a simple university lecturer whose salary had remained the same for the last two years: Rls 120,000 was worth US$1,700 the year earlier but had now sunk to a mere US$800; and the value of the rial was dropping daily. Two years later, his salary would be worth only US$200. Meanwhile, prices steadily increased and the government was too busy to think about the salary of its employees.

I had to get used to the change in our lifestyle—we could no longer buy anything we wanted. We lived in a smart part of town whose inhabitants were pretty well off but even though the rent was exceptionally low we couldn't afford to live up to the standards of the area. Nor did we dare move out. I realized I couldn't afford to keep in touch with my friends and I busied myself with activities that didn't involve socializing: reading, swimming, experimenting with chemicals or my microscope.

Just before the summer holidays, after Mum had finished her second semester nursing exams, she came home from university with tears in her eyes. Dad tried to console her while they discussed the new situation in whispers. Something was wrong. Determined not to be left out of whatever it was, I asked her what had happened.

Mum explained that the much-anticipated Cultural Revolution had finally begun. At the beginning of the year, Khomeini had declared that the universities must be 'cleansed' from Western, imperial and communist influences. He said that we should not be afraid of the sanctions and military invasions but rather of the pro-West attitudes of the universities. No one believed he meant what he said until, in June 1980, it was declared that students could not go back to the universities for the next academic year. They had to wait until the Cultural Revolution and the 'cleansing' were complete.

'Every time I think I'm finally following my dream, something horrible happens,' Mum told me, sobbing.

'Ever since I've been a child I've wanted to become a doctor. But then I was pulled out of school and forced to marry!' She would never forgive her father for this.

'And when I wanted to begin again, I got pregnant,' she went on though she made sure I wasn't offended.

'I don't mean I didn't want you but I did have to wait a little longer. When I finally managed to begin again it was too late for medicine. And now I can't even study nursing!' she said, and burst into tears again.

'Mum, they might open the universities soon.'

'They won't—they're following the example of the Cultural Revolution in China.'

She was right. She had to wait two years before she could go back. Mum fell into a deep depression from which she emerged only when the Ministry of Education announced that students could apply for jobs as teachers while the universities remained closed. This hope of a new career was the only thing that saved Mum.

To make things worse, on 22 September 1980, the Iraqi army, led by Saddam Hussein and backed by almost every country in the world, attacked Iran by land and air.

Childhood was over.

PART II

*If you want the ultimate pleasure
step on a landmine*

(Autumn 1980–Summer 1988)

*Autumn 1980*

A dog runs to fetch his bone. Suddenly, he freezes. The screen goes blank, and then across it appear a few words in the largest possible typeface accompanied by the threatening voice of the narrator. 'Dear citizens, the sound that you are about to hear is the Red Alarm, meaning that we are being attacked by air. You should turn off the lights and begin moving towards your shelters NOW!' Then the alarm began, deafening and continuous, and our hearts leapt into our mouths. Mum clutched little Golnar, grabbed the torch and began to run towards the stairs. Dad leapt up to turn off the lights while Madar pulled me by the hand towards the cellar, whispering prayers in Arabic. The blasts began before I could reach the stairs; the sound made my knees tremble and slowed my reflexes. It was the anti-aircraft missiles shooting in the air at random to keep away the Iraqi planes. Dad joined us, took my other hand and shouted angrily, 'Be a man, Arash! Your sister needs you downstairs!'

I tried, I tried very hard to overcome the invincible fear within me, I tried hard to be the man Dad expected me to be but I couldn't. I felt like throwing up. I didn't want to die under tons of rubble: I was only 10. I was not supposed to be running for my life: I was supposed to wait and see if the dog finally got his bone.

Once we were in the cellar, the fear was replaced by a sense of expectation. We were in the dark; I couldn't see but I could hear. I heard Dad struggling to light the candles we had been stocking in the cellar since the air raids began. I could hear Madar whispering in Arabic: 'Allah is the protecting guardian of those who believe. He bringeth them out of darkness into light . . .' I could hear Golnar sobbing and Mum trying to catch her breath. Through the thick walls of the cellar I could also hear the muffled sound of the blasts. Above all, I could hear the pounding of my heart.

Dad managed to light the candles and turn on his radio. We listened to military marches while we waited for the threat to pass. The war was not 'cool', not like those films which hailed it as an opportunity for the valiant to prove themselves and which always ended with the death of the bad guys. I wasn't feeling valiant at all. My knees wouldn't stop trembling.

Dad decided to distract us with a game, a traditional one. The first person recites a verse from a Persian poet and the second has to recite another that begins with the last letter of the previous one.

Dad: 'I wish there was a place for me to unload / Or a final ending to this longest road' (Khayyam).

Mum: 'Dead is whoever does not live by love / Bury him by my command even if he breathes' (Hafiz)

I: 'Seek no kindness of those full of hate / People of the mosque with the church debate' (Hafiz).

This took my mind off the crisis but it didn't help four-year-old Golnar; she did't know any poetry and found it hard to stop crying.

Finally, after what seemed an age, the narrator's voice interrupted the military marches on the radio. 'Dear citizens, we are happy to announce that the threat has passed and the sound you are about to hear is the White Alarm. You can now leave your shelters and return to your habitations.' We heaved a sigh of relief. We would live another night.

The Iranian Army was considerably weakened and most of its experienced commanders had been executed. Hence, Saddam Hussein considered this an opportune moment to attack Iran and seize control of the Persian Gulf. Casting aside the 1975 agreement between Iran and Iraq that had ended the war between them and resolved their border disputes, he declared war. Announcing that the Iraqi army would reach Tehran in three days, he launched a full-scale attack. Iran, caught by surprise, couldn't react quickly enough and several cities in the southwest were captured, most notably Khorramshahr, one of the most strategic sites in the war.

Khomeini retaliated by appointing Bani-Sadr as his Commander-in-Chief and declaring that there was no shortage of manpower in Iran. The people were asked to join the Basij and fight against the invaders: 'A country that has 20 million young people has 20 million soldiers.' This was the beginning of the institutionalization of the Basij, an army of volunteer militiamen formed a year ago.

Hundreds of thousands enrolled; after two weeks of training, they were sent to the front to stop the Iraqi advance. Although the newly formed Basij and the Revolutionary Guards had very little training, they surprised Saddam Hussein with their courage. Thousands of them died in the first weeks, fighting heavily armed Iraqis with their bare hands, among them a 13-year-old boy who tied several grenades to his body and ran under a tank as it rolled into the city. The tank exploded and blocked the way for other tanks for a while. It was then that Khomeini called upon the nation to follow the young martyr's example. 'Our leader is this 13-year-old child who, with his little heart that is worth more than hundreds of tongues and pens, threw himself with his grenades under the tank of the enemy and destroyed it, and drank from the chalice of martyrdom.'

Suddenly, disputes over the structure of the government faded away as the war took over the nation. Saddam didn't expect such a firm resistance and the war that was expected to last only three days turned into eight bitter years of incessant fighting and destroyed the resources of both countries.

The bombing of the cities; news of the front dominating all conversation; teachers continually emphasizing the greatness of our soldiers' sacrifice and the importance of our support; the military marches played on TV all day; pleas for donations for the soldiers; buses and trucks rushing through the streets, collecting offerings from the people and ferrying volunteer soldiers to the front; the government's increasing pressure on women to wear the hijab; trying to understand how to divide a three-figure number by a two-figure one in class; my classmates discussing the latest films they had watched on their Betamax video players; listening to them and yearning for a time when we could have one as well; Mum beginning to teach the fifth grade in a school in North Tehran . . . that was my life in 1980.

And then it happened. The Cultural Revolution wasn't over for us. The expulsion of university lecturers and professors had begun and Dad, Dean of Faculty and Senior Lecturer, was clearly not an advocate of the Islamic government.

Once again, it was a while before I understood the cause for the new tension at home. Some of it I overheard as Dad discussed the situation with his friend Hormoz, another lecturer at the Iran University of Science and Technology. The most painful part was that they were being tried by their students, now turned into Islamic hardliners. Actively involved in these trials and bearing witness to the 'un-Islamic tendencies' of the lecturers was a young man whose name may now ring a few bells. He had charted his course and nothing was to get in the way. Twenty years later, he would be one of the most talked-about political figures in the world: Mahmoud Ahmadinejad.

I didn't know him at the time but I knew his supervisor, Hamid Behbahani, who was Dad's colleague and friend. A senior lecturer in Transport and Traffic, he went on to become Minister of Transport in Ahmadinejad's cabinet. He seemed a decent enough man at the time, and not an Islamist at all. He had just completed his PhD in the US and, unlike the pro-Khomeini lecturers, he shaved and wore a tie. As soon as the Cultural Revolution began, however, he changed. He decided to follow the rightful objectives of the Islamic Revolution, claiming to be repenting his sinful past. Apparently, his repentance bore fruit: he moved up the political ladder fairly swiftly and, eventually, became a minister. Ironically, he seems to have been a more honest person during his 'sinful past'. He was accused of plagiarism in 2009 after one of his papers was published in an international journal. Naturally, this caused a scandal in academic circles. Though Behbahani always remained respectful towards Dad, it was obvious when he was questioned that their friendship was over.

The trials were ruthless and handed out a variety of sentences. Some of the professors and lecturers were expelled without any chance of appeal; others were demoted; yet others acquitted. Hormoz was expelled because of his ties with the Tudeh Communist Party. But Dad's case was more complicated. Everyone knew him as a sceptic but no one could prove his ties with any communist, monarchist or pro-Western front. Then, one of his students stepped in to testify that he was a communist. The jury was told that Dr Hejazi had said in one of his classes that engineers had to think not only about the economic justifications of their decisions but also about the impact of their efforts on society. This, according to the student, amounted to communism. And the judge agreed. Right through the trials Dad never hesitated to defend democracy and his liberal ideas but he never accepted the accusation of being a communist.

The atmosphere in our house was terrible. Dad tried hard to hide his fear of losing the only job he loved but he couldn't control his nerves, couldn't stop grumbling or fussing or shouting at us for the simplest mistakes. Mum spent her time studying the textbooks she had been assigned for her fifth-graders, as she had no background in teaching and teacher texts were unavailable.

Uncle Muhammad, who worked for National TV, was facing a similar ordeal: National TV, too, was undergoing the same 'cleansing' process. Uncle Muhammad had already published several books expounding his socialist ideas. His wife and daughter had left Iran for France a few months earlier but he decided to stay, saying, as he always did: 'A lamp should bring light to the home before it shines elsewhere.'

He stayed with us: he couldn't afford to rent a place while paying for his family in France. Neither could he stay with my grandparents. Hadj-Agha refused to accept him: first, because he had obvious socialist beliefs; and second, because he had married an Armenian Christian woman. Hadj-Agha could never accept having a non-Muslim daughter-in-law.

It was the night before Dad's last trial session, and he had to prepare his final defence. He began to write but he was too devastated to put his thoughts to paper. Under the circumstances, it was extremely difficult to defend the ideals for which he had fought so hard: freedom and democracy. He paced about the living room in a state of great nervous agitation and Golnar and I realized he was best left alone. Mum tried to be there for him but Dad preferred to be on his own. Then he began striding about the house, shouting, swearing and cursing at every single step he had taken for this Revolution, punching the walls, grinding his teeth and holding his head between his hands. I took Golnar to the garden and tried to distract her. By the time Mum called us in, I had managed to convince Golnar that our garden concealed a hidden treasure which we could find if we first drew a map.

When we went inside, Mum and Dad were dressed up, ready to go out.

'Can you take care of your sister until Uncle Muhammad comes?' Mum asked, 'He should be home any minute.'

'Of course,' I answered, a remark that couldn't be further from the truth. I had no idea what to do if the Red Alarm went off.

'Where are you going?' I asked, hesitantly.

'Dad needs to go out. We have to take care of an important matter.'

'Can I come too, Mummy?' asked Golnar.

'No darling,' Mum answered, caressing her hair, 'Children aren't allowed there.'

I turned on the TV. The children's programme was about to begin. I decided to do my homework while I waited, an essay on the life of Iranian villagers near the Caspian Sea where winter would never come and where people worked all day, either fishing or in the rice fields, and where the houses were built on frames that prevented the damp soil from ruining their foundations.

When the children's programme began, I put aside my homework and tried to watch the story of the two brothers fighting over a ball. But I couldn't concentrate. What would happen tomorrow? What was Dad writing in his defence? And *why* did he throw it away? I left Golnar in front of the TV and crept into Dad's office to look for his papers. I heard the door of the house open and then Uncle Muhammad talking to Golnar but I carried on searching. I finally found Dad's papers in the dustbin but they weren't his defence: they were poetry. I knew Dad wrote a poem once in a while but I couldn't understand why he was doing so on such an important night.

I still remember a verse:

*The bodies of our own offspring*
*we are forced to devour.*

When I left the room to greet Uncle Muhammad, he wasn't there.

'Where did Uncle go, Golnar?'

'He left,' she answered, her eyes fixed on the screen. 'To look for Mum and Dad, I think.'

So we were alone again and I was in charge: a 10-year-old boy guarding his sister against all the evils of the world. If there was an air raid I would have to pick her up and run to the cellar. That I could do. But where had everyone gone? What if they didn't return? We knew that Dad may not return at all. Those at the front could be killed, and those in the cities could be arrested. I tried to convince myself that they wouldn't arrest Dad a day before his trial.

Nothing happened, though. Mum and Dad returned after an hour and Uncle Muhammad a little later, holding two gift-wrapped boxes.

'Happy birthday, Golnar!' he shouted as he gave her one of the boxes. Then, as the rest of us stood there, gaping, he handed the other box to me. 'And this is for you Arash, so that you don't feel left out!'

Smiling, Golnar kissed Uncle Muhammad and began to unwrap her present while Mum and Dad continued to look bewildered.

'Why didn't you tell me, Pari?' Uncle asked Mum.

'What didn't I tell you?' she asked, with raised eyebrows.

'That it's Golnar's birthday today!'

'But, it isn't. Not for another six months,' said Dad.

Then it was Uncle's turn to gape in astonishment.

'It isn't? But Golnar said it was!'

Golnar shook her head. 'I didn't say it was my birthday, I said, "I think Mum and Dad have gone to buy me a birthday present!"'

Mum frowned. 'And why would you say that?'

'You said you were going to do something important, and that I wasn't supposed to go with you. That means that you wanted to buy me a present and surprise me.'

Yes, what could be more important than buying Golnar a birthday present six months before her birthday!

Everyone burst out laughing. I hadn't heard genuine laughter in our home for months and this came as such a relief.

We immediately decided to buy a cake from the shop around the corner and celebrate Golnar's four-and-a-half-year birthday. A huge burden seemed to have been lifted from Dad's shoulders; he even brought out some home-made vodka from the cellar. I was, meanwhile, completely immersed in the Persian dictionary—my first—that I had just received from Uncle Muhammad. I think he bought it to stop my incessant questions about the meanings of difficult words and phrases such as 'social reform', 'imperialism', 'sovereignty of the jurisprudent', 'scrutiny' and so on. That dictionary became my bedside companion for many years, satisfying my passion for words.

The next day, when Dad came home from the trial his eyes were sparkling.

'I kicked their arses!' he declared. 'Last night, when Golnar said that the most important thing we could do was buy her a present, I was so relieved! She was right!'

Mum wasn't sure if 'kicking their arses' was the best strategy for Dad and whether it really deserved such a wide grin.

'What happened, Jalal?'

'I told them: if they sack me, they'll be doing me a great favour because then I can spend more time with my family, I can set up a private consultancy that will be much more lucrative than teaching, or I can easily go back to England since I already have job offers from there.'

'And what did they say?'

'They were taken aback. I said I didn't care if I was sacked. It was they who would have to answer to the academic world for firing one of the only Iranian scientists in material sciences who had papers in peer-reviewed international journals.'

'You didn't say anything about your ideology?'

'I just said that I was being tried because I believed in freedom, and that I will continue believing in it.'

Then he looked into my eyes and finished his story. 'Arash, remember, never become too attached to anything and never become too detached from what you love. And . . . never be a coward.'

When it came to making the final decision, no one quite dared expel Dad. He was a distinguished academic who had become a member of the Academy of Science before he was 40. It would be bad publicity for the Revolution. But he was demoted from Dean of Faculty to Senior Lecturer. Dad didn't mind; he never really wanted to be a manager; he only wanted to teach and carry on with his research. Some of the students who had testified against him, when they realized he was going to remain an influential figure in the university, tried to make up for their betrayal. But Dad told them never to talk to him except for matters related to their studies, though he promised that he wouldn't be vengeful. He wasn't. He loved his students, even the ones who turned out to be traitors.

However, the Cultural Revolution did succeed in sacking several prominent lecturers. For the rest, Ahmadinejad decided to finish the mission when he seized the presidency for his second term in 2009.

Uncle Muhammad was also expelled and soon informed by a friend in high places that he was under observation. He was advised to leave the country before an arrest warrant could be issued. He could not ignore the warning this time and immediately left for France.

He never returned.

By 1981, the war was entering a new phase. Every day we heard about the conflicts between President Bani-Sadr, who believed in strengthening the Iranian Army and limiting the power of the unorganized army of the Revolutionary Guard, and Khamenei, Rafsanjani, Beheshti and Prime Minister Muhammad Ali Rajaii, who insisted on the inadequacy of conventional military strategy and the need for the full participation of the Guard. On the other hand, the leaders of the People's Mujahideen were beginning to question the increasing power and authority of Khomeini and the other clerics. The war would make little progress with so much internal division.

Khomeini was openly critical of Bani-Sadr's strategy and preferred to support the Revolutionary Guard and the Basij rather than the Iranian Army. Bani-Sadr obviously opposed this stand, and that was the beginning of his downfall. Khomeini officially ordered Bani-Sadr to support the Revolutionary Guard. Bani-Sadr was politically isolated. Although he attempted to join forces with the People's Mujahideen, it was too late.

We children really thought that we had a say in all this. We were divided into two groups: those who supported Bani-Sadr; and those who supported Rajaii. None of us really knew why we had chosen one or the other: we had no idea about the real source of this conflict. But it was exciting to 'play' politics. During our breaks, our groups took up position on opposite sides of the yard and screamed slogans in support of our preferred leader. I didn't know which one to support, so I moved between the two groups and my vote could easily be bought with a bit of candy or half a sandwich. This proved to be lucrative business as each group tried hard to recruit more supporters. Instead of supporting our favourite football teams, we supported our favourite politicians. The supporters of Rajaii said he was a true believer in Imam Khomeini and the ideals of the Islamic Republic and that Bani-Sadr was a traitor and a coward. The advocates of Bani-Sadr shouted that he had the votes of the people and 11 million votes meant he had the right to rule the country.

I ate a lot of free sandwiches at that time but then the head-master forbade political demonstrations in school and I went back to bringing my own sandwiches.

In June 1981, Khomeini reclaimed the power of Com-mander-in-Chief. This was the signal for Bani-Sadr's opponents to attack. Bani-Sadr escaped the police who had come to arrest him on a charge of treason. After a few days, he was impeached and disqualified in the Islamic Parliament in his absence. After a month of living in hiding, Bani-Sadr and Rajavi, the leader of the People's Mujahideen, fled the country and ended up in Paris. It was only later that Rajavi settled in Iraq with his supporters.

This was the final bullet in the head of our dying democ-racy and the official launch of the reign of terror: the govern-ment outlawed all political parties except its own, the Islamic Republic Party.

Why do I remember all this? Because we children were ineluctably doomed to know what was going on in our country. But we were also confused. We weren't entirely sure that believing in Khomeini was the right path; even as 10-year-olds we could understand and condemn the violence that came next; even we could feel the terror spreading.

Ahmadreza was a 16-year-old boy and a neighbour of my Aunt Sediqeh. Whenever Madar came to Tehran to visit us, she would spend a few days with Aunt Sediqeh before returning to Qom. Whenever I could, I accompanied her; there, I would spend time with my cousins Kazem, Soussan, Soheila and their neighbour Ahmadreza. He was our mentor and the neighbourhood favourite. He was finishing high school and his range of interests and knowledge was considerable. After a game of football in the street, he would buy us ice cream and talk to us about everything, from his problems in studying geometry and biology to explaining how a wind was created. Sometimes we sat on the doorstep as he read to us and then quizzed us about what we had just heard. A faint moustache was making an appearance; a beard seemed far off. He was funny, energetic, kind and wise, and everyone anticipated a bright future for him.

It was the middle of June, 1981. I had finished my exams and the summer holidays had just begun. Elementary school was over and, in the long break before I began junior high, I was free to go with Madar to Aunt Sediqeh's.

When we arrived, my excitement dissolved into anxiety as soon as I saw the tearful faces of the neighbours standing at their doors as well as two uniformed Committee members strolling in the street, asking everyone to go home. Madar took my hand and dragged me towards Aunt Sediqeh's house but no one opened the door. One of the neighbours, a woman in a black chador, her eyes red from crying, came to us and whispered that my aunt and all the children were at Ahmadreza's house.

'What's happened? Why is everyone crying?' asked Madar.

'Ahmadreza . . .' the woman sobbed.

'What's happened to Ahmadreza? Is he ill?'

She looked around to see if the two Committee members were watching, then whispered, 'He was executed last night.'

Madar slumped to the street and began to wail. I simply stood there, aghast. Why would someone execute a schoolboy? It couldn't be true. And then I remembered Azadeh.

We went to Ahmadreza's house. Aunt Sediqeh hugged Madar, sobbing. Kazem and Soussan had been crying silently; they grabbed me by the hand and pulled me to the corner where we all sat beside my other cousin, Soheila. Almost the same age as Ahmadreza, she had been his sweetheart. We all knew it. He'd follow her around with lovesick eyes even though she was not allowed to return his affections. It was a traditional neighbourhood and it would have been considered immodest for a girl to be 'involved' with a boy.

Soheila was sitting in the corner, staring into space. Every now and then a tear would fall, tracing a wet path along her dry cheek.

Ahmadreza's mother was wailing and cursing everything and everyone, including Imam Khomeini, Ayatollah Guillani, the Jurisprudent Judge, and Asadollah Ladjevardi, Head of Tehran's Revolutionary Court and chief of Evin Jail where Ahmadreza had been executed.

'Soheila, what happened?' I asked.

Soheila said nothing.

'Soheila, it can't be true!' I cried. 'Ahmadreza was the best! What will happen to *you* now?'

This question finally penetrated her silence. Perhaps she was thinking the same thing, regretting never having told Ahmadreza how much she adored him, how much she loved to hold his hand, even if only for a second. Later, I came to know that Soheila had always dreamt about the day when Ahmadreza would finally come home with his family and ask for her hand . . .

We listened to taped recitations from the Quran:

*When the sun is folded up*
*When the stars fall, losing their lustre*
*When the mountains vanish*

*. . .*

*When the oceans boil over with a swell*
*When the souls are sorted out*
*And when the girl is asked*
*For what sin she was slain . . .*

'My heart is broken, Arash . . .' said Soheila finally and began to weep. I sat there with her and we cried together for what seemed like an age. Time had stopped, and we felt that we could bear the loss as long as we could shed tears for him. But then came a time when all our tears ran dry. Soheila took our hands and we silently left Ahmadreza's house forever. There was a photograph of him on the table, surrounded by black candles; his eyes seemed to follow Soheila with so much desire, as if he were trying to say, 'Don't go Soheila, at least wait until the candles have burnt out . . .'

Soheila explained everything to me that night. Ahmadreza had been a supporter of the People's Mujahideen. Though it had a significant number of official members, its main power lay in the support from the youth who were, quite simply and in most cases, fond of its revolutionary rhetoric. The People's Mujahideen had also been a key supporter of Khomeini during the Revolution.

A few days after the impeachment of Bani-Sadr and his going into hiding, supporters of the People's Mujahideen had organized a huge demonstration in the streets. But the crowds were confronted by a massive police crackdown. Most of its leaders had already fled Iran; those in the streets were mainly its young supporters. Thousands were arrested during that demonstration on 20 June 1981; hundreds were condemned to death in collective trials and executed within hours. There was no question of either providing them with legal help or of allowing them a chance to appeal. Later, when a foreign reporter asked Ladjevardi why they had been deprived of their rights, he answered: 'The crimes of these people are so clear that no lawyer would dare to defend them. Were they to do so, they, too, would be charged with the same offence.' It was then that Ladjevardi was awarded the title of 'Hangman' by the people. Many years later, after he had retired, he was killed by an anonymous assassin's bullet. People felt no sorrow or regret when they heard the news.

Next day, the names of all the executed prisoners were published in the afternoon newspapers and it was only then that hundreds of families discovered their loss. More names were published the day after and yet more the day after that; this went on for some time. Families with missing children formed long queues at the news-stands every afternoon, waiting to buy the paper and skim fearfully through the names of the hundreds who had been executed the night before, searching for mention of their children. A woman breathed a sigh of relief: although her 16-year-old daughter was still missing, at least her name was not on the list. Another woman shrieked and fell to the ground, having come across the name of her son. People gathered. Some shouted in anger, others tried to silence them lest a policeman arrested them, too.

The boys were shot instantly; the girls were given a few more hours. Islamic law forbids the killing of virgins. Therefore, each girl was forcefully married to one of the guards. After he had raped his new wife, she was eligible for execution.

Years later, I had an employee, Ali, who had been a guard in Evin Prison in the 1980s. After a nervous breakdown, he had picked a fight with Ladjevardi and hence been sacked. He recounted many blood-curdling tales from that time, repeatedly asking for God's forgiveness as he did so.

'They usually executed them in batches,' he once told me, while we drove to Isfahan on a business trip. 'I was one of the guards who had to be present during the executions, although I wasn't in the firing squad. One night, about 24 young prisoners from death row were to be shot. When the squad began to fire, a 17-year-old girl who, miraculously, hadn't been hit, threw herself to the ground and feigned death as she lay there in the blood of her slaughtered peers. To save the bullets, the victims didn't receive a *coup de grâce*, and because of time constraints and the sheer speed and volume of the executions, no doctor was brought in to verify whether the youngsters were really dead.

'They put the bodies in a huge trailer to take them to the cemetery. I was asked to escort it in a police car, and a city truck moved behind the trailer to wash the road clean of the blood seeping from it.

'When we reached the cemetery, we found a mass grave dug and waiting for the bodies. The girl had escaped as soon as the trailer had stopped. But overwhelmed and paralyzed by the darkness of the huge graveyard, she simply squatted behind a bush and waited for us to leave.'

Ali slowed down the car and wiped the beads of sweat off his forehead.

'She didn't know there'd be a body count.'

I looked at him, surprised.

'The officer accompanying the trailer soon found out about a missing body and he realized what might have happened. He sent all the guards to look for her. They found her soon enough and dragged her towards the grave while she howled and begged the officer to spare her life.'

I asked him to pull over. It was too risky being driven with those trembling hands. He obeyed and took a large gulp from his bottle of water.

'You don't have to tell me this, you know,' I said.

'No, no! I have to, now that I've begun.'

He took a deep breath and finished the story.

'The guards kept her standing over the grave. The officer took out his gun and pointed it at the poor girl's forehead. I was watching, and she turned towards me and begged: "Please . . ."

'That was her last word. A blast . . . and she fell, like a young tree cut down, into the pit.'

Ali's lips were trembling. He took another gulp of water.

'I simply stood there, watching. She had been raped and beaten. She had seen her friends die around her. She had faced the darkness of the graveyard. She had looked into the eyes of her executioner . . . And she had looked at me and asked for my help . . . She was only 17. My daughter is 17 now.

'I wish I had said something . . . I wish I had protected her . . . I wish I had died trying to save her life . . . But I simply stood there and watched. That's why I'm never going to see a good day again.'

He told me he rarely slept without seeing those imploring eyes in his nightmares. He suffered from an anxiety disorder so acute that it could only be quelled with opium. His wife and children had left him and he had never managed to find a proper job since he left the police force—until I employed him as the company's driver. And this misery followed him to his death: one day, he simply drove his motorbike into a few cement-filled barrels placed across the street as traffic barriers. Comatose for two weeks after that, when he finally regained consciousness he could recognize no one and was completely paralyzed. He died a few months later.

Ahmadreza's family never got a chance to say goodbye to him, not even to his body which was buried secretly. They only received his clothes, his wallet and his will, and that too after they had paid the cost of the bullets used for his execution.

Soheila eventually recovered from the trauma. She studied hard and became a successful GP.

But she never married.

Thousands were executed and thousands more were sentenced to 7–10 years' imprisonment. No country condemned these arbitrary executions at the time. Reagan was designing his Star Wars defence initiative while the rest of the world was steeling itself for what was to become the final decade of the Cold War. In the meantime, Iranian youth were being massacred, either by their own government or while trying to defend their country against Saddam Hussein (who thought he was destined to repeat the Arab conquest of the Persian Empire). The world remained silent. And there were no camcorders then to provide the international media with journalistic scoops. No one cared about the collective murder of these juvenile prisoners.

The people of Iran said nothing either. It was as if the country had been reduced to silence. Parents silently watched their children being butchered and didn't take a single step to stop it, largely out of fear for their remaining children.

The executions went on for several years. Ayatollah Guillani signed the death sentence of his own two sons, who were supporters of the People's Mujahideen, without a moment's hesitation. 'The Revolution will no longer tolerate any opposition,' he announced to anyone who cared to listen.

Overnight and in retaliation, the People's Mujahideen turned into a terrorist group. On 27 June, Khamenei, Khomeini's delegate in the Supreme Council of Defence, survived an explosion from a bomb hidden in a tape recorder and placed beside him at a press conference. His right arm was permanently paralyzed. The following day a bomb exploded in the general assembly of the Islamic Republic Party and killed Muhammad Beheshti, one of Bani-Sadr's most feared opponents, along with 90-odd other members, each a prominent political figure. Khomeini declared that nothing would change: 'Kill us. It will simply awaken our nation.'

A presidential election was held in less than a month's time and, on 15 August 1981, Prime Minister Rajaii, supported by Khamenei and Rafsanjani, became President without much competition. But he was destined to be so for only 15 days. On 30 August, Prime Minister Javad Bahonar and he were killed in another explosion, this time in his office.

The People's Mujahideen accepted responsibility for this attack as well.

In the next election, Khamenei, promoted to the rank of 'living martyr' on account of the failed assassination, won the election to become Iran's third president in a single year.

Ahmadreza's death marked a turning point in my life. I lost my faith in the Revolution and in religion. I stopped praying, fasting and observing my religious duties. I came to the conclusion that Khomeini was definitely not sent by God. Even if he had been, this God was nowhere close to being either merciful or compassionate. When someone loses his faith, he is confronted by a confusing range of emotions: on the one hand he feels a sense of liberation but on the other he feels alone and isolated. In my case, I had to continue living a dual life: a public life at school where I pretended to be a wholehearted supporter of the Revolution; and a personal one at home where I was to discover a world of diversity and variety that would have been lost to me had I obeyed the strict instructions and censorship of the state.

Madar, too, could no longer see Khomeini's face in the moon.

In the summer of 1981, after our final exams, our school announced that all the fifth graders due to begin junior high the following year had to go to summer school. The classes began about 15 days after the death of Ahmadreza but by now I had become so familiar with death that it no longer held its old mysteries or terrors. We had all lost members of our families, either during the Revolution, in the purges afterwards or in the war. We had grown desensitized; the word 'death' no longer disturbed us, neither did the news of the delivery of yet another dead body to the neighbourhood. We were the children of the Revolution, preparing ourselves to defend it when the time came.

Contrary to my parents' idea, summer school was not about preparing for junior high at all. In accordance with a quote by Prophet Muhammad, parents and teachers were encouraged to teach their children archery and swimming in preparation for the jihad, the holy war. The regime had decided to interpret 'archery' as 'military training'.

We had to be in school every morning at 8. The day began with Quran classes: we were taught how to read the verses correctly, how to translate them and understand their true meaning. Those who were thought to have good voices were forced to take extra classes in recitation, and in the music that accompanied the verses during the readings. I never had a good voice; so I was spared.

After the Quran classes we had Islamic training, where we learnt about the Sharia, its law and practice. We were taught how to fast, how to pray and how to enter the lavatories with our left feet first.

Then we had political classes: the teachers taught us, 11-year-old children, that America was the Great Satan, Israel the embodiment of evil on earth and Saddam Hussein the envoy of the Devil sent to destroy Islam. We were told that the executed had been 'corrupters on earth'; they had waged war against God and execution was the minimum punishment they deserved. We were also taught to spy on our parents, friends and family and encouraged to inform our teachers if we noticed our older siblings indulging in any suspicious activities. We were also told about the advantages of martyrdom, the highest honour for a Muslim, and that we had to pay the utmost respect to our compatriots being martyred in the war against Iraq. We were encouraged to nurture an exclusive desire: to join them as soon as possible. Our teacher convinced us that if we were fortunate enough to be killed on the battlefield while fighting for Islam, then our spirits would be received on the spot by houris, beautiful women who resided in Paradise and whose job was to provide every conceivable sexual pleasure for those who were privileged enough to enter Heaven.

According to our teacher, the exquisite houris would embrace us and, even while we were still soaring to Heaven, begin to make love to us. This language was not specific to our teacher but was common propaganda. Now that all potential competition had been wiped out, the Revolutionary Guards and the Basij had entered the war, body and soul. But because of the sanctions against Iran that deprived them of modern artillery against the Iraqi troops armed to the teeth with the latest in military hardware, a completely new strategy was devised: soldiers became the living shields that guarded the country, forming barriers of flesh against the barrage of the enemy.

More than a million people, between 13 and 60 years of age, but mainly in the 16–25 group, volunteered to go to the front to fight the 'heretic Saddamists': the Iraqi army, as it had been labelled by our government. Most of them received only two weeks' military training before they were dispatched to the front with Russian AK-47s, wearing Basij uniforms and sporting headbands that bore the slogan 'O Hussein'. Like Imam Hussein, they were ready for martyrdom. The commanders used them as human shields against the advanced Iraqi artillery. When Iraq's ground forces attacked, they would be confronted by thousands of soldiers who weren't afraid to die. The Iraqis would open fire, the young Iranians would fall to the ground and thousands more would step up to take their place. The more the Iraqis killed, the more volunteers joined the Basij. The new strategy did indeed work a lot better than Bani-Sadr's plans for conventional warfare. The Iraqi army was paralyzed.

Unexpected attacks across the border took Saddam by surprise. How could it happen? The Iraqis ensured that the land taken from Iran was made impregnable: they planted thousands of landmines along a new and deadly border that stretched for 1,458 km between Iran and Iraq. There was no way of clearing those mines. We didn't have sophisticated minesweeping equipment, true but we had soldiers. A lot of them.

The night before that attack, the volunteers gathered for communal prayers. After their prayers, they listened to stories about Imam Hussein and his followers and their courage. Though they knew they would die, they fought against evil until their very last breath.

Operations were to begin early in the morning. The first task was to clear a path through the minefield for the tanks and the troops. It was then that the commander would appear before the troops and give a sermon on the joys of martyrdom, the pleasures of being accepted into God's presence. Then he would ask for volunteers to run through the minefield, thus triggering off the mines and clearing the way for the tanks.

Surprisingly, there was no shortage of volunteers. Soldiers fought to be chosen as one of the martyrs-to-be. So much so that the commander was almost spoilt for choice. The shouts of joy from the Chosen Ones echoed through the battlefield. Those who were left out would cry and implore to be sent instead.

The Chosen Ones said goodbye to their compatriots, asked for their sins to be forgiven, handed over their last will and testament to a trusted friend and then waited for the order to go forward, their eyes glowing and their faces shining with joy. The 'testaments' all followed the same pattern. First, praises to Allah and the Hidden Imam and Khomeini for giving them the privilege of martyrdom. Then, a request to friends and families to be loyal to the ideals of the Revolution and Imam Khomeini. And, finally, mention of more mundane matters, such as debts that needed to be cleared.

The commander reassured them of their instant reception by the houris, and then gave the order to proceed. Almost all the volunteers would be killed. At the very least, they would lose a leg. But the vital path would be opened up in the fastest and most effective minesweeping operation ever seen.

The story of the houris was supported by another legend. Much in the manner of the odd UFO spotted in the sky, rumours of an extraordinary sight began to spread among the troops. A man, in a white mask and cape, and riding on a white horse, appeared before the soldiers and led the Iranian Basij to victory against the Iraqi infidels. All the soldiers were convinced that it was the Hidden Imam himself, although no two persons could come up with the same description. Even Imam Khomeini implied in his speeches that these sightings were authentic. 'Our army is fighting the American Saddam under the Hidden Imam's support. Our nation will conquer the world of heresy by the grace of the Hidden Imam's flag . . .'

When Al-Mahdi, the Hidden Imam, himself was fighting for us, wouldn't it be sacrilege for us to not join him? But it didn't last long. The sightings of the mysterious white horseman grew less frequent and the story of the houris faded away. There was no need for them any more: enough blood had been shed to incite every man to fight for his country.

And the faces of the cities had changed. At the entrance to each alley you would find a *hijlah*, literally a 'wedding bed' but, in fact, a memorial stand with the photograph of a young soldier who had just been killed at the front. Set up near their homes by their families, these had to remain for 40 days after the death of the loved one, especially if she or he had died young. The local authorities were kept busy too, changing the names of the streets and alleys to honour the war martyrs: Shahid (martyr) Salehi, Shahid Fakouri, Shahid Hassani, Shahid this, Shahid that and Shahid the other . . .

If you walk in Tehran today, it will be difficult to find a road, a street, even a tiny alley, that doesn't bear a martyr's name. Sometimes disputes broke out among the inhabitants of that street or alley over the choice of martyr for its name: which family would have the honour of seeing their son's name up on the wall? People no longer cared about Paradise; it was dignity, revenge and the feeling that they were responsible for the safety of their families that pulled them like magnets to the front.

Ironically, most of those who took over the Revolutionary Guard after the war, and the majority of those who claim to be members of the Basij today, have never been to war. Those who did so were killed, maimed or lost their health or their minds. They bore not the slightest resemblance to the Basij who shot Neda and the others, nor to those who tortured and raped the detainees. Had it not been for the courage and sacrifice of the real warriors, none of us would have lived to see this day.

We were all being prepared for martyrdom that summer and most of us couldn't wait till we had the chance to meet our houris, even though we were still a few years away from puberty and wouldn't have known what to do with the beautiful women had we met them.

In the afternoons at our summer school, it was either military training or swimming lessons. Military training entailed how to use, dismantle, clean and mount assault rifles; target practice; learning to be part of a unit; war strategy; and hand-to-hand combat.

The swimming lessons were not as aggressive.

All Iranians hate the 1980s. It was not only that death and the fear of death pervaded the hearts and minds of us all but also that time itself seemed to have stopped. The sanctions against Iran combined with the steep fall in the price of oil and the high costs of the war had reduced the country to a miserable state. Its remaining resources were spent in buying weapons on the international black market (no country was permitted to sell arms to us directly). The economy was plummeting and many would have starved if it hadn't been for the strategic planning of Prime Minister Mir-Hussein Mousavi. He decided to ration everything so that no one would be left with nothing. Milk, bread, cigarettes, eggs, meat, chicken, rice, oil, petrol: everything that could be was rationed. And it worked. The worst side effect was the long hours in queues to buy the things we needed.

Those who still had money began to leave for the US or Europe or any country in the world that would accept them. In less than a year, about 4 million Iranians emigrated. Those who didn't have the money to do so tried to send their young sons away to avoid conscription. For the law had been changed and as soon as a boy reached the age of 15, he was not allowed to leave the country; conscription was mandatory, as was being sent to the front at 18. The statistics therefore were devastating: one in three sent to the front was killed. Families were prepared to sell everything they had to give their sons a chance outside Iran. There were also those families whose sons were already 15 or a little older. Amir was one of them.

Amir was the son of my father's friend Ahmad. They had both been students at the University of Birmingham. Amir was four years older than I. After the war flared up, his parents tried hard to send him away before he turned 15 but they failed to get a visa for the UK in time. There were financial issues too. They couldn't afford to pay for his journey and upkeep in the UK. Before they could sort everything out, it was time for Amir's fifteenth birthday. Their time had run out. And Amir no longer had the right to hold a valid passport.

One night, Amir and his parents came over to seek Dad's advice. Amir was devastated at the knowledge that he was no longer able to leave the country. His mother said he had stopped eating, talking, studying, even watching TV. He was also having recurrent nightmares about going to the front and dying.

Dad spent hours trying to talk to Amir but he couldn't stop crying. Dad told him that a real man wouldn't cry in fear lest the others consider him a coward. But Amir didn't care; he didn't mind being a coward as long as he stayed alive. I was getting really annoyed and bored. There were a million people at the front, around the same age as Amir, fighting with their bare hands. They were giving up everything, their future, their safety, their arms and legs and lives, to keep us safe and to prevent the enemy from destroying our country. And this young man, who wouldn't even be asked to go to the front for another three years, was sitting here and crying because he was having nightmares about a summons from the army. I was disgusted.

Dad tried telling him that the war might even be over in three years but Amir's tears refused to stop. 'What if it's not?' No one could reason with him; and now that I look back, despite the resentment I felt at the time, I think perhaps his fear was justified: not everyone is supposed to be a warrior.

They finally left quite late that night, clutching a cucumber in case they came across the night guards. Soon after, Amir sank into depression and threatened to commit suicide. The psychiatrists warned his parents that something terrible might happen if they didn't send him abroad as soon as possible.

Amir's father sold his car, converted all his savings into cash and then negotiated a deal with a smuggler who charged them a fortune. Amir took nothing with him but a rucksack and the huge amount of cash his parents had given him. He bade farewell to them and set off on his illegal journey across the border. The smugglers took him by car to a place near the border and then handed him over to another team. They walked for days in the mountains of Azerbaijan, slept in tents and did not light fires lest they attract the attention of the hundreds of border patrol officers who were under orders to shoot anyone who tried to escape. They crept among the herds of sheep and moved ever closer to the border. At the frontier they bribed one of the patrols to let them cross and, after a few weeks, Amir was finally on Turkish soil. The smugglers arranged his transport to the UK where he claimed asylum.

In an ironical turn of events, Amir's father found he could no longer live on the low salary he received as a civil servant and decided to set up his own enterprise in order to raise enough money for the huge expenses of his son. Luckily it took off and in a few years he became a very rich man.

On the other hand, not all of those several thousand families who tried to smuggle their children out of Iran enjoyed the same good fortune. Hundreds were robbed, left alone in the mountains or murdered by the smugglers for their cash. Some were shot or arrested by the police, others were mugged in Turkey. I remember wondering why Amir preferred to face the unknown dangers instead of accepting the more familiar fate: of going to the front in three years and trying to help his country.

But when I turned 15 myself, I understood. It wasn't the fear of death or war as it was the longing for freedom that made Amir want to leave Iran.

And that made all the risks worthwhile.

Nothing can be all bad or all gloomy. There's always a ray of light, even at life's darkest moments. From what I've described so far, our life at the time may be summarized thus: war, fear of death, oppression, execution, military training, lack of individual freedom, no entertainment, inquisition, boredom, waiting for many hours in many queues . . .

But that's not the whole story. We had our diversions too. First of all, in a society starved of entertainment, the numerous queues outside the shops became a chance to socialize. As the eldest child in the family, I was in charge of waiting in most of the queues. Only when Madar stayed with us did I escape this task; she volunteered to replace me in the lines. Boys and girls, ordinarily seized by the police if they walked or talked together, had a chance to meet and talk in the queues; soon, the queues turned into a rendezvous for lovers. Women had a chance to find 'proper' spouses for their children; men had a chance to debate current political events. As the police never suffered the indignity of queuing, some of these discussions turned into heated debates on the legitimacy of the government. Men would

107

begin to shout at one another, trying to prove their point. These quarrels turned into an ongoing social event. Wherever there were no policemen in sight, people would start a debate: in the queues, in the doctors' waiting rooms, in the taxis, on the bus . . . until it became unbearable and you would see the sign 'No Political Debates' put up by irritated shop-owners, taxi-drivers and bakers, who were tired of these never-ending discussions that led nowhere.

The young boys and girls were not to enjoy their freedom for long. The police were quick to respond to these 'illegal interactions' in the queues and separated the lines into one for the men and another for the women. Not that it helped much, for the boys and girls always found a way to sidle up to one another and begin a conversation.

This wasn't our only entertainment. Dad, a little concerned about the kind of education I was getting at summer school, tried to arrange other forms of 'edutainment' that could counter the brainwashing. One of them was discussing books. Every week, Mum, Dad and I decided on a novel. And on Friday mornings—our weekend—we discussed it around the breakfast table. It was a time-consuming but rewarding form of entertainment, a primitive form of the book club.

Another was the book *Heliat-ol Motaghin* ('The Ornaments of the Righteous'). Written by one of the most prominent Shiite clerics in the sixteenth century, the ruling mullahs considered it recommended reading for every believer. We, too, read a chapter every night after dinner but our purpose was rather different: it was not so much a source of Islamic manners as it was an encyclopaedia of jokes. It kept us in stitches for hours.

'It is not recommended that virtuous Muslims wear clothes of wool; clothes of cotton are recommended.'

'You must wear your underwear while seated. Woe to whoever wears his underwear while standing, as he will face sadness in the next three days.'

'When you take off your clothes, you must say: "In the name of Allah". If you do not, the Jinn might wear them.'

'Whoever wears shoes will be safe from tuberculosis.'

'Don't drink water while you are standing.'

'Don't have intercourse with your wives on Wednesday nights.'

'Don't talk while you are having sex because the conceived child will be born mute.'

'A rug left in the corner is better than a woman who cannot bear children.'

'Don't have sex under a fruit-bearing tree, because the child conceived will grow up to be a hangman.'

'Don't let your moustache grow long lest it become the den of Satan.'

'Don't lie on your back in the bathroom.'

'Don't say hello to people from other religions unless they greet you first. Don't shake hands with them and, if you do, wash your hands afterwards.'

'Laughing too much kills your heart.'

'Don't keep dogs as pets.'

Chess, backgammon, board games and cards were other ways of passing the time. All of these had been banned after the Revolution as a pretext for gambling, a cardinal sin in Islam. But people didn't care; they only had to be careful to keep it secret.

Something else that made our life tolerable in those days was jokes. Iranians are master jokers, especially in the telling of political jokes. They can create a joke out of the most surprising and improbable incident, particularly if stupidity is involved. After the Revolution, the butt of the national joke-making machine was Ayatollah Montazeri, vice-leader of the Revolution. He, unlike Khomeini, was a simple person with a good heart and thus easily incorporated into popular jokes:

> Once Montazeri visited the Louvre Museum in Paris. The curator gave him a pair of shoes and said, 'In order to show you our utmost respect, we are offering you the shoes of Louis XVI of France?'
>
> Montazeri put on the shoes and said, 'Thank you very much but these shoes are a little tight. Would you please give me the shoes of Louis XVII.'
>
> Montazeri was on his way to Tehran on a helicopter. After a while he asked the man sitting beside him, 'Are you feeling hot, Sir?'
>
> 'No,' the man answered.
>
> 'Captain,' Montazeri shouted to the pilot, 'none of us are feeling hot. Would you please turn off the fan on top? The noise is disturbing us!'

We had no pubs, bars or restaurants to go to but what we did have was time to travel. Iran is the land of holidays: Thursdays and Fridays are the weekends but that's not all: we have 13 days of Norouz and another 20 days through the year dedicated to religious ceremonies, either mourning for the anniversary of the death of the Prophet and the Shiite Imams or celebrating their birthdays or other religious events such as Fitir (the first day after the end of Ramadan), Qurban (celebrating the day when God asked Abraham to sacrifice a lamb instead of his son, according to the Islamic tradition) or Qadir (the day when, according to the Shiites, the Prophet appointed Ali his successor).

There is another holiday commemorating the anniversary of the Revolution, one the anniversary of the nationalization of oil, one mourning the martyrs of the Revolution. Later, one more mourning the death of Khomeini although that was not until 1989. And that's still not all: a working day between two holidays is usually included in the holiday. Out of the 365 days in a year, we work for only 220—a little more than seven months!

Dad used these holidays as an opportunity to open our eyes to our own country. We usually travelled in our old Peugeot 304 for the brand-new Ford had been sold to cover day-to-day expenses. Thanks to those trips I am familiar with almost every corner of Iran.

One of the most beautiful places we went to was, of course, the Caspian Sea. The Caspian Sea has a lasting effect even on those who have seen it only once. The drive twists up to 10,000 feet through the snow-covered mountains of Alborz. The roads are narrow and dangerous, inclining either to the stone face of the mountain on one side or down into the vast and mist-covered pits on the other. If you travel in any season other than summer, you are likely to drive almost the entire way through the clouds that crown the Alborz. Up in those mountains you are filled with a sense of immense loneliness and more than a little fear, as also by a sense of freedom. The Alborz are crowned by Damavand, the Olympus of Iran, and you cannot pass it without feeling an overwhelming sense of humility, especially if you know the stories associated with it.

According to Iranian mythology, the evil King Zahak is chained in a cave in the heart of Mount Damavand, waiting for the time of his release when he will destroy life on earth. It was also from this peak that Arash the Archer shot his last arrow. Legend has it that he is still there, waiting to help those who have lost their way in the mountains.

111

It's hard not to be awed by Damavand, a mountain painted white with snow, its peak obscured by clouds. No wonder the Iranians believed it to be the abode of Mithra or Mehr, the Aryan God of Light and Covenants, and the starting point of his daily journey around the world on his fiery chariot. It was also believed to be where the mythical king and sage Kay Khusro, my favourite Iranian mythological character, disappeared after defeating the arch-enemy of Iran. I think of him whenever I look at Damavand, and now, sadly, at its photographs.

Prince Kay Khusro was born at a time of brutal wars between Iran and its neighbouring country, Turan. The struggle had been carrying on for centuries. As the son of Prince Siyâvash he was destined to be involved in the violence. Siyâvash, trying to bring peace to both lands, had left Iran for Turan. There, he married the daughter of Afrasiab, King of Turan, and built a utopia. Siyâvash succeeded in stopping the war for a few years but then Afrasiab, poisoned by paranoia, ordered the execution of Siyâvash and his daughter Farangis who was, by then, pregnant with Kay Khusro.

Siyâvash was killed but Farangis survived. Kay Khusro was born in Turan and grew up among the shepherds until he was summoned back to Afrasiab's court and received as a prince.

After a few years, an Iranian hero ventured on a quest to find the son of Siyâvash and bring him back to Iran to become the rightful king. When Kay Khusro heard the story of his grandfather's atrocities and the cruel death of his father, he fled Turan, his birthplace, and became king of Iran. He then led the army of Iran in the wars between Iran and Turan and finally, after many years, defeated and slew Afrasiab and ended the war once and for all. But he refused to occupy Turan and returned to Iran. Then, having seen how power corrupted and how it had polluted the judgement and consciousness of those who possessed it, he renounced his throne. He had caused the death of everyone he loved in his pursuit of justice and peace: his grandfather, his uncle, his friends and his godfather. Power was not worth such a terrible price and, like Yudhishthira in the Mahabharata, he embarked on a journey towards Mount Damavand. He disappeared among the peaks and all his companions died. It is said that he will come back at the end of time to lead the Army of Light in the final battle between Good and Evil.

For Westerners, although its origins lie far earlier, the story may be a reminder of the legend of King Arthur. There are also many parallels with the Mahabharata and these stories probably share the same origins.

Many years later I wrote *Kay Khusro*, a novel. In it, the time has come for Kay Khusro to reveal himself and wage war against Evil. But he, wandering through history, is tired. He has neither the will to fight nor the desire to live. But he cannot die. A young woman finds him and takes care of him and, in return, Kay Khusro takes her back to the time when he was forced to wage war against his grandfather and his motherland. The novel was published, ironically, only a few days after Neda's death, when I had already left Iran in anticipation of arrest. Shall I share the same destiny as Kay Khusro who was forced to flee his motherland? My bones tremble at the very idea . . .

I feel a sense of unity with my roots whenever I see Alborz. Most Iranians will take advantage of any excuse to drive once more among those cloud-draped peaks. The southern side of the Sierra, facing Tehran, is almost bare except for a few plantations here and there. But when you reach the peak and begin your downward journey, everything changes in a matter of minutes. Before you know it, the snow along the mountainside is replaced by menacing dark forests. This is the path to the everlasting paradise of the North, the strip of land confined by the

Caspian Sea in the north and the Alborz in the south, where winter never comes and the air is filled with a pleasant humidity very different from the stifling variety one finds by other seas. The air is clear and possessed of a healing power. Even in your saddest times, a whiff of it and you feel a sense of joy seeping into your skin. In my imagination the Garden of Eden was a place perhaps very like the North, if not the North itself.

And then there is the sea itself. Swimming in it was a unique experience, although less so after the Revolution when men and women were no longer allowed to swim together. While men were allowed unrestricted access, women could swim only in designated areas, concealed by huge black curtains. Families could no longer go for a swim together. Mum told me that when she wanted to swim in the women's area in her swimming costume, the female guard told her to wear a T-shirt over it.

'Why? Isn't this area for women only?' Mum had asked.

'It is indeed,' the guard answered, 'but should you drown and be carried away by the water, the lifeguards who look for you will be men. You don't want to be in an inappropriate outfit that reveals your body.' Mum laughed as she told us the story and guessed she would probably be past caring what she was wearing by then!

But I also had a chance to visit other places, like the ancient ruins of Persepolis and the tomb of Cyrus the Great, the first Persian Emperor from 2,500 years ago. It was impossible to feel anything but nostalgia in those places. Cyrus and his successors, Kambys and Darius, created the largest empire the earth has ever seen, stretching across Egypt, Libya, Mesopotamia and many other parts of Europe and Asia.

When I stood before the tomb of Cyrus, Dad told me that Alexander, whose invasion had brought an end to the Persian empire, burnt everything in Iran until he reached the tomb of

Cyrus. He intended to destroy it, too, but curiosity overcame him and he decided to visit the final resting place of the Great Cyrus, the inspiration for the Greek writer Xenophon's recently published *Cyropaedi*, a biographical paeon in praise of Cyrus. On arriving at the tomb, he read the inscription, Cyrus' last testament:

> O man, whoever thou art, from wheresoever
> thou cometh, for I know thou shalt come,
> I am Cyrus, who founded the empire of the
> Persians. Grudge me not, therefore, this
> little earth that covers my body.

At these words, Alexander was ashamed of the destruction he had wrought in Iran and decided to bring it to a halt. It was already too late for Persepolis, the huge palace of the Achaemenid kings. The palace, the gardens and the unrivalled library of 40,000 books—a summary of all human knowledge at the time—were razed to the ground. It took the Iranians nearly a thousand years to rebuild the library. By the end of the Sassanid Empire (seventh century AD) it had again become one of the world's largest but, sadly, it was destroyed again, this time by Arab invaders. According to many historians, Caliph Omar declared: 'If the contents of these books are in accordance with the Quran then we don't need them, and if they contradict it, they should be destroyed. Either way, these books have to go.'

The Iranians are still proud of that era of ancient glory and are perhaps a trifle over-zealous in expounding its triumphs and virtues. Perhaps it's because some foreign force has thrown up an obstruction whenever Iranians have tried to establish their proper place in the world and its history. First it was the Greeks, then came the Arabs, then the Mongols, the Turks, the Russians and, indeed, even the Shah himself. Tales of our ancient glory serve as a symbolic reminder of who we were, what we believed in and how much we have contributed to the progress of human history. Now it's the fundamentalist religious regime which is trying to strip us of our true identity. In defence, therefore, we are beginning to revive the ancient   symbols of a more auspicious time.

I also paid more than one visit to Isfahan and its magnificent architecture conceived at a time when architecture was considered the most transcendent form of art among Muslims. We visited the golden shrine of Imam Reza in Mashad; faraway Bakhtiari and Qashqai villages in the deserts, the homes of nomadic pastoralists; and, of course, Dehaghan, the village of my grandfather before he moved to Tehran and before my father was born. We belonged to one of these nomadic tribes who at some point in history decided to stop migrating and inhabited Dehaghan, a fertile plane between the mountains that lay waiting to be cultivated. My grandfather and his brother, Uncle Habib, who was killed during the Revolution, came to begin a new life in Tehran around 1915.

Dad, a founder of the Iranian Foundrymen's Society, one of the first scientific societies formed after the Revolution, also took me on a visit to the war zone along with a group of foundry engineers. They had been invited to inspect the Iranian fleet of US-manufactured warships and to discuss whether replacement rudders and propellers could be made in Iran itself. Sanctions prevented the import of spare parts.

Dad didn't tell Mum where we were going for she would never have allowed it. But Dad strongly believed that I, too, needed to see the war zone. We travelled via Ahvaz to Imam Khomeini port, a crucial and immensely important location that was Iran's closest port to Iraq. We passed by Shush, site of the ancient city of Susa and now within the occupied province of Khuzestan but we couldn't get to it through the barbed wire that demarcated the war zone. I could see the tanks and the troops in the distance but we didn't linger long; an Iraqi attack could happen at any time and it always began with the bombing of roads leading to the Iranian front. Nothing serious happened that day, though. Dad's group visited the site, decided that it was possible to manufacture the propellers and returned to Tehran to begin the design process.

All that travel broadened my mind and I have always appreciated Dad's efforts to make me see my country better. I continued with my travels through Iran right up to the day when I was forced to leave. Iran is a land of great diversity with different ethnic groups, languages, dialects, professions and religions living in harmony; where you can ski in the morning and bathe in the sea in the afternoon and find yourself on the sands of the desert the day after.

I may never see the North nor breathe its healing air nor drive up the winding roads of Alborz nor feel that life is truly worth living as I sip the ice-cold water from a spring amid the remorseless heat of the never-ending desert. But I don't ever have to feel that I never knew my homeland. I feel pain and regret, of course, but what is life worth without pain and regrets?

*Autumn 1981*

Despite the excitement of beginning my first year in junior high school, I was distressed and under considerable pressure. A lot had happened during the summer and I wasn't the same person any more. I no longer believed in the ideals of the Revolution and I knew I was going to face an even more controlled environment. The hijab had become obligatory for women everywhere and men were not allowed to wear short-sleeved shirts. The Committee patrols roamed the city and arrested women who still resisted covering their hair. They were backed by an over-zealous crowd of fanatics who had decided that they could take the law into their own hands; they unleashed chaos in the city with their knives and buckets of black paint. The knives were used to hurt or threaten women who didn't wear headscarves or whose hijab wasn't completely covering their hair; the paint was used to paint the arms of those men who wore short-sleeved shirts. The patrols had another mission: to make sure that no officially unrelated boys and girls appeared outdoors together. According to the Sharia, only siblings and spouses were allowed to go out together, although first cousins were sometimes allowed as well. Anything else was considered a manifestation of 'moral corruption' and was intolerable to the government.

This decision had created a dramatic, and in many instances comic, situation. Naturally, boys and girls wanted to meet and mingle and no law could control the instincts that attracted the sexes. All that the teenagers really wanted was a chance to step out with a friend of the opposite sex, take a walk, go to a park, have a coffee or an ice cream, and, in extreme cases, hold hands. And they did so, despite the regimentation. The most frightening sight for a boy and girl walking together was a glimpse of Tharallah ('blood of God', a title originally used for Imam Hussein) Patrols' four-wheel-drive Nissans. These vans were constantly on the move around the city, usually carrying two male and two female officers, looking for incidents of 'moral corruption'. The seized were treated differently, according to the extent of the 'felony' and according to the officers' judgement; they could let the person off with a verbal warning or they could insist on an arrest.

Married couples always carried a copy of their marriage certificate, in case they were stopped and questioned. Brothers and sisters always carried their birth certificates, to prove they were born of the same parents and were indeed siblings. The problem lay in unmarried couples going out together. They would have to spend a lot of time memorizing one another's family history. Seized by the Tharallah, they would claim to be either siblings or cousins. To verify their claims, the officers would question them individually.

'You say you're his sister. What's your mother's name?'

'Where do you live?'

'What pictures have you got on the wall of the living room?'

'When was the last time you went to see your grandmother?'

'What does your father do after dinner?'

'What colour are your dinner plates?'

If they gave the same answers, they would be released. God forbid that they gave different ones. They would be arrested on the spot and kept in detention until their parents claimed them; sometimes, they were even forced to pay a fine.

Public workplaces were forced to implement a 'selection policy' (*gozinesh*) before hiring a new employee. Each of the shortlisted candidates had to undergo a verbal or written exam to test their Islamic and political knowledge. If they cleared the exam, the employers were allowed to hire them; if not, no matter how suitable the applicant was in all other respects, no public organization was allowed to employ him or her. This 'selection' soon entered popular culture through our jokes.

'Who killed Imam Hussein?'

'I swear by God, Sir, it wasn't me!'

'Do you know the Twelve Imams?'

'Yes, of course.'

'Tell me their first names!'

'We're not on a first-name basis yet.'

'Would you enter the restroom with your right foot or left foot?'

'If it helps in hiring me, I'll enter with my head!'

'Tell me three names that end with Allah.'

'Roohallah, Nasrollah and Cinderella!'

The unfortunate consequence of these 'selections' was that they deprived thousands of employment simply because they didn't know the correct method of entering the lavatory! There were even stricter rules at school. Our hair was not allowed to grow longer than an inch and we weren't allowed to wear jeans or sneakers, both symbols of Western culture. Expensive clothes weren't exactly illegal but they were frowned upon as was the possession of fancy stationary or even a stylish satchel. Nevertheless, it was much easier for us boys than it was for the girls. They were not allowed to grow their nails nor use any kind of make-up; they could not wear jeans or coats or any other clothes that hinted at their figure nor any colours other than black, gray and dark blue. The cuffs of their trousers could not be too tight and plucking eyebrows or removing facial hair was an unforgivable crime.

I didn't care. In fact, I was almost happy with the new dress code for boys since it meant that I wouldn't feel like an outsider—because of my simple clothes—in my upper-class school. What really repelled me was the pretence of believing in the Revolution and the Sharia. Any hesitation in responding to religious questions, rousing the slightest suspicion among the Tutors of Islamic Manners about my loyalty to the Islamic Republic or the Supreme Leader or giving any impression that I belonged to a family with lax Islamic foundations would result in my expulsion from school or place my parents in jeopardy.

On the other hand, I was raised in a family in which dishonesty was considered the ultimate vice or dishonour. That principle had been engraved upon my subconscious since I was a child and I wasn't sure that I could succeed in this game of pretence. Having witnessed my father's trial, the expulsion of Uncle Hormoz and the plight of a lot of other friends, I knew that it was a matter of life and death. I also remembered losing Ahmadreza to the firing squad because he, too, hadn't hidden his beliefs.

I finally decided to damn it all to hell. It was a new school and no one knew me. From the very first day, I followed a two-pronged strategy: frequented the prayer hall and prayed at noon. I enrolled in extracurricular Islamic classes at the Islamic Manners Department. I also became a member of the school's

Islamic Association. At the same time, I studied hard and made friends. I would not come under too much scrutiny were I considered a good student. I also knew that if I could build a strong circle of friends irrespective of their class or background, then no one would hate me enough to spy on me.

My strategy worked. My religious efforts endeared me to the Islamic Manners Department and I soon came to be known as one of the most intelligent students in the school. In reality, it had less to do with intelligence and more to do with hard work.

On the other hand, by inviting all the outcasts to join our circle, my close friend Farhad and I succeeded in breaking the practice of gangs and exclusive groups who picked on those less privileged in one way or another: those who were physically weaker or overweight or poor. We turned the class into a unified body of friends who supported one another, no matter what.

But there was a downside to all this. I got so carried away that my main objective—to remain invisible—was forgotten. I had become so popular among the students and the teachers that I was unanimously voted class rep. That popularity felt so good that I completely forgot its beginnings as a strategy for survival. Now I had a responsibility towards maintaining our solidarity. I was convinced that I was the champion of the underprivileged and I had to make sure that I deserved the trust of those who had voted for me.

But I was out of ideas. It was a school after all. After the hours spent in class or in Islamic activities, there wasn't much time for anything else. Then I happened to watch a film that proved inspirational. I don't remember the title; made in Yugoslavia, it was about a class of children, almost our age, who had formed a cooperative. I began planning our own cooperative the moment the film ended. I discussed it with Dad. He was excited and stayed up all night with me, developing the idea.

Next day, I requested my classmates to stay behind after school. I then gave them a long speech about my idea and we put it to a vote. It was a unanimous victory. We formed a central committee and began implementing the plan right away. Within the week we had officially launched 'The Class 1/3 Cooperative'.

The idea was simple: we would take care of one another. Everyone contributed a few pennies to the class fund every week and we appointed one of the students as the 'Banker' to keep track of every contribution. By the end of the year we promised to reimburse everyone. The fund was used to give loans to those students who were in serious financial trouble and who couldn't afford to buy their stationary, or who had to walk long distances to and from school because they didn't have money for the bus.

We also formed a consultancy group, headed by Farhad, from among the brightest students. They were to give tutorials to those students who needed help with their lessons.

There was yet another group dedicated to environmental issues long before the environmental crisis made the headlines. We collected scrap paper from around school, in the streets or at home, and sold it to the recyclers. The income went into the fund which, after a while, grew substantial enough to pay for such treats as birthday presents for students.

News of our cooperative spread like wildfire and we were chosen as the best class only three months into the year. In the meantime, I attended my prayers and asked my classmates to do the same every afternoon. I remembered what had happened to Aunt Marjaneh and I certainly didn't want to be considered a socialist or leftist. The Islamic Manners Tutors couldn't hide their joy at the sight of an entire class voluntarily appearing at the prayer hall, and they loved me for having such a positive influence on my classmates. At the end of the first term we were told that we were going to receive the highest honour possible for any Iranian: we had been invited to the residence of Imam Khomeini, to listen to one of his speeches.

I must confess that I was excited at the prospect of another chance to meet the man I had once adored. Despite all the news of executions and imprisonments, I had never succeeded in convincing myself that Khomeini himself was responsible for those crimes. I had seen him and I was sure that a man as kind and as intelligent as he would never do such a thing to the people, to those who had given him their unstinting support. I couldn't blame him for Ahmadreza's death, no matter how hard I tried; I felt that, had he known, he would have stopped the executions. Meeting him was one of the best memories of my childhood. Now I had an opportunity to meet him again and make sure that I hadn't been wrong about him all along.

Khomeini lived in a large house in a district called Jamaran in North Tehran. From several miles off, all the roads were controlled by the special guards and our Islamic Manners Tutor had to show an authorization before being allowed through. When we reached his home, we were taken into a room for a security check. We handed over our belts, shoes, wallets, watches, keys and glasses and were then further searched by the security officers. Only then were we allowed to enter the meeting hall.

I had already seen the hall several times on TV since it was from here that the Imam gave those lengthy speeches that were broadcast almost daily. It seemed smaller than I had imagined. We were asked to sit on the floor and wait for him to come. We weren't alone; students from several schools arrived in clusters. The girls were taken upstairs and made to sit on a balcony above us. A man with a huge beard appeared and explained what we were supposed to do. I, as the rep, had to make sure that our class behaved according to his instructions.

Then the Imam appeared on a balcony and began to wave at us. This was the sign we had been waiting for. All of us rose to our feet and, throwing our fists in the air, began to shout.

O KHOMEINI, YOU ARE MY SOUL!
O KHOMEINI, THE DESTROYER OF IDOLS!

We repeated this slogan for precisely two minutes until the bearded man motioned for silence and for us to sit down.

The Imam sat on his chair and began his speech. And I found myself completely unable to pay any attention to what he was saying: he was so very boring. Not a word beyond what he had been repeating these last three years: the US was our main enemy, Israel was Satan's representative on earth, we had to keep our solidarity, Islam was our only refuge, the Islamic Republic of Iran was the only righteous government in the world, the Iranian soldiers fighting the evil Saddam were the true warriors of God, the martyrs of the war were the highest honours a nation could receive, we were all preparing the path for the coming of the Hidden Imam and so on and on and on . . . I tried to look at him but from that distance I couldn't see his face. His eyes were downcast right through the speech and I wondered why he didn't look at his audience.

Every once in a while we received the 'sign'—someone would shout, '*TAKBIR*!' whenever the Imam said something important (such as 'We will defeat the world of heresy with the power of Islam'). The sign meant we had to shout: '*Allah-o Akbar*! Khomeini is the Leader! Death to those against the Rule of the Jurisprudent! Death to America! Death to the Soviets! Death to Israel! Death to the Hypocrites! Death to Saddam!' And then, just as suddenly, fall silent again.

I coordinated the class, I shouted the slogans, I gave the signs. But I only had one thing on my mind: to get close to the Imam and look into his eyes.

All at once I had an idea and I shared it with a friend sitting beside me. I knew about the secret security guards but I believed they wouldn't be too harsh. Not that I cared about them: I *had* to see the Imam and I was ready to bear the consequences. We knew when the speech was nearing its end: the Imam began to wrap up with a few verses from the Quran and a prayer for the nation and the warriors of Islam. According to our instructions, as soon as he said, '*Vassalam-o alaikom va rahmatollah va barakatehi*,' (Peace upon you as well as God's compassion and blessing), we were to stand up and shout our slogans for the last time.

It was then that I gave the signal to my friend. While the audience was busy shouting and Khomeini was waving from the top of the balcony before rising to leave, my friend and I wriggled through the crowd until we were directly beneath him. Then my friend held his two hands together to give me a leg up and, in an instant, I was standing on his shoulders, climbing my way up to the Imam. My friend pushed me up with what seemed to me to be superhuman strength while I was using all of my own to pull myself up. Suddenly, my arms were seized in a pincer grip and, before I realized what was happening, I was standing on the balcony only a few steps away from the Imam. The man who had pulled me up was of intimidating proportions and I could tell from the look in his eyes that I was in serious trouble. But the cameras were on us and broadcasting the scene live on TV so he let go of my arms quickly enough. My acrobatic feat had startled the Imam and he stood for a few seconds with his right arm frozen in a wave. There was no time to lose. A couple of steps and I was in front of him. He turned to look at me and I, my heart almost leaping out of my mouth, looked into his eyes and said, 'Hello! I'm Arash.'

I don't know why I expected him to remember me. I had grown up since my last visit, and he had seen so many people over the course of these last three years. But being forgotten wasn't what bothered me. He stuck out his hand. At first I thought he wanted to pat my shoulder and shake my hand, as he had the first time I met him. But no, his hand was turned downward, a clear sign that I was supposed to kiss it. I looked into his eyes again but saw no trace of the sparkle that had enchanted me that first time. I looked around me. The crowd was still shouting their slogans. I had no choice: I bent and kissed his ring.

My tutor came forward after the Imam had left the balcony trying to apologize for my inappropriate behaviour and promising that I would be punished. But the chief of Khomeini's household said that it was perfectly all right; that my unexpected behaviour had lent a certain human touch to the ceremony; that everyone would love to see how the Iranian children would do anything to kiss the hand of their beloved Leader. They suggested that I be encouraged and rewarded.

I didn't care either way. I had not only lost Uncle Habib, Azadeh, Ahmadreza and Uncle Muhammad but also the Leader I adored. That was the last tie between me and the Revolution. I hated myself for my hypocrisy, for betraying myself and for betraying the cherished memory of the wise man who had once taught me not to bow before anyone other than God.

I couldn't pull out of the Islamic Association at school for that would raise too much suspicion. But I decided to use my influence and prevent my classmates from being brainwashed. The first thought that came into my head was to use my parents' strategy: get them to read.

The libraries in the schools had been 'purged' of every book that was deemed 'inappropriate'. Ours had only religious books and 'approved' fiction and non-fiction: hundreds of volumes of the Quran, individual chapters (*surahs*) of the Quran, prayer books, books by the official writers of the system, stories about the lives of the prophets and Imams.

It was time the students broadened their horizons.

We found a broken bookshelf in a ruin outside school and dragged it into class. We bought a lock for it out of our fund and then I made an official announcement: the next step in getting closer to the ideals of the Revolution was to act according to a saying of the Prophet: 'One hour of reading is more blissful than 70 hours of prayer.' I asked everyone to bring a good book from home and donate it to our library; whenever they wanted their books back, they would be returned.

In less than a week we had more than a hundred books. I contributed quite a bit by donating those I had most enjoyed reading: the ones by Tolstoy, Stevenson, Twain, Nesbit and some on the history of science which Dad had given me. Every student could borrow two books a week if he were a donor and one if he weren't. We also decided to write short stories instead of our usual essays during our creative-writing classes, fed up as we were with the standard topics placed before us: 'Which is better, Knowledge or Wealth?' 'Describe an Autumn Day.' 'What Should We Do to Help the Revolution?' 'Your Love for Imam Khomeini: Describe It!'

Dark clouds loomed over our fates in less than a month. Apparently, this time I had gone too far.

The first storm was raised by our teacher of creative writing. We had been told to write about 'Bravery' and I had written a short story about a sheep dog. One day, a shepherd got lost and a pack of wolves attacked his flock of sheep. His sheepdog herded them towards the village while he tried to keep back the wolves. He fought hard and was finally wounded and killed. But, by then, the sheep had already reached the village and were saved.

My teacher didn't like the story. He claimed I had plagiarized it, which made me furious. 'Why do you think I have stolen this story?' I shouted, 'I've written it myself!'

'An 11-year-old cannot possibly have written it!'

'You have to prove I stole it. Where did you read this story?'

'I don't know where but it's definitely not by YOU!'

He was beginning to lose his temper but changed tack soon enough. 'And you weren't asked to write a story. You were asked to write about bravery!'

'This is bravery, isn't it?' I responded, 'Giving up your life to save the others'!'

But the teacher wasn't interested in my opinion. He gave me 10 out of 20 and asked me to sit down.

I didn't realize there was a conspiracy afoot until two weeks later when I was summoned by the Tutor of Islamic Manners.

'We haven't authorized the setting up of a library in your class,' he said.

'But we simply wanted to encourage our classmates to read more books!'

'There's the school library if they want to read.'

'But there are a lot of good books in our class library that aren't available in the school library.'

'There is a good reason for that,' he smiled, 'They aren't good books.'

I didn't know what to say. I had only just realized the enormity of what I had done.

'This book, for example, *War and Peace* by the communist Tolstoy.'

It was my turn to smile, 'Tolstoy wasn't a communist.'

'He was. All Russian authors are communists.'

'But he died long before the Communist Revolution!' I insisted.

The teacher raised his eyes and looked straight into mine: 'And why do you know so much about the Communist Revolution? Perhaps you are a communist? Perhaps your parents are communists?'

Oh God! I had ruined everything!

'No, no. I am a true believer in Islam and the Revolution.'

He raised his eyebrows. 'Then why do you have this book about this cursed Darwin and his stupid theory of evolution in your library?'

'Darwin? Stupid?' I hadn't known that Darwin was a forbidden topic too.

'Yes, Darwin claims that our ancestors were monkeys. That's stupid!'

'But . . .'

'Whereas the Holy Quran teaches us that Allah created Adam and Eve from clay. Darwin is going to burn in hell for corrupting the minds of people.'

I decided that silence was the best strategy.

'Listen, Arash. It is never too late to correct your mistakes. Next week we will have a nice book-burning ceremony in our courtyard. You can invite your classmates to bring all the inappropriate books and we will celebrate the destruction of heretic ideas.' He handed me a list. 'These are the books in your library that have to be destroyed. The rest you can keep.'

*The Adventures of Huckleberry Finn, Tom Sawyer, Treasure Island, War and Peace, 1001 Nights, The Little Black Fish* and, of course, *Fahrenheit 451* were only a few of the titles that were sentenced to be burnt at the stake.

I cried all night. I couldn't believe that we were going to have an actual *book-burning ceremony*. When I had read about the book burnings in Nazi Germany I had thought they were a myth. No one could celebrate burning books. But now . . .

I had to save the books no matter what. I got together my classmates and told them that we had to shut down our library as a result of 'technical problems' with the school; that everyone should take their books back. When the Tutor of Islamic Manners came to our class at the end of the week to collect the doomed books he found the bookshelf empty.

This bit of cleverness on my part didn't entirely avert the threat. The Tutor didn't say anything but that was the end of his support for the class and for me. He bided his time, waiting for his turn to catch me out. And so he did, a month before the final school exams.

'I've been checking on you, and I'm concerned about your loyalty to the Revolution,' he said as I stood before him in his room.

Fear overwhelmed me and I found myself unable to say a word.

'You could be a spy of one of our numerous enemies.'

'But . . . I am not! I am loyal . . . !'

'Well,' he said, holding out a sheet of paper, 'this is your chance to prove it. We need to know about the students' families and you will help us to do so.'

I looked at the sheet of paper: it contained a list of religious and political questions.

'Any child brought up in a proper Islamic environment will know the answers to these questions. If they don't, we will know that their families are not faithful to the Revolution and we will act accordingly.'

I was supposed to spy on my classmates!

'You will ask each of them the questions and record each of their answers.'

I had no choice but to agree. Later, I could try and come up with a way out of this horrible situation.

'All right, Sir, I'll work on it.'

He smiled, and I knew it wasn't over.

'There's something else.'

What else?!

'After the final exams, a caravan of schoolboys is being sent to the front to join our valiant Basij. We want YOU to be on that caravan.'

'ME?!' My knees began to tremble.

'Yes, this way you will prove your loyalty,' he answered, handing me another sheet of paper.

'Ask your father to sign this approval form. You've had enough military training and you'll receive more when you enlist.'

He laughed when he saw the fear in my eyes.

'Don't worry, you youngsters won't participate in any operations. You won't have to fight. You'll help in the kitchen and can come back in time for the next academic year.'

It was time I talked with Dad.

Dad decided to act, and act fast. First, he came to our school and talked to the headmaster who was a decent man. He asked him not to bother me before my exams were over. Then he moved heaven and earth, including contacting all his friends in high places, to get me out of the impasse. As soon as I had finished my last exam, he had me transferred to another school before the Tutor of Islamic Manners could find out.

'You will remain silent here!' said Dad, with 'the look' in his eyes. 'No more heroic activities! No more libraries! No more cooperatives! No more pretentious behaviour! And no more HYPOCRISY! You will stick to studying and friends and sports!'

No problem.

I saw Farhad again, 18 years later. When I didn't return to school the following year, my friends were told that I had failed all my exams and been expelled. Apparently, the Islamic Manners Department was so furious with my getting away that the school decided to ruin my 'leader' image.

But as Farhad said, it didn't really matter. 'When I heard that you'd become a publisher, I thought it was inevitable. You were always concerned with making other people read!'

During the summer of 1982, Mum, who believed I really needed some time off, insisted I take tennis lessons. She thought I'd got too involved with studying and reading and that I needed to think more about some sort of physical training. But, only a day before I was to begin my tennis lessons I received an offer from my grandfather Hadj-Agha: Would I come and work for him during the summer holidays?

Perhaps I made a mistake by saying yes to him. Perhaps I lost my only chance at learning how to play tennis and thereby joining the bourgeoisie. My friends and the children of my family friends went skiing every winter but my parents couldn't afford the kit. So I missed what was for many Iranians the best opportunity for some fun in an environment rather more liberal than that of our daily lives. Tennis was an alternative opportunity and my parents were offering it to me. Had I chosen tennis over bookselling that summer I am convinced that my life would have turned out completely different. Tennis and skiing were social markers that differentiated the upper classes from the rest, the elite from the mob, the happy from the striving and, of course, the complacent from the fighters. I wanted to be a fighter. And Dad had asked me not to be a hypocrite.

Pretending to a class and lifestyle different from my own would be the absolute manifestation of hypocrisy. The decision to work for Hadj-Agha had another, more significant, effect on my life: I fell in love with the business of books.

My day began early in the morning. I had to take the bus and be at the shop by 9. Then Hadj-Agha's assistant would unlock the door. My job was to look after a stand of discounted books outside the shop, mainly novels and books for children. Most of the sales happened in the afternoon, so I usually had all morning to sit on my stool and read or watch the passers-by; a highly educational pastime, especially when I decided to play Sherlock Holmes and guess their identities. I soon developed a good sense of the character of every stranger who went by, merely through a combination of their behaviour and their clothes. I could tell if someone in an old coat was poor or simply careless about his appearance; sometimes, I could even tell how much money he had in his pockets.

Afternoons inside the shop were just as interesting. Hadj-Agha was against electronic calculators and preferred that I do the sums by hand. Hence, my arithmetic skills swiftly improved and I could soon calculate any discount without putting pen to paper. I also learnt how to negotiate. When the customers saw me, they assumed I would be easy to bargain with. But when they realized I had read every book on the stand and that I could explain why each book was an important buy, and a good one at that discounted price, they would inevitably end up making a purchase. Soon I ran out of my stock of discounted books and I asked Hadj-Agha to order more. His main intention in hiring me had been to help him get rid of his unsold stock. When he realized how lucrative the sale of discounted books could be, he decided to expand. And this time he offered me a place *inside*.

I was officially a bookseller—and a successful one, too.

This job gave me the opportunity to engage in long religious discussions with Hadj-Agha even though I was no longer religious. I raised such a lot of questions that sometimes he would be quite furious with me. I was finally asked to stop talking nonsense or else I would be fired.

It also gave me the chance to meet several of the mullahs who came there. I would listen to Hadj-Agha's heated discussions with them, especially when he, very carefully, criticized the idea of the Rule of the Jurisprudent. One day I heard him telling a mullah: 'God asked the Twelfth Imam to go into Occultation. It means that God didn't want him to rule the Muslims for the time being. This concept can be interpreted to mean that God didn't want the State to be mixed up with Religion until the time is right for it to be so. In the meantime, the people should be ruled by the laws of man and religion should be practised individually, as a private matter. I believe Shia Islam is the most secular religion in the world!'

The mullahs obviously disagreed, although with the utmost respect.

If I hadn't worked for Hadj-Agha that summer I would perhaps have not been able to set up a publishing house many years later nor turn it into one of the most innovative and successful publishing companies in Iran. Destiny plays its own tricks. That summer, all I wanted to do was work and make some money. And overcome my frustrations.

Nothing more.

Throughout 1982 and 1983, silence was my language at my new school. I studied hard, I made one or two friends, I didn't participate in any of the collective or extracurricular activities unless I was forced to. My family really wanted me to take up sports; so I enrolled in a karate class near school and took lessons three afternoons a week. Something within me had died. I had lost my ambition, my motivation, my drive to change the world and my appetite for socializing. Karate was the one thing that gave meaning to my life. It was an individual pursuit and no teamwork was involved unless there was a competition and our club was participating. I think I made quite rapid progress. I learnt how to master my body and thoughts, how to be tough and to withstand—as well as inflict—punches and kicks, I learnt how to study my opponent and how to be patient until he showed his weakness, and I learnt how to play with the fear I could sense in my opponent, no matter who and how strong he was. I was promoted to yellow belt and then to orange belt but a blow below my abdomen put me in hospital for two days. Thereafter my parents, concerned about the lack of safety precautions in class, wouldn't let me continue. That was the end of my martial arts life though not of my enthusiasm for them. I practised at home for a while but it was difficult without an instructor and soon I gave up; although I did watch every single martial arts film I could get hold of, no matter how mindless it may have been.

At the time, the only outlet left to schoolboys for an expression of our individualitiy was our hairstyles. But the following year, at the height of the 1980s' craze for fancy hair, we were suddenly told by the headmaster that we had to shave our heads. I resisted for a few days; I loved my hair and thought of myself as a little Samson, much more secure with my long locks. But after I was prevented from entering school one morning I was forced to give in: I went to a barber's shop and surrendered myself to the razor's edge.

The loss of my hair had a devastating effect on me. It had been the last sign of my individuality, and its absence pushed me further into my corner of solitude and isolation.

Meanwhile, Mum's troubles were just beginning. She had been transferred and was now working as a librarian at a girls' high school. There, she was facing the same problems I had with my small class library but on a much bigger scale. She was given a list of the books that needed to be 'purged' from the library— books sentenced to the flames—and she was trying hard to save a few. But this wasn't the only thing that was destroying her. The primary cause of her suffering was the periodic police raids carried out on the school and the arrest of students who were branded 'anti-Revolutionary', either communists or supporters of the People's Mujahideen. She began to object to the arrests but only succeeded in further compromising her own situation. Her actions raised the suspicions of the Islamic Department and they began to exert pressure. Had it not been for the reopening of the universities that allowed students to return to their courses, she would have been in even greater trouble. As it was, she instantly resigned and returned to her studies.

By the end of 1983, we moved to a new and much smaller house. We could no longer afford the rent on the large house and, in any case, the owner had returned from abroad.

*1982*

On 24 May 1982, after several years of fear and sorrow, a wave of joy swept the country. 'Khorramshahr is liberated!' This announcement didn't have quite the same effect on the public as 'The Shah is Gone!' but the joy was comparable.

Khorramshahr was one of the last and most strategic Iranian territories still occupied by Iraqi forces. Iran had taken the offensive and, with the support of millions of untrained volunteer Basijis at the front, had succeeded in forcing the Iraqi armies to retreat from most of the occupied lands, which now included the port city of Khorramshahr in Khuzestan province.

Saddam Hussein was now forced to retreat behind the official border as well as to confess that continuing the war was no longer plausible. The latest defeats had left the Iraqi army too demoralized and damaged. At the same time, Israel had invaded Lebanon. Saddam Hussein suggested to Khomeini that they should stop fighting and send their armies to help the Lebanese and the Palestinians. Backed by Saudi Arabia and other Arab states in the Persian Gulf, he even offered Iran US$70 billion by way of war reparations and the complete evacuation of his forces from Iranian territory.

A complete and total victory seemed in sight for the Iranian troops who had fought with nothing more than their old-fashioned rifles and their bare hands. They had sacrificed their lives, their limbs, their families and their youth in defence of their homeland. Now the enemy was offering a truce. Peace seemed so close.

But Khomeini was intoxicated with the idea of a total victory. He had destroyed all his potential competitors within Iran; he had gained immense popularity among the young as the 'Father of the Nation'; and, as the Vicar of the Hidden Imam, the Shia considered him the holiest man on earth. Now, the retreat of Saddam Hussein could prove his righteousness.

It was at this moment that he made the biggest mistake of his life.

To the surprise of everyone in the country, even his closest friends, Khomeini declared that the liberation of Palestine from the occupation of the Israelis would not be possible until Iraq had been liberated from Saddam Hussein. Therefore, Iran would not accept the truce unless Saddam Hussein was arrested and tried; the government of Iraq paid US$150 billion by way of war reparations and released all the imprisoned Shia in Iraq. Declaring 'The road to Quds [Jerusalem] passes through Karbala,' Khomeini further insisted that Karbala and Najaf, two of the most sacred cities for the Shia and located in southern Iraq, must first be liberated.

But after a few days he changed his mind.

'There are no conditions except that the regime in Baghdad must fall and be replaced by an Islamic Republic.'

This decision turned a defensive war into an absurd, ideological one that continued for another six years, during which up to a million Iranian soldiers were killed, hundreds of thousands more maimed or rendered homeless and the Iranian economy shattered. It would take years to rebuild the country. Iraq fared no better, with an estimated 160,000–240,000 dead and 375,000 casualties.

I thought things couldn't possibly get worse nor life any gloomier when another series of blows fell across our fortunes.

Hormoz and Reza Company, Dad's close friends who had been expelled from university two years earlier for their affiliation with the Tudeh Communist Party, were at home when I returned from school one day in February 1983. They were playing backgammon and chatting and everything seemed 'normal', although I knew that was far from the truth. Dad never came home so early and Hormoz and Reza had suddenly appeared in our house after several months' absence.

I said hello, left them and waited for Mum to come home from university.

She, too, returned earlier than usual. I asked her what was going on. She motioned for me to be quiet and said she'd explain later. Then she joined Dad and his friends. I went to my room and tried to help Golnar who had recently begun school and was learning the alphabet and numbers. A little later I was called to join the grown-ups for tea and I noticed that the three men were working hard at repairing something while they chatted. It was our toaster! It had been broken for a while and a new one was not to be found in the shops; Iranian industries were not producing toasters and they couldn't be imported either because of a combination of customs regulations and sanctions. Dad was in love with toasted bread. Both his friends were electrical engineers: it made sense to ask them to try and fix it. It also gave me an excuse to stick around: I, too, wanted to learn how to fix a toaster.

But the atmosphere was too tense. All of the leaders of the Tudeh Party had been arrested during the past two days and now the police were looking for all other members and affiliates on the grounds that they were spying for the KGB. Hussein, another mutual friend, had already been arrested and Hormoz and Reza knew they were being pursued. Although Dad had never been a supporter of the Tudeh Party—rather, he was one of its more serious critics—they had turned to him for help because they could no longer trust anyone within the Party.

They stayed until late. Hormoz stayed overnight. Despite Dad's insistence Reza Company would not. He claimed there were important matters he needed to take care of before making his decision.

Just before he left, he asked Mum for a plastic bag into which he carefully put all the pieces of the toaster. Then he handed it to Mum and said, 'Well, Pari, I think I'll need to come back in a few days with my tools. I can't fix it without them, and I need to buy a spare part for it as well.' He laughed. We all knew there was nothing wrong with Dad's tools. It was the anxiety that prevented him from concentrating.

He never returned to finish the job: he was arrested as soon as he got home. That was the last time I ever saw him. The disconnected pieces of the toaster remained in our cupboard for many years, a symbol of the lives that had come apart after the Revolution.

Hormoz fled the country through the mountains, entrusting his wife and two children to Dad. I never saw him again either. It took his wife and their two children six months to get their passports and another six months to get visas to Germany, where Hormoz had finally ended his journey. During that time they had no contact with Hormoz other than a few phone calls every couple of months, less than two minutes long and made from public phone booths. They also had enormous financial problems; all their savings had been used up after Hormoz's dismissal from university, and his wife had been fired because she was married to a 'traitor' and had not filed for divorce. The night before their departure, she called Dad and thanked him for everything he had done for them in Hormoz's absence. Dad offered to take them to the airport but she declined.

By now Dad had lost most of his friends. Hussein and Reza Company were sentenced to seven years in prison and Hormoz was in exile. A few years later, just before Hormoz died of cancer, Dad and he met for one night in Germany, the better part of which they spent drinking and smoking and telling jokes. Just like old times. As if nothing had happened. They bade farewell in the morning, knowing that it was the last time they were seeing one another.

Hussein's wife didn't have the luxury of joining her husband. She, too, lost her job at university but, after a year of knocking on every possible door, was recruited again by the order of Prime Minister Mousavi in 1984. She took care of her son on her minimal income for the seven years her husband spent in prison, and she never ceased to support Hussein.

Over the next few months, 5,000 leaders and members of the Tudeh Party were arrested. Most of the leaders were paraded on TV, confessing to the crimes deemed most atrocious by the Islamic Republic: spying for the KGB, propagating mistrust towards the regime, corrupting the minds of the young with destructive ideas, treason, subversion and conspiracy to overthrow the regime. A year later, one of the most influential members and ideologues of the Party's Central Committee, Ehsan Tabari, announced that, after reading the works of great Islamic thinkers in prison, he was now 'repudiating' the works he had written over the past 40 years. According to Ervand Abrahamian in his *Tortured Confessions*, Tabari realized that his entire life's work had been 'defective', 'damaging' and 'totally spurious' because it had all been based on unreliable thinkers: Freemasons nourished by the Pahlavis, secularists, Western liberals and Marxists linked to imperialism and Zionism.

There were rumours about these confessions being made under torture. Most of the activists had been members of the Tudeh Party for many years and had endured long-term imprisonment during the Shah's regime. But they had never confessed to spying or treason. Now Tabari, after 50 years of being a party theoretician and the author of several books defending Marxism and defying religion, was repenting and declaring himself a strong believer in Islam.

After the death of Khomeini and the ascension of Khamenei to the position of Supreme Leader in 1989, Noureddin Kianoori, Secretary General of the Tudeh Party, wrote him a letter which became available to the public only 20 years later. In it he describes the tortures endured by him, his family and other members of the party; how his daughter and wife had been tortured in front of him and how he had been beaten, chained up and forced to witness the execution of his friends. He simply wanted the new Leader to know what was going on in Iranian prisons, assuming that he would care. Khamenei never responded, and it was soon evident that he was going to follow the legacy of his predecessor to the letter.

Tudeh's top leaders were sentenced to long-term imprisonment; the second tier of membership was executed; others were sentenced to between 7 and 10 years. This was the end of the Party: the last vestiges of plurality in Iranian society were wiped out. Now Iran had only one party and that wasn't even a registered one: 'There is no Party but Hezbollah (Party of God); there is no leader but Ruhollah [Khomeini].'

Imagine yourself in an Orwellian environment. There is a war going on that you no longer believe in but you are being trained every day for the honour of being one of its martyrs. Your childhood friends have all left the country. You have never had a chance to discover the opposite sex. You are not allowed to express any signs of individuality lest you arouse suspicions. Anyone around you who dared criticize the regime is in prison or in exile or has been executed. There is a formidable horror hanging over every tomorrow. What have you got to help you cling to your sanity?

'I want a VCR!'

This was the first time I had asked Dad for anything in many years, and I knew it wasn't a reasonable request. Nearly a year ago, the sale of VCRs had been banned in Iran and the video clubs all shut down. But I really wanted one. I had lost confidence in my schoolmates, karate no longer interested me, I couldn't participate in any extracurricular activities, the TV showed nothing but Khomeini's speeches and I had grown horribly afraid after the arrest of Reza Company and Hussein and the exile of Hormoz. Films offered the only escape route; and I think that I would have lost my mind if Dad had not agreed to buy a VCR.

I knew our financial situation wasn't very good, and I knew that Dad was under observation for any suspicious activities. But I wanted that VCR and, to my surprise, Dad agreed. I don't know if it was to gratify the only wish I had expressed in the last three years or if he, too, needed some diversion for his exhausted mind.

Getting hold of one wasn't easy. You had to locate a smuggler and he wouldn't answer your call unless you were recommended by a 'safe' source. And the options were limited: a second-hand T-7 or T-20 Sony Betamax.

The most important thing was the price: about Rls 1,200,000, roughly US$2,000. In other words, a fortune. And it had to be paid in cash. Dad's salary had recently been increased to about US$600 a month, ever since his promotion to Reader because of his immense scientific contributions, his books and his papers which had been published in several prestigious international journals. Even with the raise he could only afford to pay the rent and daily running costs of the home. I had no idea how he was planning to pay for a VCR; when I heard the price, I found myself embarrassed to have asked for it at all. But he was determined to buy one.

The smuggler told Dad that he would come to our home at night, during Khomeini's TV appearance. That was when the roads and streets were under the least surveillance since the police dutifully watched their leader. All four of us sat in the living room, excited, listening to Khomeini's speech and trying not to look at the clock.

At the sound of the doorbell Dad opened the door. A middle-aged man, his hair brown and his moustache extending from one ear to the other, came in, looking around carefully. The first sign of anything suspicious and he would leave. Then he saw us, smiled and greeted everyone and sat down, putting the carton he was carrying on the table. Unwrapping the black plastic bag from around it, he brought forth the box of a T-20 Sony Betamax. I was almost faint with excitement: I had dreamt about this moment for many years.

'Would you please instal it for us, sir?' asked Dad.

'Of course,' the smuggler answered with a smile, 'but first the money.'

Dad brought out his briefcase, pulled out a bundle of banknotes, counted them carefully and handed them over. When I saw the look in his eyes, reflecting all his financial concerns, his worries about paying the rent, I wanted to cry out, 'Dad, forget about it. I don't want it any more.' But I couldn't. I wanted that VCR. For the first time in my life, I wanted something so badly that I couldn't care less about the rent, the electricity, gas, food, clothing . . . I said nothing but I have not forgotten that look on Dad's face.

My journey into the world of cinema had begun. I borrowed as many films as I could from friends and family. One of Dad's friends gave me five which made my life worthwhile and I still remember them: *Indiana Jones and the Temple of Doom*, *Magnum Force*, *Buona Serra Mrs. Campbell*, *Rocky* and *First Blood*.

I could never have believed that life could be so delightful. I watched the films a thousand times over. I memorized every left hook Rocky received from Apollo, shouting every time with anxiety, hoping that this time Rocky would win. After I'd memorized the entire film, I got bored with it and began watching only the last 15 minutes, the fight between Rocky and Apollo. I've lost count of how many times I watched it. I grew angry that Apollo won the match on points although Rocky had fought so hard. Until I discovered the truth: it wasn't the win that Rocky was after. Not being knocked out for one more round: that was his ambition. And that was what I had to do. Make sure that I wasn't knocked out.

Watching films became far more important than school work. After a year, we could afford to rent videos and Dad called a distributor who came every week and loaned us five films. We didn't have any choice in the number since, for security reasons, he couldn't carry more than five at a time. He hid them in his long coat, especially tailored with five large pockets that could hold the cassettes without being visible. I could watch 250 films a year. We watched the demonstration copies of the latest Hollywood releases even before they were screened in the US. It was the only thing that made me feel that life was still worth living.

But when I finished junior high and prepared myself for senior high, my life in limbo was over. I had to face several new challenges, the most important of which was survival: to survive the knockout for just one more round.

There weren't enough high schools in Tehran back in 1984. Most of the teachers were untrained students who had joined the education system during the Cultural Revolution and had decided to stay on rather than return to university. There were few schools with qualified and experienced staff, and it was absolutely important for Dad that I enrol in one of them. We had finally settled on Razi High School, formerly the Lycée Franco-Iranian Razi. The name of the school had been changed from Razi (after the Iranian physician who discovered Ethanol and distilled it for medicinal purposes) to Shohada (martyrs) but everyone still called it Razi.

It wasn't easy to get in: the number of applicants far exceeded the number of seats. Despite the fact that it was a public, and therefore free, school, only those who volunteered to 'donate' a large sum to the school's funds or those recommended by people with influence were accepted. We didn't have any money; so Dad asked one of his friends in the Ministry of Higher Education to write a recommendation for me. My grades in junior high helped as well.

For senior high school we had to opt for a specific direction in our course of studies: Maths and Physics; Experimental

Sciences; Human Sciences; or Professional Training. There was another option available but only for girls: Housekeeping, during which they learnt how to cook, sew, take care of future husbands and children and how to keep the house clean. I chose Maths and Physics, although I should have chosen Experimental Sciences since I was planning to go to medical school. If it were left to me I'd have chosen Human Sciences as that has always been my passion.

Things were about to get serious. We were only four years away from the National University entrance exam or the Concours. Every year, more than a million graduates, of whom 50 per cent were girls, appeared for the National University entrance exam but only about 100,000 of them were accepted.

Once, in the biology class, in the first year of senior high, our teacher gave us a long and boring lecture on how different plants were fertilized. After a bet with my friend, I raised my hand.

'Yes, Arash,' the teacher said.

'Excuse me, Sir,' I exclaimed, 'I'm intrigued. Why are we supposed to know these things? Does it in any way help us in our future careers or personal life?'

I had expected quite a violent reaction. Teachers usually didn't tolerate doubts about their lessons. But he simply smiled.

'Well, there's the simplest explanation in the world,' he chuckled, 'If you don't learn what I'm teaching you, you will not pass the Concours.' Then he stopped smiling. 'If you don't pass the Concours, you have to do your military service, and you know what that means . . .'

Yes, everyone knew but he explained nonetheless.

'Before you know it a street will be named after you because you will have become a martyr.'

He was right. Out of those 100,000 places offered by the universities, 40,000 were kept for former Basij members who had returned from the front or those who had lost a father, brother or son in the war. Fifty per cent of the applicants were usually boys, who were then conscripted and sent to the front if they didn't succeed in getting into higher education courses. The odds of being killed were one in three. This simple statistic was enough to create enormous anxiety in all of us who were beginning high school. Only 30,000 of the boys would be able to go to university. 470,000 others had to go to the war, of whom 156,000 would die. One thing was for sure: in this life-or-death competition, only the best would survive. It was only then that I understood why my friend Amir had been so petrified and so anxious to get out of the country.

But there was a more serious and more immediate challenge staring me in the face. I had just reached puberty. The male hormones pumping into my veins were pushing me not so much towards survival as they were towards sex.

Tehran is a large city, the largest in the Middle East and the sixteenth largest in the world. Knowing that I may never see Tehran again makes my heart bleed, although it is the same feeling that makes me appreciate its mysteries. It was in senior high that I really got to know Tehran; until then, I only knew the districts where I lived or where I went to school. When I turned 15, my fears of the unknown gradually turned into a craving for adventure. Exploring the streets with my friends became a daily thrill, second only to finding a girlfriend, of course. Having a girlfriend had assumed extreme importance and whoever had succeeded in acquiring one was considered a hero. However, it was easier said than done. We had almost no opportunities to meet girls, let alone build the simplest forms of friendship with them. I say 'almost no opportunity' since we had devised a variety of ways of overcoming this hurdle.

The first solution and the easiest one was the old-fashioned way: convince a friend who had a girlfriend to convince her to convince another girl to meet you. But not all my friends had girlfriends, and I wasn't rich enough to bribe any others with a pizza from the canteen.

Another was telephone dating. Both boys and girls used this long-range communication to connect back then since they had no Internet or Skype, no chat rooms, no online forums, no email and no Facebook or Twitter.

However, the most adventurous way of meeting girls was the 'street chase' game. There was a high school for girls about two miles away from ours. After school, we'd linger in the street until the girls began to appear on their way home. Then we'd choose the most interesting group, usually the one that showed the slightest interest—a look, a smile, even a meaningful frown —and then the long walk would begin. Walking on opposite sides of the street—we didn't want to be spotted by the police patrols—we'd begin by talking loudly, trying to attract their attention, and then gradually draw closer. If the girls were not interested, they'd quicken their steps, a move that told us to go to hell. But if they were, they continued at a leisurely pace and we drew closer and closer until we were able to exchange a few words. That was it, unless a boy in our group and a girl in theirs grew more interested and exchanged phone numbers; otherwise the game ended as soon as the girls began to say their goodbyes and take their separate ways home.

I loved the adventure, although I never tried to find a girl-friend through these street games. Rather, they gave me the opportunity to stay on the streets, meet people and explore unknown districts and alleys in Tehran. The city was my real girlfriend, a warm city, full of mystery, full of the unknown. Confined in the north by the enchanting Alborz Mountains and in the south by the endless desert, it is one of the most beautiful places in the world. This huge metropolis was not much more than a village when the first ruler of the Qajar dynasty, 200 years ago, decided to make it the capital of Iran because of its unique strategic location. Since then, the city has continued to grow, both in area and in the size of its population.

It is also a city of paradoxes. Because of the huge migration from other places in Iran, you can find extremely 'rich' people settled happily in the 'poor' areas where they can identify with the culture; and you can also see people now come down in the world but still living in posh neighbourhoods. There was no such thing as town planning when the city began to grow and it's hard to say whether any district has an identity of its own. The city is made up of vast numbers of blocks of buildings standing beside one another and each possessed of very little aesthetic value. But if you have lived here long enough, Tehran will open up and show you her inner beauty. And that was what I glimpsed on our long walks and journeys through it.

Sometimes we walked north along the popular Vali-Asr Avenue where one could see the large number of trees planted by the Shah's father, ending in the beautiful old and narrow roads of Darakeh, a small village that got absorbed by the city in the course of its unplanned expansion. We had to cross Darakeh whenever we wanted to go to the Alborz Mountains for a long trek. Although we had to pass the gates of hell—Evin Prison— before we were allowed to enter that paradise.

Every Friday we went to the mountains. I hung on to this liberating tradition for more than six years, until the mountains, too, were haunted by Committee members and the police. Many young people discovered that the Alborz Mountains offered an opportunity to meet in a freer, less oppressive environment.

No one who is ignorant of captivity can enjoy freedom. It's not enough to know that you are free to do whatever you want. For the first time in their history, since the 2009 post-election protests in Iran and the police crackdown, the Iranian people have made sure that everyone living in freedom in any part of the planet knows about what is happening in Iran. Neda and many others died while trying to break the walls of their prison, not with their fists but with their lives. Their eyes were gazing at a distant future where they could live free of all restrictions. I no longer feel that Neda's dying gaze was asking 'How did it come to this?' Rather, I feel her trying to say, 'Look! All of you living free without knowing what freedom is, look! All of you taking what you have for granted, look! Freedom is the most precious gift in the world. Somewhere in the world, under a sky the same colour as yours, there's a young girl ready to die to win what you already have. Enjoy your freedom, appreciate it, I am dying to make sure that you will never forget that you are free.'

Neda brought a gift to the entire world: a message of joy.

The same was true of us whenever we went to the Leopard's Den (Palang Chall), high in the Alborz, via the village of Darakeh. We had to cross a long road that passed the haunting landscape of Evin Prison, a sight that sent shivers down our spines. A long wall across the mountain showed us the extent of the prison. No one could say how many people had been executed behind that gloomy wall, how many were rotting in solitary cells, how many were shrieking for help while being tortured to confess to crimes they had never committed. I usually held my breath to slow my pounding heart until the prison was out of sight. Then, as if that terror did not exist, the road turned into a small alley confined on either side by clay walls and covered by the green leaves of mulberry trees, a dusty street that made you feel that time had stood still for 200 years and that your life was not stained with a myriad shades of fear. The place had no memory of the Russian Tsar's invasion of Iran nor of the two world wars and Tehran's occupation by British and Russian troops, the coup by the Shah, aided by the US, against his own people in the 1950s, the Revolution and the bloodbath, the hundreds of executions that had taken place just around the corner, the thousands of bombs that had fallen from Iraqi planes onto the land, the hundreds of thousands of Iranians who had died defending the borders of their country. None of this. Darakeh had no memory; there was no past nor any future. Only the road towards the cloud-covered heights. It was during these weekly mountain treks that I learnt how to enjoy the present; how not to think of the destination but only of the journey.

A huge group of us, boys and girls, met there every week. We walked along the narrow paths, climbed the rocks and had our breakfast in a restaurant on top of the mountain. The scrambled eggs and sausages after our long climb was the ultimate pleasure. We talked, we laughed, we had serious literary or philosophical discussions, we chatted about music without a care in the world. As if no policemen were lurking at the foot of the mountain to make sure we acted according to Islamic Good Manners or to see that the girls were keeping their hijabs intact. I made a lot of friends up there, although I have had no news from any of them over the years. After a few years, the police realized the mountains had to be patrolled. Each week we lost at least one member of our group until only I remained. Eventually the loneliness of the mountain became unbearable and I, too, gave up. We did revive our excursions after Khatami won the election in 1997. But I was too busy at the time and I couldn't afford to lose a day in the mountains. When I did, I found that a new generation—Neda's generation—had emerged and claimed the mountain for their own. *Our* mountain was *theirs* now.

And, unlike us, they would never have to give it up.

I also discovered the power of music in my first year of high school. All of a sudden, a wave of smuggled cassettes made its way into the country. There was both Iranian pop—banned since the early days of the Revolution—and Western pop and rock.

Most of Iran's pop musicians had fled to the US immediately after the Revolution; there they had reconvened and continued to produce their music. Los Angeles formed the heart of this activity and cassettes smuggled out of there began to warm up the secret parties of Iran. I, however, was more interested in Western music. It was in 1983 that I first heard Pink Floyd's 'The Wall', a song that changed many lives. I thought Roger Waters should have written the song for us Iranians, since I couldn't understand why someone educated in a liberal system in the UK should complain about not wanting 'thought control'. Nevertheless, being one of the few boys at school who knew English well enough to make sense of the words, I was forced by my friends to transcribe the lyrics from the low-quality recordings to which we had access. There was no way for us to locate the original lyrics and, given the poor quality of the recordings, I'm not sure I did a very good job. Michael Jackson had just become the biggest hit on the pop scene, Madonna was on her way to becoming the queen of pop and breakdancing had overtaken Iranian schoolboys and girls, as it had everywhere else in the world. Anyone who didn't know how to breakdance was immediately an outcast. At home, I must have watched *Breakin'*, the cult classic, at least a hundred times as well as spent endless hours in front of the mirror, practising Michael Jackson's moonwalk. I never became a particularly good dancer but I learnt enough to be eligible for an initiation into my classmates' secret society. We'd close the doors and curtain off the classroom in- between classes and challenge one another to dance. This was our main diversion at school until our secret society was discovered. The leader was expelled and the rest of us received serious warnings: if we were seen dancing again, we would be expelled too.

But we really didn't care any more. All of us felt that our days were already numbered. The war had reached its peak and we were convinced that we'd soon be sent to the front and die there. There was nothing we could do to delay this death other than study and get into university. We had unconsciously written off 'the future': it didn't exist. And when the future doesn't exist and you are too young to have a past to cling to, you are left with only the present. And one of the most important aspects of living in the present and not looking towards the future is that the word 'consequences' ceases to exist. That's why we had turned into daredevils who would do anything for a moment of excitement; anything for the thrill of knowing that we were challenging a tyrannical system.

And while we, the little blind mice, tried to challenge the mad elephant of a regime at the same time as we groped our way amid the mountain of books on Chemistry, Physics, Literature, Algebra, Geometry, Islamic 'Insights', Arabic, English and Biology, time flew by and the new year drew closer. New Year's Eve 1985 marked the date when I would no longer be allowed to

161

hold a passport to leave the country. As soon as I turned 15, I would be 'on call' in case the army needed me, even though 15 was still three years short of the legal age for military service.

Mum and Dad fought over me constantly. Mum insisted I leave the country while there was still time; Uncle Muhammad, who lived in Paris, had offered to take care of me. Dad, however, believed that a 15-year-old boy needed a family more than anything. He was certain I'd pass the Concours successfully and would not be packed off to the front.

I was not sure what I wanted. I was scared at the thought of the front; the Concours terrified me too. And the freedom I would enjoy in France was definitely tempting. At the same time, I didn't want to be a coward like Amir. There were millions of boys in the same situation. Then again, a lot of my friends had already left or were preparing to leave before the New Year and I really envied them. Whenever Mum and Dad quarrelled over me, I only grew more confused.

'I know Arash doesn't want to leave Iran,' said Dad. 'It's his country, isn't it, Arash?'

'Don't put words into his mouth!' Mum would say, before I had a chance to open my mouth. 'I'm sure he wants to leave. Don't you, Arash?'

I trusted both of them, and I was sure neither of them had the slightest idea about what I really wanted. I didn't want to go to the war, nor did I want to be sent out into the unknown world alone. I wanted all of us to leave: Mum, Dad, Golnar and I. But that was out of question. Dad would never agree to leave Iran. He loved his country.

Finally, they reached a compromise. We would go to Turkey during the Norouz holidays. There, we would decide. If we agreed that I was better off in Iran then we would return together. If not, I would stay back.

Knowing my father and his stubborn nature, I was sure that this was only his way of keeping Mum quiet for a while. I think Mum knew that, too, but perhaps she thought she would be able to convince Dad when we saw that freedom was possible and I could live a life without horror and war.

I was so sure we'd all return together that I didn't say good-bye to any of my friends. We took the coach to Turkey; after many hours of driving, we arrived at the border an hour before midnight. We joined the long queue of travellers who wanted to get through the ordeal of passport control and enter Turkey. We were told it usually took several hours before the Iranian passport control officers could check the backgrounds of all the passengers and let them cross the border to wait in yet another lengthy queue behind the booths of the Turkish passport control. However, I alone had a unique problem: if I didn't cross the border before midnight, I could no longer leave the country. Dad began anxiously to explain the situation to every person ahead of us in the queue, imploring them to give up their places. Although they were all exhausted after their long trips, they all allowed us to go ahead.

When the passport control officer took our passports, checked my age and looked at his watch it was 11:57. Almost a hundred people had gathered behind us, waiting to see if I could cross the border in time. 'Let the boy go!' shouted some of them while others patted Dad's shoulder to keep him calm.

'The background check will take at least 15 minutes,' the passport police finally told Dad: 'There's no way your son can make it in time.'

Dad was furious, biting his lips to stop the words from leaping out. Mum had frozen, and I realized I was the only one who could speak. 'Officer, if you kindly put that exit stamp on my passport in time, I promise you that I will wait in No Man's Land until you have checked my background.'

The officer chuckled and looked at me over the top of his glasses. 'What horrible crime could you have committed anyway, young boy?' he said, stamping my passport. 'No need to wait in No Man's Land.'

The crowd burst into applause and cheers as we stepped over the border and entered No Man's Land.

I was free . . . for two weeks at least.

After waiting for many hours in the long queue outside Turkish customs we crossed the snow and mud of the border. It was 2 in the morning when we finally got into our coach again, this time on Turkish soil. The moment I climbed back into the coach the difference was apparent. Despite the wet clothes, the muddy boots and the exhausted faces, it was obvious we had entered another land. Women were removing their headscarves and putting on make-up, and men were insisting the driver take them instantly to a supermarket to buy alcohol. Since everyone had had a really hard time at the border, the driver agreed to take us to a bar nearby so that we could wash and have coffee or a drink. Moreover, everyone in the bus insisted we celebrate the New Year as well as my escape in the nick of time.

It was the first time I had ever been inside a bar. Everyone ordered beer, bottles of vodka or whatever spirits they could get their hands on. They all insisted—since I no longer needed to do military service—I be allowed to drink a pint, or at least have a sip. And I did, excited at the thought of telling my friends that I had drunk beer!

But the party was soon over and the driver summoned us to the coach. It was time to go. Everyone got in with their bottles. And then the real party began. The driver took out an illegal cassette of Persian pop music and played it while the passengers drank and danced.

We were in the middle of nowhere, driving through the dark along the twisted, snow-covered mountain roads near Erzurum, close to Mount Ararat. We were all dancing and singing, happy to have left the land of restrictions. I, feeling the warmth of alcohol coursing through my veins for the very first time, had no idea I was drunk.

It was pitch black outside. There was a steep drop on the left and a wall of rock and snow on the right. The road was frozen. I didn't care. For the first time in my life, I was not worried about a thing and I believed I had earned it. I simply sat there, soaking in the sight and sounds of song and dance and revelling in the kind of happiness that lasts for a brief time. Then, as if to show us once more that everything in life is temporary, it passes away, leaving behind traces of a pleasant memory, the hope to carry on and the promise that, some day, it will be back.

Our trip from Tehran to Istanbul took four days, most of it through Turkey. After the initial outburst of joy, most of the journey was dominated by the unbearable sounds of the Iranian passengers drinking day and night, singing and dancing, intoxicated with their new—and temporary—freedom. No matter how much I enjoyed this freedom, I resented being on that coach. The first day of celebration was exciting but soon I grew bored. I was curious to see everything I could in this new country, in the outside world; I thought it might be my last chance to see a place in the world other than my own . . . And Turkey was such a beautiful country. However, until we said our goodbyes at the Istanbul coach station and took a taxi to our hotel, there was no chance to discover any of it. But then, as soon as we had settled in our room, the mysterious and enchanting atmosphere of Istanbul beckoned me.

Istanbul is, in my opinion, not the most beautiful capital in the world but certainly the most exotic. As soon as you enter the city, you can feel and smell its unique quality. The only city in the world located on two different continents, Istanbul is, literally and virtually, the bridge between the East and the West, between Asia and Europe. And it has reconciled the paradoxical attributes of these two continents: the exotic, fairy-tale ambience full of modesty and Oriental warmth on the one hand, where any of the young lads passing by could be Aladdin with his magic lamp, and the modern, Western lifestyle on the other, with its aspiration of 'progress' for all. This grew even more obvious when you noticed that the young Aladdin was not clutching a magic lamp but a Walkman playing Michael Jackson or Madonna. Walking along the narrow Oriental-style alleys that open into modern highways creates a certain feeling in the soul that compels one never to forget Istanbul. The Western bars sit right beside traditional coffee houses, and modern skyscrapers beside the 1,500-year-old Hagia Sophia, a Byzantine church transformed into a mosque after the fall of Constantinople to the Ottoman Turks in the fifteenth century. The church-mosque itself shows how different identities can merge to create a new one, the very paradoxical identity of Istanbul. In ancient Greek, Istanbul means 'the city'. And what an appropriate name. As if trying to mark the very essence of a utopia that no one has ever defined in the literature on the subject: the convergence of paradoxes.

I didn't want to lose any time: I wanted to see everything while Mum and Dad debated my fate. I knew the outcome in advance and I didn't want to waste any time. We went from street to street; we took a boat and crossed the famous Bosphorus Strait that marks the boundary between Asia and Europe and stepped into the Asian part of the city. We walked in the traditional Bazaar, where Dad bought the latest fashionable jeans for Golnar and me; we ate delicious kofta while Dad smoked the narguile; and we all listened to Turkish pop songs played on the latest stereo systems.

Before I knew it, our time was over and we were on the same coach, going back along the same road with the same travel companions. They were all astonished when they saw me on the bus and couldn't believe that after all the stress and strain of getting me out of Iran I was on the way back. And voluntarily too.

'Arash loves his country,' Dad explained proudly 'he has no reason to leave it. He wants to stay with his family.'

True, I loved my country but I had very good reasons for leaving it too. For one thing, I didn't want to die or lose a leg running across a minefield, shouting '*Allah-o Akbar*'. Nor did I want to look over my shoulder after every two steps in case a Committee patrol appeared out of nowhere to seize me because of my hairstyle, my new jeans or the Michael Jackson's *Greatest Hits* cassette. I had bought the cassette in Istanbul hoping to be able to smuggle it across the border and impress my friends back in Tehran by being the one who owned the *only* original Jacko tape.

The dancing and drinking resumed on the coach, although this time something was different. When we left Iran, the celebration had been by way of an explosion of several year's suppressed need for fun, released in all too short a time. On the way back, the dances and the songs had a touch of sorrow and nostalgia. It was the dying breath of that freedom: glimpsed, enjoyed and now to be lost once more.

This time I wasn't disgusted at all. My heart bled at the sight of those young boys and girls approaching what they called 'the prison' even as they sang songs about the beauties of their homeland. A woman, about 26 years old, with long black hair and beautiful, sad eyes, wearing a white T-shirt and tight jeans, stood in the middle of the bus and asked everyone to be silent for a moment. Then she spoke. 'Listen, friends, I always dreamt of becoming a singer. I had joined the Opera of Tehran after graduating from high school when the Revolution happened and women were banned from singing. Now I'm only able to sing when I'm alone.'

She stopped to catch her breath. The whole bus was listening in silence.

'Now that we are approaching the border,' she continued after a slug from the bottle of vodka in her hand, 'I've got the feeling that I will never have the chance to sing in public again. Will you be the only audience I will ever have? Will you let me imagine that this small coach on this slippery road is my stage and you are my public? Will you clap for me when I finish?'

No one spoke. Her romantic little speech had left everyone speechless. She took the silence as consent, gave the bottle to her friend, opened her arms and began to sing a song by Dariush, the famous Iranian singer.

> *Amidst all these alleys, connected to each other,*
> *Why is our old alley, the dead-end alley?*

The entire coach burst into tears, not only because of the lyrics but also because of the enchanting and heavenly voice that suddenly filled the bus. The intense emotion of her performance and the tears running down her face created an effect that none of us would ever forget.

> *Amidst all these alleys, connected to each other,*
> *Our old alley is the dead-end alley.*
> *The clay wall of a dried garden,*
> *Full of memorial poems,*
> *Stands between us and the great river,*
> *Always flowing, like existence itself.*

*The sound of the river is always in our ears,*
*It is the lullaby for the sweet dreams of the children.*
*But this alley, whatever it is, is the alley of our memories,*
*If it's thirsty, if it's dry, it is ours, it is our alley.*
*We were born in this alley, we are spreading roots in*
       *this alley,*
*And someday, just like Grandpa, we will die in*
       *this alley.*
*But we are in love with the river as well,*
*We can't wait behind the wall,*
*We have been thirsty all our lives,*
*We shouldn't just sing the songs of regret,*
*Take my tired hand,*
*Let's bring down the clay wall,*
*One day, some day, sooner or later,*
*Together we will reach the great river,*
*We will bathe our thirsty bodies*
*In the clear pure water of the river . . .*

The coach fell silent, breaking into applause only when the tears had dried. The last few hours of the trip were spent in silence as everyone tried to finish the last drops of vodka before we arrived at the border.

That song enlightened me. I didn't cry. I didn't sob. While we were crossing the border, I was extremely worried about my Michael Jackson cassette. I had given it to the driver who had promised he'd smuggle it in for me. At the same time, my mind was elsewhere. I had just realized why Azadeh, Uncle Habib and Ahmadreza had died; why Hormoz was never going to see his friends again; why Reza Company and Hussein were in prison, why those young men volunteered to run over the mines; and why Dad had insisted I return to Iran. If everyone gave up, who would tear down the clay wall between the great river and us?

When I stepped over the border and re-entered Iran, I had already made up my mind. I would never think again about abandoning our little dead-end alley.

Other than studying and spending time out with friends, the most important event in my first year at senior high was having my first girlfriend. I met her in the old-fashioned way: my friend Kaveh and his girlfriend arranged a meeting. We met on a bus; it was the only place we could talk freely without being persecuted by the Tharallah Patrol in their 4WD Nissans (nicknamed '4 Welgard-e Daiouth', loosely translated as 'Four Wandering Dicks').

She was a beautiful girl, tall, fair and blue-eyed, qualities uncommon in the Middle East. She said that her great-great-grandfather was Russian, hence her unusual colouring. She also explained that her parents were overprotective and would never allow her to meet a boy.

The four of us tried to sit in a coffee shop at some point for a coffee and chat but the owner threw us out: the Committee would shut down his business if they found out he allowed unmarried couples in his cafe.

We began to walk in the streets and quiet alleys, trying to find out more about one another. Trying to be charming and amusing yet staying constantly on the alert is not easy. If we spotted the shadow of a 4WD patrol, we would separate and walk alone, pretending that we had nothing to do with one another.

After an hour or two, we decided we liked one another and exchanged phone numbers. She explained that I must never call her but that she would call me whenever her parents were not home. Then we went our separate ways.

Our secret phone calls and dates went on for two years, during which we fell in love. Was it the real thing or only an infatuation? How could we tell? None of us had had the opportunity of meeting anyone of the opposite sex and we thought our relationship was unique. Whatever the truth of the matter, it was the most beautiful feeling. Whenever she had a chance, she called me and we talked for as long as possible. Sometimes, when her parents were not at home, she invited me over for a chat. More than once we lost track of the time and were almost caught by her mother. But we always managed to save ourselves in the nick of time. She'd hide me in the basement and I would leave the house as soon as an opportunity presented itself.

While I was experiencing my first romantic encounter, the country was still at war. One by one, my schoolmates dropped out to volunteer for the Basij and go to the front. The soldiers were exhausted, the sanctions had devastated the economy, the price of oil was dropping fast and Prime Minister Mousavi was trying hard to find some balance between the low GNP, providing for the essential needs of society and putting enough funds aside for military equipment and the cost of the war.

He did a brilliant job. No one starved and the army, superior in numbers despite its lack of proper artillery, stood up to the better-equipped Iraqi forces. The war had turned into an exhausting war of attrition, consuming lives and resources on both sides. Iraq received support from the USSR, France, the UK, Egypt, Saudi Arabia and the US; the only countries that supporting Iran were North Korea, Libya and China. However, over the previous two years, the army had launched several offensives, most of which had failed. Iran was never to repeat the feat of liberating Khorramshahr. It did, however, retaliate with its own missile attacks on Iraqi cities after Iraqi air raids on Iranian cities. This counter-attack succeeded in putting an end to the 'war of the cities' for a while.

In the meantime, Khomeini insisted on continuing the war until Saddam Hussein was successfully overthrown. 'It is our belief that Saddam wishes to return Islam to blasphemy and polytheism,' he said, 'if America is victorious . . . and grants victory to Saddam, Islam will receive such a blow . . . that it will not be able to raise its head for a long time. The issue is one of Islam versus blasphemy, and not of Iran versus Iraq.'

But Khomeini's propaganda wasn't as effective as in the early days of the Revolution; people knew he could have ended the war two years ago. But when, at the end of 1984, Saddam upped the ante, the situation changed. He began with another massive air and missile campaign against Iranian towns, including Tehran. This was followed by attacks on Iranian tankers, oil refineries and terminals. By the time he began to use chemical weapons against Iranian troops, the people of Iran had had enough. Once more, they rallied to the support of the troops, to their own children at the frontline. A new wave of volunteers moved into the war zone. US President Ronald Reagan had already said that the US 'would do whatever was necessary to prevent Iraq from losing the war with Iran,' and this, too, fanned the flames of hatred. The Iranians believed the US had always intervened in Iranian affairs, and this latest declaration further renewed support for the war.

Khatami was Minister of Culture at the time and everyone was aware of his liberal ideas on freedom of speech and his resistance to any form of censorship. He failed to secure free-dom for the media and the only available sources of informa-tion were three state-owned newspapers and TV. We had no access to any other information; even BBC Radio was hard to get because of the enormous jamming waves sent out by the government. However, Khatami was successful in resisting any censorship on books, and that provided us with a chance to get hold of several brilliant translations of international literature, a gift that we took for granted at the time but which, too, was not to last for long.

Ebrahim left early in the autumn of 1985 to enrol in the Basij and went to the front after two weeks' military training. He was religious but not a zealot. We were good friends and he put up with all our rebellious activities. He was two years older than the rest of us, but, because he was Jafar's cousin, we often spent time together. He always left at the sound of the azan to join the rest of the students in the prayer hall. I had given up going to the prayer hall ever since I had confronted my conscience.

Ebrahim wasn't the only one who went to the war from our school. Every week the authorities came to enrol Basiji from among the students. They told all the 15-year-olds that they no longer needed their parents' approval: in Islam, 15 is considered the age of majority for boys. Every week we had a farewell ceremony for our friends who were going off to war. When it was Ebrahim's turn to leave, he hugged each us and asked us to forgive him for any unintended hurt he may have caused us. I was trying hard not to cry. We all knew he was walking to his doom. He had only received two weeks' training and even he knew that the odds against his return were very high. The Basij were usually the frontline of any offensive. However, his eyes were shining. I had never seen so much joy on a person's face.

It was not long before he returned: in a coffin, only two months after he set out. Another friend who had been with him at the time told us that he had been shot in his stomach in an intelligence-gathering mission. Why had they sent a 16-year-old boy to gather intelligence? The answer escapes me.

His funeral procession began from the schoolyard. We all followed his coffin. Some of the students were crying; we, his closest friends, could not. As soon as he left, we knew that we had lost him forever. When you lose someone so dear to you, the sorrow runs so deep that tears do not come.

Our Islamic Manners teacher, Mr Moradi, couldn't stop weeping. He was one of our most hated teachers. Always nosing into the students' affairs, always threatening to disapprove our entrance to university if we didn't follow the rules, if we wore jeans, if we didn't cut our hair short, if we didn't pray . . .

But now he was genuinely upset. As Ebrahim's friends, we had been given the privilege of walking immediately behind the coffin. Immersed in sorrow as I was, I could feel his torment as he walked beside us. 'How graceful has God been to Ebrahim!' I heard him murmur, 'How lucky he has been to receive the highest honour of being a martyr!'

I felt an uncontrollable rage bubbling up within me and could stay silent no longer.

'It wasn't luck, Mr Moradi!' I shouted.

He turned to me in astonishment, his eyes red from grief. Everyone around us fell silent. The coffin continued its way on the shoulders of the students.

'He made a choice! If you think you envy him, why don't you volunteer to go to war instead of staying and encouraging teenagers to go . . . instead of torturing us with your threats?'

When I realized I had better shut up, it was already too late. My friends pulled me away before I could say any more but not before I had seen the look in Mr Moradi's eyes, swollen from crying. That look made my blood turn cold. I knew how vengeful he was. Everyone knew that he would never forget, that he would never forgive.

We all went to Behesht-e Zahra, the public cemetery, on the buses provided by the school. We were there when Ebrahim's body was washed and shrouded. We buried our friend, came back home and went back to school the next day as if nothing had happened. Our hearts were hardening already. But something had changed. Mr Moradi didn't come to the school that day or the day after. While we were attending Ebrahim's wake at the mosque, I looked around to see if I could spot Mr Moradi and apologize to him for my rudeness. But he wasn't there, which was most unusual.

Ebrahim's was neither the first nor the last funeral we attended that year. Most of our friends who had gone to the front returned home in less than three months: dead. But Mr Moradi was still missing. I asked about him but no one knew where he was and I slowly grew more and more relieved. Perhaps he had been transferred; if so, I could stop worrying about retribution.

Mr Moradi came back five months later, also in a coffin. The ceremony began from the schoolyard once more and ended beside his freshly dug grave at Behesht-e Zahra. Apparently he had enrolled in the Basij the day after Ebrahim's funeral. I couldn't help thinking I was responsible. Had I sent him to his death? That sense of guilt has never left me. Mr Moradi, the teacher I hated the most, taught me the most important lesson of my life: that words *can* kill.

A street was named after Ebrahim shortly after his death but Mr Moradi was deprived of the privilege. By the time he died, we were running out of streets.

Mr Moradi, who was from a small village far from Tehran, had no one to make sure he was remembered.

I was forced to break up with my girlfriend. Her parents found out about us and compelled us to end the friendship. Then, worried about their daughter indulging in another such relationship, they made her drop out of school and marry an older man. All my attempts at convincing them to let her attend school were in vain. They hung up on me when I telephoned and threw me out of the house. Finally, her mother threatened to call the police if I didn't stay away. That was the end of that. Ladan tried to call me a few times, crying, begging me to marry her so that her parents wouldn't make her marry that hateful old man. But I couldn't marry her: I was only 16.

I never saw her again. But 20 years later, when I had become a well-known writer and publisher, she sent me a letter. She had two children and lived with her husband in a small town far from Tehran. She had finally managed to finish high school, 20 years later. She knew the diploma would be of no use because her husband wouldn't let her work or go to university. She explained that she had done this only for me; she was sure that I would never have recovered from the guilt of bringing about the end of her education. She was right. But even knowing that she had finally finished high school was no consolation.

The next two years passed in much the same way: secret parties, studying, attending friend's funerals, school trying to brainwash the students, the students trying not to be brainwashed . . .

One important thing happened, though: I bought my first computer, a ZX spectrum computer with 48 kilobytes of RAM and no hard drive. The world of computers mesmerized me instantly. Instead of studying, I spent most of my free time learning BASIC and playing computer games. I must have been one of the first users of personal computers in Iran.

Boom! We heard the sound of the explosion just as we reached the cellar. It was March 1988. The sound was so close. Another house was destroyed. Madar began to pray, calling on the Prophet and naming all the Imams and saints one by one. We all heaved sighs of relief. We had survived another rocket attack and some other family had died. We were sorry for them but there was no time for compassion. It would take the Iraqis only a few hours before they launched another missile at Tehran.

The Iraqis had relaunched the 'war of the cities'. The first missile landed in Tehran immediately before New Year's Eve, Norouz. The Iraqi army had not made any advance on land and Saddam had therefore decided on a diabolical strategy. He began by using cyanide bombs in the second wave of his chemical attacks against Iranian troops and even against his own people, the Kurdish villagers of Halabja. Thousands of civilians were massacred in the blink of an eye and thousands more suffered long-term effects from which most died over the next few years.

This was followed by a new series of missile attacks, every few hours, against the major Iranian cities. It wasn't like the aerial bombing of the cities in 1980 at the start of the war. There was no time for anyone to seek refuge in a shelter. When TV or radio announced the Red Alert, it was only a matter of seconds before we heard the explosions that destroyed houses and left dead bodies in their wake. Iran began a counter-attack on Baghdad and the other major Iraqi cities within its range. The citizens realized with sinking hearts this war of the cities could go on for a long time. They began to leave the cities for the small villages outside Tehran, particularly in the North, where they were protected from the Iraqi missiles by the high mountains of the Alborz. Schools, universities and public offices were shut down so that everyone could run for their lives.

It would have been my fault had anything happened to us at that time. The more Mum and Dad insisted that we leave Tehran, the more I resisted. The National University entrance exam was only three months away and I was by no means prepared. My time over the past three years had been spent in rebellion rather than in preparation. I told Mum and Dad that the next three months were my only chance at catching up; I was staying in Tehran no matter what. My room was in the basement and I felt I'd be safe there. I encouraged them to leave me behind and go North. They didn't agree, of course. Even Madar left her home in Qom and joined us, to make sure that we were all right.

I spent the next three months studying under siege. People were dying all around me, the Iranian troops were exhausted by the Iraqi chemical attacks and the US Navy had recently entered the war on the Iraqi side, bombing Iranian oil platforms in the Persian Gulf.

Two days after I attended the Concours, the US navy shot down an Iranian civilian aircraft and killed all 290 passengers, including 66 children. The US claimed to have mistaken it for a warplane. No one in Iran believed this story, even for a minute, and it came as the final blow against the fragile forces of Iran. On 20 August 1988, Khomeini declared that Iran would accept UN Security Council Resolution 598 on a ceasefire.

> Happy are those who have departed through martyrdom . . . Unhappy am I that I still survive . . . Taking this decision is deadlier than drinking from a chalice full of poison. I submitted myself to Allah's will and took this drink for His satisfaction . . . You know that I had made this pact with you, to fight to my last drop of blood and my last breath but my decision today is only based on expediency discernment. I have defaulted on all my promises, only hoping for God's forgiveness, and if I had any honour, I have now traded it with God.

I heard the news of the ceasefire from Dad. I was standing in front of the door of our house, waiting for a friend. Suddenly, Dad's dark-blue Peugeot 304 turned into the narrow alley and screeched to a halt. He jumped out of the car, flushed with excitement and smiling from ear to ear. Crushing me in a bear hug, he shouted: 'Arash, the war is over!'

I had an acute sense of déjà vu. We were replaying a scene from 10 years ago, when Dad jumped out of the same car and shouted to me that the Shah was gone. I didn't know whether to be excited or worried. The last time I had seen Dad so happy, things hadn't turned out quite the way he'd hoped. The Shah was gone and the first instalment of Dad's dream was fulfilled but that had led to the establishment of another tyranny, far more cruel than that of the Shah and with a million deaths to its credit so far. What would happen now? Dad's dreams usually came true but usually also with dire consequences.

The war was over but we had lost a lot: so many friends gone and so many horrors witnessed. It was hard for us to be completely happy. The war had taken away part of my youth. We were neither happy nor sad. We were confused. No one could be quite sure that the future would be any brighter.

PART III

*You rebuild the country,*
*I will rebuild my pocket*

(Summer 1988–1998)

The summer of 1988 was the best summer of my life. The war was over and I was no longer afraid of falling bombs nor of being brainwashed to run through a field full of landmines. The Concours results had been declared and mine were good enough to secure me a seat at the prestigious Iran University of Medical Sciences.

That was also the summer that I met Maryam.

Maryam was the sister of Mehdi, a schoolmate. That summer it seemed as if the world was opening up before us. I met Maryam at Mellat Park, Tehran's Hyde Park, and it was love at first sight for me. She was not looking for a boyfriend, however, and our relationship began with us being good friends. It was five years before we would realize that we loved one another and take our relationship more seriously. That summer, I began to take pains about my appearance again. I wanted to enjoy my life and there seemed to be no reason why I shouldn't: I was going to be a medical student, a dream come true for any teenager. And, most important, the war was over.

It wasn't long, though, before the Committee's 4WDs took to patrolling the streets again, arresting youngsters for flouting the restrictions governing the interactions between the sexes. No severe punishments were doled out to us, however, and we were let off with no more than warnings after a few of the girls burst into tears. Another day, we were on our way to the mountains when we were stopped by the police. Apparently my hairstyle was 'Western'—I simply hadn't cut it recently—and I was to be given an immediate haircut. But only one side of my head was shaved! I looked like something out of a science fiction film, a creature from another galaxy! I was left with no option but to come back to town and shave the rest of my hair.

Nevertheless, these were mere pinpricks compared to events in the political sphere. New horrors were on their way: Khomeini was about to launch his last and bloodiest campaign.

While we were enjoying ourselves in the parks, at our secret parties and in the mountains, the regime decided—now that the external threats were taken care of—to turn to internal security issues. Over the past eight years, thanks to the war and to the extreme national security measures, most of the internal opposition movements had been suppressed or rendered inactive. But in the summer of 1988, the People's Mujahideen, now a terrorist organization based in Iraq, launched a massive offensive against Iran. The Revolutionary Guard discovered the plot, however, and trapped and massacred the invading troops near the border.

A few years later, during my military service, we were taken by bus to that same spot. The commander enthusiastically explained how they had opened fire from the top of the mountain and slaughtered thousands in this very valley, where we had set up camp. Most of the dead, both boys and girls, had been barely 20. To set an example, he said, they hadn't spared a single life. Even those who tried to escape had been shot. No prisoners. No wounded.

I couldn't help but imagine the field covered with the bodies of 18-year-olds. Most of those 'soldiers' had escaped Iran in search of freedom. The PMO had recruited them by holding out the false hope of overthrowing the Islamic Republic and then sent them off to fight alongside the Iraqi infantry. They had no access to any information about events in the outside world. Masoud Rajavi, their leader, was their only source of news, and they had been trained to worship him like a god. Trapped in yet another orgy of brainwashing, they were the burnt generation. A generation that was promised freedom but was given only death.

This was the situation when Khomeini, trying to discourage the rise of any domestic rebels, declared that all those members of the opposition who were being detained in Iranian prisons, who still did not believe in the Islamic Republic of Iran or in the values of the Revolution, would be executed.

The executions began in the summer. Between 3,000 and 30,000 political prisoners were executed and buried in mass graves at the Khavaran cemetery outside Tehran. The actual numbers were never revealed and perhaps never will be. Only the government has the figures and it has no plans for their disclosure. The Revolutionary Court set up branches across the prisons to try the political prisoners all over again. Those who convinced the judges that they had changed their attitude and repented were either released or allowed to continue with their sentences. Those who did not were executed.

The prisoners were divided into two main groups: Mohareb (Warriors against God) and Mortads (Apostates). The Mohareb were mainly PMO members or affiliates and the Mortads mainly communists. The tribunal had a different set of questions for each group.

'The trials were short and decisive,' Dad's friend Hussein told us. 'No lawyers were allowed. We were tried, one by one.'

Hussein was one of the few survivors and he told us all about it some months later, after his release. Though quite a few of Dad's friends had gathered at our home to welcome him back, there were still many missing, most notably Reza Company. He had not been as lucky as Hussein.

'We knew something horrible was going on but we had no idea of its scope. Inmates were summoned to the court in groups. Some of them returned. Most of them didn't. No one knew what happened to those who didn't. Having lived in the prison for the past few years, we knew we had to prepare ourselves for the worst.'

No one dared mention Reza Company. But Hussein had not forgotten.

'Reza and I were summoned in the same group. Sitting outside the judge's room, we discussed our strategies. He said he was a true communist. And since he was already serving his sentence for that crime, there were no reasons to renounce his beliefs now. But I'm a coward. I don't care about communism any more. I only wanted to see Heidi and my son one more time.'

Heidi took his hand. No one said a word.

'Reza went into the room first. I could hear him shouting, that these questions were irrelevant and that this was like the Inquisition. He said he wouldn't answer. That, according to the Constitution, no one was allowed to enquire about anyone else's beliefs. Then, everything went silent . . . And a few minutes later, another name was called . . .'

He took a big gulp from the glass of water.

'You don't need to explain everything,' said Heidi.

'I want to. Or else I'll die,' he said. His hair had turned grey over the past few years and his 'four-square' moustache was now white. But what struck me most was the look in his eyes. I couldn't find a single sparkle of life in them any more, in those eyes that had always shone with authority.

'By the time it was my turn, I had already made up my mind. I entered. They didn't let me sit. The judge, a middle-aged, man with a beard, calmly asked me my name, age, profession, conviction and the date for my release. Then it was time for the real questions.

'"Are you Muslim?"

'"I was born a Muslim. I never renounced my religion."

'"But you were a communist, weren't you?"

'"I was a member of the Tudeh Party but I never renounced Islam."

'"Are you still a communist?"

'"No. I've learnt a lot about my mistakes in prison."

'"Do you believe in the principles of the Islamic Republic and the values of the Revolution?"

'"I do."

'"What will you do when you are released from prison?"

'"I'll spend most of my time with my family. They have suffered a lot because of my involvement in politics. My son, who was only two when I was arrested, has been deprived of my presence during his childhood. I'll try to find a decent job. I'll never even think of getting involved in politics again."

'The prosecutor seemed pleased with my answers.

'The room had three doors, including the one through which I had entered. While he finished writing his report, the man pointed to the left door and I assumed he meant I was supposed to leave the room through that door.'

He found out later that the prisoners were divided into two groups: those who exited through the left and those who went through the right.

'Quite a few prisoners were standing outside in the corridor. No one knew what was going on. Most of them had told the prosecutor that they still believed in their original ideals, that they had not repented. I looked around for Reza but he wasn't there. Someone told me that they took prisoners away in groups of five to seven, and that they had already taken Reza away.

'Finally, four other prisoners and I were taken out and made to board a lorry waiting outside. As soon as the lorry began to move, the officer accompanying us told us that we were going to be executed. And that we had better use the short time we had left to make peace with God.

'They took us to an open space, where the firing squad was waiting. The squad commander asked the officer for our death sentences. The officer said he had not yet received them. But he asked the commander to proceed with the executions. The orders would arrive in a few minutes.

'But the commander protested and said that he would not proceed unless he had the official orders.

'"I have executed a hundred people today!" he shouted, "Two I killed while I waited for their papers only to learn that they weren't supposed to die!"

That commander had saved Hussein's life. When the papers arrived they realized that he was not meant to be there and so he was taken back to his cell.

'That was how Reza Company died.'

Hussein kept his promise to the prosecutor: he stayed away from politics for the rest of his life.

A few months later, Grand Ayatollah Hossein-Ali Montazeri, Khomeini's designated successor, resigned in protest against the arbitrary executions. Khomeini accepted his resignation immediately. Yet another coup was under way: the Constitution was changed and the post of Prime Minister dropped from the government. Absolute power was now vested in the Supreme Leader. Further, the Guardian Council, whose members were chosen by the Leader, was given the power to vet and veto any candidate seeking elected office.

Once Montazeri resigned, the jokes we had so enjoyed making at his expense ceased and he became one of the most popular clerics in Iran. He was put under house arrest in Qom for 10 years and banned from teaching or publishing in the national papers. Nevertheless, he managed to publish his memoirs online, exposing the scope of the regime's oppression and cruelty. He played a significant role in the post-election protests of 2009, mobilizing the religious sector of society in which he was held in high esteem. When he died later that year, millions of Iranian protesters attended his burial ceremony. It was a way of showing their opposition to Ahmadinejad's government at the same time as their solidarity with Montazeri and his views.

Montazeri was once asked by a reporter why he stood up to Khomeini, thereby giving the latter an excuse to remove him from power. He could just as easily have waited a few months for Khomeini's death. Then, as leader, he could have implemented his more liberal and democratic ideas.

'What if I died before that?' he replied. 'How would I explain my silence to Allah?'

Going to medical school is—or was, back in 1988—a dream come true for so many young Iranians. Given how tough the competition was, securing a place meant that you ranked among the brightest and the best. On my way to enrolment I felt I was walking on air. As, I am sure, did the rest of my classmates. I was convinced of my future fame as the one who cured cancer or perhaps eradicated AIDS. Although after some thought, I decided what I really wanted to be was a psychiatrist and cure schizophrenia. The Nobel Prize didn't look so far off either . . . All the girls would fall in love with me . . . I was going to be rich and famous and respected . . .

No more school, no more struggling with those irrelevant subjects, no more Islamic Department. I was finally free.

Our very first class brought us crashing back to earth. Although the medical college was co-ed, the boys sat on the left and the girls on the right. We were not allowed to speak to one another, even if it was about our studies. The canteens were separate as well.

The Islamic Association of Students had only one purpose: to spy on the students. The student rep, chosen by the Islamic Association—voting was not an option—had the same mission.

The girls had their own student rep although she was subordinate to her male counterpart. If any of the boys wanted to communicate with any of the girls, he had to contact the male rep. The male rep would discuss the problem with the female rep and she would pass on the message to the girl. And vice versa.

A conversation between the male and female rep was certainly worth watching. They could not look into one another's eyes: that would lead to sexual thoughts and those would in turn lead them to sin. So they sat back to back and addressed the wall instead!

This problem was solved over the next two or three years: the reps got married and thus resolved their conversational problems. The Islamic Association of Students was, in an ironic twist of fate, gradually integrated into the National Bureau for Enforcing the Unity of Students and began to advocate freedom of speech, secularism and democracy. By the time we graduated eight years later, in 1996, most of my hardliner, pro-government and religious classmates had turned into liberal advocates of democracy.

I could tell I was a different person as soon as I began classes at university. I was no longer the coward I had turned into during high school. It was as if some invisible hand had turned on a 'liberty' switch in my head. I wore jeans and T-shirts while my classmates wore suits, carried Samsonite briefcases and practised calling one another 'Doctor'. I let my hair grow—which was going to create so much trouble for me later—and decided to be as funny as I could, to make as many, boy and girl, friends as possible and to break all the rules.

As it happened, university turned out to be worse than high school. The sanctions meant that we had minimal access to textbooks and the library had no money. We had no choice but to buy the books on the black market until some publishers identified the gap and decided to exploit the lack of copyright restrictions to their advantage. They began to reprint the textbooks and then sell them at a significantly lower price than the original editions. But these textbooks, once we managed to get a few, weren't really that useful since the lecturers tested us only on what they had said in class. If you walked into a lecture, you'd find all the students with their heads bowed, taking down every single word uttered by the lecturer.

My friend Mehdi and I decided to *listen* to the lectures and then read the relevant chapters from the textbooks. We were medical students, after all, and not scribes! But when we had our quarter-semester exams we found out the hard way that there was no beating this particular system.

It was then that my first publishing idea struck me. Why not release the students from this burden of taking notes? I shared my idea with Mehdi and a few other friends and they all loved it: we would record the lectures and then divide them among the students for transcription. Then we could photocopy the transcripts for distribution.

And we did it. Mehdi and I acted as both editors and transcribers. Although it was not long before everyone grew fed up of my horrible handwriting and asked me to resign as transcriber and be content with being editor and publisher. Thus began my first step in the direction of my lifelong passion: publishing.

But the problem lay in recording the lectures. Most of the lecturers preferred to see the students writing copious notes. It gave them a degree of deniability and hence they were loath to allow recordings. We needed to be particularly clever in choosing a spot for the tape recorder; close enough to be effective yet not obvious enough to court discovery. My friends transcribed the lectures and I edited them. This involved translating relevant portions from the textbooks and adding them in parentheses, then photocopying relevant images and, finally, putting together the pages. Mehdi would rewrite the entire lecture in his excellent handwriting and we'd create an interesting cover for the handbook. Then we'd make 200 photocopies and distribute them among those students who had registered to receive them. When I bought my IBM 80286 later that year—sold at a subsidized price to my father as a university professor—I began to type the lectures. I also taught myself page layouts and the basic principles of design.

We stopped taking notes and were able, instead, to pay attention to the lecturer. The handbooks became so popular that they remained in use over the next few years. So much so that when the lecturers decided to modify their lectures according to the revisions in the new editions of the textbooks, the next generation of students merely incorporated the changes in our handbooks instead of creating their own.

Thus passed the first year of medical school. I began to work and earned some money by being a private tutor to rich high-school students who wanted to pass the school examinations or the Concours but weren't smart enough to study and prepare themselves. I hated the job. These youngsters believed that hiring a private tutor meant they no longer needed to make any effort themselves. But it was good money and I couldn't afford to lose the job.

In the meantime, my hair grew longer and I grew bolder.

2 June 1989. Mehdi and I were at his house. We were preparing for our anatomy exam the next day when he turned on the TV for a short break and we heard the news.

> Our beloved Imam Khomeini's condition has deteriorated in the past few hours. Hereby we implore his followers and the whole nation to pray for him, asking God to cure him and keep his blessed existence for the Islamic Nation.

He had been hospitalized a few days earlier because of cancer-induced internal bleeding and no one had doubted his recovery. It wasn't the first time he had been hospitalized and the best doctors in the country tended him. We turned off the TV and thought nothing of the crowd around his house praying for his return. I was completely preoccupied with my own worries: the exam was hours away and I had a lot of ground to cover.

ssI was still in Mehdi's room at daybreak and far from confident. What the hell was *Ligamentum arteriosum* and why did I need to know about it?

Suddenly Mehdi rushed in, clutching his dad's small radio.

'*Enna Lellah va Enna Elaiheh Raje'oon . . .*' (Truly! To Allâh we belong and truly, to Him we shall return).

Ayatollah Rouhollah Khomeini was dead!

I threw aside my textbook, petrified by this simple but unbelievable piece of news. Everything was going to change.

The Imam's earthly remains were to be kept at Tehran's Grand Musalla (prayer centre) prior to the burial so that his admirers could pay their last respects and bid him farewell.

I knew I had to go.

The number of people at an Iranian funeral is in some measure a reflection of the person's righteousness in life. I had doubts about whether Khomeini had been a good man but the millions who attended his funeral did not. I went to the Musalla early in the morning but couldn't get closer than three miles from the body. But I was patient, unlike the weeping thousands who jostled and trampled one another to get just an inch closer to their Imam. A dozen died over those three days, trampled under the feet of the multitudes thronging for a last glimpse of their leader. Their numbers swelled by the minute. As if all of Iran's 60 million had erupted in a spontaneous pilgrimage towards Tehran. The police couldn't control the mourners; it was the people themselves who took on the responsibility of maintaining order.

Buffetted by the crowds, I kept asking myself what I was doing there. I wasn't an admirer, nor was I the sort who attended funerals unless it was absolutely imperative that I do so. Then why, instead of staying at home and watching events unfold on TV, had I risked my life in the midst of this teeming crowd? Didn't I blame Khomeini for Ahmadreza's death? For Reza Company's? For Ebrahim's? Even for Mr Moradi's?

Why was I there?

I didn't try to get close to the coffin. Abandoning my fate in the hands of the crowd, I let it carry me towards my destiny. I seemed to be floating on the angry waves of a river in full spate.

I was lifted by the flood and, often, my feet lost touch with the ground. Suddenly I found myself a few yards away from his lifeless body. The white shroud, the black turban kept on his chest, the glass coffin . . . Why had they put him on display like that? Those hands, those feet, those clothes, kissed and admired for 11 years . . . adored, respected, worshipped, feared . . . but never loved.

And I knew, then, why I was there. I was the only one who had *loved* that man. I felt a lump in my throat. He had saved me when I most needed consolation. He had always been there for me, in my thoughts. His actions, his decisions, his vanity, his cruelty, had broken my heart. But can a child hate Santa Claus when he finds out he isn't real? The tyrant had reverted to my childhood guardian angel, the one who assured me with his deep, kind eyes that I needn't worry about Azadeh.

I bade farewell to the last remnant of my childhood and made my way back through the crazed crowd, wondering what the future held in store. Nothing would be the same, that was certain.

To everyone's surprise, the Council of Experts chose Ali Khamenei, President, as the Supreme Leader. He wasn't even an Ayatollah but was immediately granted the title.

Rafsanjani, who won the presidential election, was the one who convinced the Council of Experts to do so. Imam Khomeini, he claimed, had once told him that Khamenei was the best choice for the position of Supreme Leader. They believed him without asking him the obvious: if Khomeini intended to appoint Khamenei as his successor, why had he not announced it or discussed it with anyone but Rafsanjani?

Rafsanjani began rebuilding the country by trying to repair's Iran's relations with the world and by initiating serious industrial reconstruction. Loans were made to manufacturers to build new factories and to expand Iran's industrial base.

That year, Agha-djoon, my grandfather, died.

Life took a dramatic turn during my third year at medical school. It was our last year at University. Clinical training at the hospitals would begin in the fourth year, then internships in the sixth.

Three things happened at the same time. First, a difference of opinion broke out among the advocates of the Islamic Republic as did the first signs of a reformist movement. Dr Abdolkarim Soroush, a pharmacologist and theologian and one of the brains behind the Cultural Revolution, had undergone a startling metamorphosis. He claimed in an article that theology was not a science—despite the government's insistence—since it was based on predetermined principles. As a point of view, it was fiercely criticized by one of the clerics and lecturers in the religious school. This exchange of opinions took everyone by surprise, especially us students. We found it hard to believe that a free debate was possible in Iran's fundamentalist regime.

Second, my hair: I had decided to let it grow as a protest against the 'doctor' stereotype. One could be a good doctor even if one had long hair and wore jeans. But the university didn't approve. I was summoned by the Disciplinary Committee and given a stern warning.

Third, my lecture on 'the healthy personality'. Some of my classmates and I had been invited to give a lecture on a medical topic of our choosing. I chose 'The Characteristics of a Healthy Personality'.

To my surprise, there were more than 500 people in the audience. I began my lecture with the seven contemporary icons of psychology: Gordon Allport, Carl Gustave Jung, Carl Rogers, Viktor Frankl, Abraham Maslow, Alfred Adler and Jean Piaget. I explained how Frankl developed his school of logotherapy after surviving the concentration camps, and how Allport believed that a wholesome person always tries to push boundaries and step beyond the limits. I described Maslow's pyramid of needs and Jung's struggle to achieve self-realization.

While I was speaking, I heard a noise at the back of the hall and noticed a few members of the Islamic Association moving about. I carried on, describing how a wholesome person takes nothing for granted, how he or she always tries to achieve more and challenges any prescribed rules.

That was it. A student with a long beard and a white shirt handed me a slip of paper. 'Two minutes to wrap up,' it said.

But why? I was supposed to speak for an hour and I was only halfway through. It was a mistake. I put it aside and continued. Exactly two minutes later, I received another note. 'Shut up! Or we will disconnect the microphone.'

I felt the old rage bubbling up. I tore up the note and continued talking about Frankl's experiences in the concentration camps, about how he set himself the task of ensuring that no one around him lost hope.

And then my microphone went dead.

'Because of a technical problem,' I shouted, 'I can't use the microphone but I believe my voice is loud enough for you to hear me.'

It was another 15 minutes before I wrapped up my speech. The beards couldn't do anything else to stop me since there were professors and lecturers present. But the look in their eyes confirmed that I was in trouble indeed.

I was suddenly afraid.

The audience realized that something was amiss, although I had done nothing wrong.

Later that day, when I was once again hauled up before the Disciplinary Committee, I learnt that I had. First of all, I hadn't begun my lecture with the name of Allah and nor had I continued with a verse from the Holy Quran.

'I forgot!' I said, 'I was too nervous!'

'You should have known that Allah's name would wipe away all fear.'

My second mistake was to have referred to the tragedy of the Jews in the Nazi concentration camps. This was long before the infamous denial of the Holocaust by Ahmadinejad.

'Recent evidence as well as research shows that the entire story about the Jews in the concentration camps is a myth created by the Israelis.'

It was the first time I had heard about this 'research' but I said nothing other than 'I didn't know'.

The last and most important accusation shook me to the core. 'The Holy Quran has explained clearly and completely what a wholesome personality is. But you made no mention of it. You went on and on about these Western psychologists, most of whom are Jews. We don't need their heretic theories.'

I felt sick to my stomach.

'Aren't you a med. student, Hamid?'

'I am,' my classmate answered, looking straight into my eyes, 'but psychology is not medicine.'

'The Holy Quran talks about spiritual well-being,' I said. 'Psychology is the science of the behaviour of the human mind.'

He peered at me over his glasses, 'And are you implying that the human mind can exist without the soul?'

This wasn't a person with whom one could reason. 'So you cut short my speech because you disagree with my views?' I asked instead.

'We cut it short as a warning to you. Do your studies, cut your hair, choose clothes more appropriate for a doctor and don't try to give any more lectures. We have decided not to let you choose a specialization. If you do not cooperate, we will stop your classes altogether.'

Unknown to us, the transformation had already begun among members of the Islamic Association of Students. The further they went with real 'science', the more critical they became of their own fundamentalist ideas. Today, the Islamic Association of Students is one of the main opposition groups within the Islamic Republic.

Madar died in 1991, the same year that Dad finally managed to buy a small flat in Tehran and we moved out of our rented home. Madar's death was a most devastating blow. She was the purest person I had known and my dearest friend. She died alone, in her small room in Qom. We had been trying to persuade her to move to Tehran and live with us but she refused. She didn't want to lose her independence. And, she'd said to me, if she died in Tehran then Dad wouldn't bury her in Qom, near the holy shrine.

According to her landlady, she suffered a heart attack during her sunset prayers. We received the news late at night and set off for Qom early in the morning. By the time we reached her rooms, the ambulance had already taken her body to the morgue. But her prayer chador and mat were still spread on the floor. Dad went to the morgue to take care of the paperwork while I sat in the middle of the room.

I could not shed a single tear.

I knew where she kept her most intimate things, and, when I opened the box, her will lay on top of everything else, including a shroud from Mecca and the deeds to the grave she had bought for herself in a Qom cemetery. She had instructed us explicitly not to spend any money for her wake.

Maryam and I were married in 1994, while we were still students. I had been working as a layout designer for the academic journal of the Iranian Foundrymen's Society; Dad was still part of its Board. At the same time, between getting married, working at the hospital and my job at the journal, I wrote my first novel, *The Grief of the Moon*, about a doctor who has grown tired of challenging Death: it is an unfair battle which he always loses. Finally, he decides to embark on a quest, to find a weapon that can defeat Death. This quest, spanning 38 years, takes him to the border between reality and fantasy. There he discovers that it is not Death that he must defeat.

Then began the all too familiar adventure of submitting the manuscript, my first encounter with the Iranian publishing industry. I believed I was a new Dostoyevsky waiting to be discovered by the literary world. Unfortunately, none of the publishers were of the same opinion. Looking back after 14 years in publishing, I must confess that I, too, would have rejected my manuscript. Finally, I thought it best to publish *The Grief of the Moon* myself. My two-year stint with journal production had made me familiar with the process. I submitted the manuscript to the Book Department of the Ministry of Culture and Islamic

Guidance—yes, we have a ministry where people go to be 'guided'—to get prepublication permission.

Muhammad Khatami had just resigned from the Ministry of Culture, protesting the passing of a resolution in the Supreme Council of the Cultural Revolution which sanctioned prepublication censorship. A publisher's office had just been razed to the ground for publishing a novel about a gay cleric and the judiciary was already trying one of Khatami's deputies for permitting its publication. Another book, *Women without Men* by Shahrnoosh Parsipour, a prominent Iranian female writer, had been banned. The author was in jail and the official who had signed the prepublication permission had been summoned to court. Ali Larijani, later Speaker of the Majlis (parliament) was appointed in Khatami's place and he made sure that all the policies approved by the Supreme Council were implemented.

Although I feared that the controversial content of my book would encourage the censors to ban it, I received my prepublication permission without any trouble.

Printing 1,500 copies would cost around US$150: all my savings. But I was determined to go ahead. I did the cover design and typesetting myself and commissioned the printer at Dad's university to print and bind it. The day I laid my hands on the first copies, fresh off the press, was the best day of my life. I was sure that all the critics in the world would discover my literary genius . . . I would sell hundreds of thousands of copies . . . I would win every literary prize . . . I would become an icon of contemporary Persian literature . . .

But I hadn't thought about distribution! By the time I realized that publishing is nothing without effective distribution, it was too late. I had no money left for marketing. No distributor accepted my book. I was ready to give them any amount of discount but it wasn't about figures. They were sure they couldn't sell the book and warehouse space was too precious to be wasted.

I kept all 1,500 in my room and began to sell them, one by one. I sold around 200 to my friends, family, family friends and classmates. Then I set out for the booksellers. Every day I'd put 50 into my rucksack and go from one bookshop to another, trying to convince the booksellers to stock a few. Though I was mostly shown the door, I did manage to sell another 300. My main problem was that I was a medical intern: I had to work 90 hours a week because I needed to support Maryam and myself. I couldn't visit the bookshops regularly to replenish their stocks. The book sold relatively well given the difficulties, and I also received good reviews. But I could spare it no more thought over the next two years.

I spent most of my time in the hospital. Back home, I worked some more. Sometimes I slept.

The two years I spent in the hospitals were among the worst years of my life.

I was a happy man when I began my internship: no more memorizing thousands of pages of text, no more terrifying exams, no more Disciplinary Committee. I could finally help the suffering, I could finally save someone's life. I did not know then that I still had to read thousands of pages to keep myself updated. I still had to endure the scrutiny of the University's internal intelligence officers. And there wasn't much I could do to help the suffering.

We were in the hospital from 7.30 a.m. until 2 p.m. We had night shifts two or three times a week and we took turns to cover the weekends. That meant that we worked about 90 hours a week. But this two-year marathon wasn't my problem. My problem was the system itself.

University hospitals were public. One of the cornerstones of the Revolution's propaganda, one with which Khomeini had appeased the masses, was that education and health care should be free to all. Health care was *not* free—anyone not covered by insurance of some kind had to pay—and, to make things worse, we were duty-bound to turn away patients thought to be in a critical condition. How often we'd have patients suffering from myocardial infarctions or serious crash injuries. They were brought in and then left unattended: their relatives were busy trying to get hold of some money. We were not allowed to approach the patients unless we received official approval from the accounts department. I couldn't believe this was true until I once put an IV line into a homeless patient who had been hit by a car and who was bleeding to death. He had no one; if I didn't try to replace the blood, he would be dead by the time the social service officer arrived to check if he was eligible for free treatment.

I was severely reprimanded by the head of ER and charged for the equipment and the medication. I paid without a thought but I couldn't afford to do this on a regular basis. So I watched patients dying in ER despite knowing I could help. This was destroying my spirits; so I went to see my rich grandfather, Hadj-Agha, to ask him to help with the fund I was trying to put together. He donated some money and that perhaps saved the lives of a few people but he refused to replenish the fund thereafter. And I realized that, while the present system was in place, one poor intern working 90 hours a week couldn't really make very much of a difference.

Something else that bothered me was the 'under-treatment' of patients by some of the consultants. They encouraged patients to visit their private clinics where they could charge much more than at the public hospital. In the public sector, the specialists worked for a fixed fee and a very small commission. There wasn't anything I could do about this but bully the consultants to pay my patients the attention they deserved. Understandably, this made me rather unpopular.

There were 'good' doctors, too, the very embodiment of the Hippocratic oath, who asked some of the underprivileged patients to visit them in their private practices. Not to charge them more but to treat them for free. But they were few and far between and not much liked by their colleagues.

Add to all of this the silence. Since the war and the mass execution of political prisoners in 1988, what one heard most was the sound of silence. Life went on, or seemed to . . . Children played in the streets, fans cheered their favourite teams, the streets thrummed with cars . . . but the eyes of the secret police were everywhere. Even up in the mountains, where the Iranians went every weekend in their cars and pretended to have a good time. This was also when the women began to push at their boundaries, to flout the more rigid constraints of the hijab. Following the decree of a collective unconscious, they began to pull back their headscarves, they began to show their hair and they wore shorter, tighter coats.

Neda would have been 12 or 13 then. She was growing up at a time when the invisible battle between the women and the system had just begun. Women were trying to gain their individual freedom by patiently insisting upon what they considered to be their rights, and the system was trying not to alienate them completely yet hoping to slow the change.

Silence and fear prevailed. No one dared say a word. Not even I, not even when I was beaten up by the Islamic goons.

I was supposed to pick up Mehdi from the main square in Yousef-Abad Street and then go to the university library to do some research for our theses. I was there at 2 p.m, in my battered second-hand Fiat 131, waiting for him, when the car's engine suddenly died. *Shit*, I thought, *what am I supposed to do now*? I got out of the car, opened the bonnet and began a check: oil, starter, petrol pump, coil, distributor . . . my face and arms were soon stained black with oil. *Dammit*, I thought, *now I'll have to take the car to the garage instead of going to the library*. I closed the bonnet and leaned on it, nervous, exhausted, sweating and furious, waiting for Mehdi to show up and help me move the car.

'Leave!' barked an authoritative voice, from somewhere behind me. I turned to see who it was and found three huge men glaring at me.

'Leave! Are you deaf?'

'Who the hell are you?' I asked, although I had the feeling I already knew. But I was too anxious to behave.

'None of your business. You can't stay here. The girl's school is going to give over soon and we're not having you here fooling around.'

'Girls? I haven't got anything to do with girls! My car's broken down.'

'I don't care. If you don't leave now, we'll break your legs.'

'Can't you see? I'm covered in mud and oil. Who would try to pick up girls like this?'

'I am going to tell you one last time. Go away! Now!'

All of a sudden, the strain of the years of repression proved to be too much and I exploded. I was too angry to control myself. If I had said yes and left, nothing would have happened.

'Go to hell! I'm not going anywhere! I'm staying right here . . .'

Before I could finish, I was hurled to the ground and beaten mercilessly. I tried to cover my face against the blows that landed on my stomach, while my attackers shouted, 'You wimp! Asshole! We didn't give our blood so that motherfuckers like you can walk the streets!' 'This one is for the martyrs!' another one yelled. As if I had killed the martyrs . . .

People passed by, ignoring the sight. No one turned around to see who was being ground under the feet of the three thugs.

They finally grew tired, or perhaps thought it best to stop before they killed me. Blood was pouring out of my mouth and nose and I couldn't move my arms and legs. One of them grabbed me, put me on his motorbike and whisked me off to the police station. They threw me into a room where I stayed for a few hours until a conscript arrived and took me to the officer.

'They've complained that you were picking up girls in front of the high school.'

'Lieutenant, Sir', I said, imploringly, 'I'm a married man. A medical student. I was waiting for my friend to join me and then go to the library. My car broke down. I was trying to repair it when your men began to beat me to death.'

The officer looked at my arms, covered in oil, and shook his head.

'They were not my men. They were the Basij.'

'I thought the Basij were fighting our enemies.'

'Now that the war is over, the Basij is fighting our internal enemies.'

'But I'm not an enemy, Sir. I'm only a student . . .'

'I understand', he said, shaking his head in sympathy, 'and I believe you. But a complaint has been filed against you. So I have to detain you and send you to court tomorrow. The judge will decide what is to be done.'

'But why? Will those Basijis come to the court as well? I want to file a complaint against them.'

'You can't. No one can file a complaint against a member of the Basij.'

'I can', I lied, 'I have friends in high places. What if Ayatollah Rayshahri hears what you've done to his best friend's son?'

I knew that Ayatollah Rayshahri, a powerful judge and cleric, was a friend of Hadj-Agha.

The officer's voice softened at the name.

'There is one thing I can do. If you sign this paper and promise that you regret disturbing the girls and will never do that again, I will let you go.'

'I'll sign nothing. I want my lawyer.'

'You've been watching too many Hollywood films, my son,' he laughed, 'Who said you were entitled to a lawyer? Sign, or go to court.'

'I want to make a phone call.'

'No phone calls. Sign or go back to your cell.'

'I'll go back to my cell.'

I knew he'd release me if I signed the paper. He needed that piece of paper so that I couldn't file a complaint against the Basij. I had been beaten, offended, humiliated. I had nothing else to lose and I was determined not to give up. Unable to stay calm, I began to curse and shout.

The conscript opened the door and said, 'Shut up, man! Do you want them to beat you again?'

I felt he was sorry for me and that I could use the sympathy.

'Hey, man, can you call someone for me?'

'What will you give me if I do?'

'What do you want?'

'Cigarettes. You got any?'

I gave him my packet.

'Call this number for me. Tell him his son's here. Tell him to call Hadj-Agha and get in touch with Rayshahri.'

To my utmost surprise, Hadj-Agha accompanied Dad to the police station. He told them that if they didn't release me on the spot, then all of them would be tried the next day for unjustified violence.

I was called from my cell and the same officer told me that I could go and that I didn't need to sign anything. But I was too furious.

'I want to complain against those men who beat me.'

'Don't overdo it,' muttered Hadj-Agha. 'Shut up and get out.'

Thus were my nerves shattered during my two-year internship. Hundreds of people died before my eyes. I could have saved some of them. As I recited the Islamic version of the Hippocratic oath during my graduation ceremony in the spring of 1996, I felt this was all a huge mistake.

Had I shown more perseverance, perhaps I would have been able to make more of a difference. But I hadn't known that corruption had permeated every aspect and every level of society.

I was going to practice medicine for another three years before I finally decided to give it up. When I decided to abandon my medical career, I could never have imagined that one day, years later, my name would appear among the top ten search results on Google when one typed in 'Iran' and 'doctor'. Not because I was a good doctor but because I had failed to save the life of a young girl bleeding to death in the street.

How could I have imagined it, then?

Google was yet to be invented.

PART IV

*Lie if you want to survive*

(1995–1999)

The smell of formalin, the sleepless nights, the strain of supporting Maryam and myself, the ongoing persecution of our generation which never had a chance to enjoy life, see the world or spend time with friends without fear of arrests, was not all that defined my life in those years. Iranian society, too, was undergoing significant changes and upheavals. The rulers of the Islamic Republic were clearly splitting into two. Rafsanjani had set up a new political party called Kargozaran-e Sazandegi (Executives of Construction) and had as its objective the re-establishment of capitalism. Apparently, as the most powerful man in Iran at the time, he had realized that capitalism was what would help rebuild the economic infrastructure destroyed during the war. In order to achieve this, he called for a more liberal approach. He was not aiming at political reform or the creation of a democracy but he was clearly advocating greater individual freedom. I remember the day when he announced that the Guards and the police should no longer harass young boys and girls if they were seen walking together. We were all amazed—and delighted—that the great taboo on the interaction of the sexes was finally done away with. It was some time before we noticed the disappearance of the 4WDs from the streets.

Rafsanjani even tried to re-introduce the practice of provisional marriage or *sigheh*, the fixed-term marriage in Shi'a Islam. The duration of such a marriage is fixed at its inception and then automatically dissolved upon completion of its term. An attempt to legitimize civil partnerships, it met with limited success.

On the other hand, the political environment was growing even more oppressive. Khamenei announced that the universities had to be 'Islamized'. This time the problem was not with the students since they had established several filtering mechanisms to ensure that no controversial student entered the universities; if they did, they were severely controlled. Once again, it was the lecturers and professors who were targeted and the Minister of Higher Education was assigned to carry out the plan.

In the course of a year, hundreds of professors with liberal, Western ideas were judged disloyal to the Revolution and forcibly retired, including Dad, who had been promoted to Professor a few years earlier and received the highest scientific honour in Iran. This broke his heart and he never recovered from the impact of not being able to teach any more. He, along with a few of his colleagues and former students, set up a research centre which, supported by the strength of his reputation, went on to become very successful. He was also appointed a member of the Iranian Academy of Science. But none of this could make up for the fact that he had been deprived of his only ambition in life: to die on the job, in the classroom.

Dad was no longer the same after his retirement. He lost the sparkle in his eyes although he became kinder, less autocratic and more outgoing. I couldn't help but feel a certain sorrow whenever I saw him groping for a new meaning to his life. He was never commercially astute and his position as managing director of a company that needed to be profitable bothered him. He simply wanted to research, whereas now he had to worry about negotiations and competition from rival companies.

Mum, on the other hand, began work as a nurse after she graduated but she gave it up a year later and returned to teaching at high school, once again as a librarian.

I decided I didn't want to follow in Dad's footsteps by putting all my eggs in one basket. So I began to think about a second career: publishing. My work with the scientific journal plus publishing my book and my bookselling background seemed to me enough preparation for founding a publishing house. I wanted to try and fill the gap in the market for a publisher who would 'think globally but act locally'. Most of the publishers I knew were stuck in the past: none of them seemed to have thought of bringing the industry up to international standards. I didn't have a business plan, I didn't have the money and I didn't have any experience in management. But I had an idea and a passionate desire to see it fulfilled.

I already knew that I would not be allowed to pursue my medical studies into any area of specialization. And in Iran, if one is not a specialist then one is highly unlikely to become a successful doctor. In the absence of a national health service, people turn immediately to a private consultant. If they have a stomach ache, they'll consult a gastroenterologist rather than a GP. There are tens of thousands of unemployed GPs in Iran who wander about the country for a few years before they decide to give up the profession and move into other careers. I knew that this would happen to me and I decided to pre-empt it.

What I didn't know was that setting up a publishing company wasn't as easy as it seemed and that the problems had nothing to do with the business aspects: they lay entirely in government-imposed regulation. Before I could do anything, I needed a Publishing Licence from the Ministry of Culture. No one is allowed to register a publishing company and begin publishing books or periodicals without it; and not everyone is considered eligible to even put in an application for it.

In the first place, all applicants had to prove that they were reputable Iranian citizens, at least 27 years old, with sufficient knowledge of publishing and at least a Bachelor's degree. At the time, being married was another precondition but this absurdity was done away with soon after. Applicants needed to have completed military service and have no criminal record or history of bankruptcy.

Once the forms were filled, the application was sent to the Security Department for a background check. If no deviant political, religious or moral activity was detected, the application was then scrutinized by a special committee. If, and only if, all these hurdles were surmounted, a provisional Publishing Licence was issued in the name of the 'Responsible Manager' of the publishing house. Licences were usually valid for a year and could be extended.

When I was thinking of setting up a publishing house, I was neither 27 nor had I done my military service. So I persuaded Dad to apply for the Licence. He was a reputable man, the author of several books and articles, the editor-in-chief of a leading journal and a member of the Academy of Sciences. I believed that the authorities would approve his application on the spot.

Dad was reluctant to apply but I insisted and reminded him that I hadn't really asked him for anything ever since the video player. He was not entirely convinced about my decision; he believed I needed to concentrate on my studies. I had to promise to see through my graduation before I began any publishing to finally win him over to my side.

We applied in 1994. Dad introduced me as his representative and then the marathon began. I went to the Ministry every two weeks to see how things were progressing and to check if I needed to supply any more documentation. I did, every time: his qualifications, evidence of his prominence in international circles, proof that he was a writer, police check, etc.

Finally, after nine months, his file was deemed complete and then sent off for a background check. The official told me that he'd call me if there was any news.

A year went by. I was about to graduate but there was still no news of Dad's file. I decided to go to the Ministry and see for myself.

It was almost three hours before I was let in.

'What do you want?'

'Has there been any development in the Publishing License application of my father, Dr Jalal Hejazi?

He looked into his files. 'Well, yes', he said, smiling, 'we had a response a while ago. But I must have been too busy to call'.

I leaned forward in my chair, 'And?'

'Unfortunately your father has not been approved. His background shows that he is not very loyal to the Revolution. It is not the end of the world, though. Ask him to come and see me. If he signs a statement that he regrets whatever he has done, the Security Office might reconsider . . .'

I left the Ministry in despair. Dad would never sign such a statement. I talked to him and I wasn't surprised when he simply smiled and said, 'Never!'

My dreams of becoming a publisher were dashed to the ground. I began to prepare for military service. I got my papers from the conscription office in April 1996 and was called very soon after.

Another two years of my life. Another two years wasted.

We had two months of military training before being assigned to our posts. A few of my classmates and I and were sent to the Montazeri Military Centre, located in a field 20 kilometres outside the city of Kermanshah in West Iran.

We arrived in Kermanshah at 6 a.m. We were going to spend the next two years in the Revolutionary Guard, the most fearsome and powerful entity in Iran. None of us was religious; although we knew how to play the hypocrite well enough to convince the authorities of our loyalty, we knew it was going to be very different in the army. In the latest parliamentary election, the more liberal Kargozaran Party had been defeated and the hardliners had taken over parliament. There were rumours that the Revolutionary Guard had rigged the results. The Guard believed itself to be the real owners of the country. It had defended the Revolution in its early days, it had defended the country for eight years during the war against Iraq and it was in charge of the huge Basij militia. It controlled the borders—customs, airports, exports and imports—and had infiltrated most economic activity, from arms manufacture to the oil industry. There was no way we could fool its men.

It was 7.30 a.m. by the time we got to the infantry base. We were searched thoroughly at the entrance and our cigarettes were confiscated. No one was allowed to smoke in the infantry, it seemed. Later I realized that the whole point of confiscating our cigarettes was to make us buy them from the smugglers *within* the infantry at a much higher price. We were told we were not allowed to shave our faces, then we were divided into three groups and sent to the three dorms. But there were not enough beds for all of us, so the commander announced that those who lived in Kermanshah could go home at night. We decided to volunteer so that we wouldn't be trapped in that base for two months.

We were trained again on the use of a gun, how to respond to chemical attacks and how to use RPG-7 rockets. We also attended war strategy classes and received Islamic training.

Hamid was one of the men who left the base with us every evening and we had become friends. When I heard his surname was Barazesh, I asked, 'Do you know Barazesh, Deputy Minister of Culture?'

He smiled and said, 'Yeah, sort of. Why?'

'I really wish I could speak to him.'

'You can if you want. He's my brother.'

With growing excitement, I explained Dad's situation regarding the Publishing Licence.

'No problem. Call me when we go back to Tehran.'

He truly performed a miracle. Two months later, when our military training was over, we returned to Tehran.

Within a few days, he telephoned.

'What do you want to call your publishing house?' he asked.

'Caravan.'

'OK, ask your father to come and get his PL tomorrow.'

227

The path that had taken two years and then petered out into a dead-end suddenly opened up again.

In Iran, everything was impossible and everything was possible. It all depended on who you knew.

It was 7 in the morning. We had just returned to the infantry base and were preparing for the morning ceremony when the Sergeant called us out and asked us to fall in line.

'In the name of Allah, the compassionate, the merciful. YOU DIRTY SCOUNDRELS! YOU WIMPS!' he bellowed. 'I thought you were educated! I thought you were doctors and engineers! Now I know that you are nothing but a rotting disease at the heart of the Revolution!'

He cursed us for 10 minutes, while we looked at one another in bafflement. What was wrong?

'You're a disgrace to your country! You think I don't know what goes on in the dorms at nights? I have eyes everywhere . . .'

Ah, he must have witnessed something truly terrible! Perhaps two boys had been caught having sex? Taking drugs?

'Don't you respect the blood of the martyrs who once lay on the same beds as you filthy animals? For this disgrace, you will do 100 push-ups and 100 sit-ups!'

We were all scared to death. What on earth had happened? I didn't sleep in the dorm so I had no clue. I looked at the others to see if they knew what the Sergeant was talking about but they were as astonished as I.

Meanwhile, the Sergeant was about to reveal the unforgivable, heinous crime.

'I have received reports that some of you pigs have been sleeping only in your *underwear*!'

'Ha ha ha ha . . . !'

Someone burst into laughter and the sound of it rippled through the courtyard. Everyone turned to gape at him. The Sergeant, too. Oh my God, I don't believe it: it's me!

'You, Dr Asshole! Step forward'.

Although I knew I was in trouble, I simply couldn't stop laughing. That sleeping in one's underwear was being treated as a national security problem . . .

I stepped forward.

'You have insulted the blood of the martyrs for which you will be punished severely'.

He called the group leader. 'You start counting, 100 push-ups, 100 sit-ups. And you', he turned to me, 'come with me'.

He took me to headquarters and told me to wait outside while he reported my crime to the commander of the infantry. I was no longer laughing but thinking hard, trying to come up with a way out of this mess. Insulting the blood of the martyrs was a serious accusation. I couldn't defend myself before the General; he wouldn't care; he'd feed on my fear and make an example out of me for the others. I decided the best way forward was to take the offensive.

I was summoned inside. The General looked at me contemptuously and said, 'The Sergeant has a complaint about you. You have insulted the blood of the martyrs.'

'Sir, I . .'

'Shut up! Don't speak until you're asked to. This is the army, not a hospital.'

I shut up.

'Do you have anything to say?'

'Can I speak openly, Sir?'

He nodded.

'My fellow soldiers and I are the ones who will file a complaint against the Sergeant.'

Both the General and the Sergeant raised their eyebrows.

'Can I speak, Sir?'

'Yes.'

'Apparently, a few soldiers have been sleeping in their underwear. But no one knew that sleeping thus was a crime. The Sergeant did not explain the rules to us but punished and insulted everyone. Further . . .'

The General and the Sergeant looked at me with ominous smiles. I realized that my case wasn't strong enough.

'I will complain against the Sergeant for having insulted the blood of the martyrs.'

The smile faded from both their faces. 'Why?' asked the Sergeant, clearly anxious.

I turned to the General and continued,

'The blood of the martyrs is sacred. The blood of the martyrs is what this glorious Revolution and the sacred regime is founded upon. The blood of the martyrs is our most powerful weapon against our arrogant enemies. It belongs to the whole nation and the Sergeant has no right to use it to his personal advantage. More important, he has no right to link the blood of the martyrs to the underwear of the soldiers. This is sacrilege! We will not let this happen again.'

The Sergeant was shocked, and the General, realizing he had to save himself, asked me to leave.

When I got back, the team had already finished the 100 push-ups. I asked them not to go through the sit-ups but to wait and see what happened.

An hour later, a new Sergeant was appointed. Ours was sent off to lead another team.

I was saved.

Two months later, when we were sent back to Tehran, I had become a First Lieutenant Doctor with three stars on my shoulder.

I was appointed as the doctor at the Corps 10 clinic in the Army of Revolutionary Guards. However, before I could begin, I was sent to set up the clinic in a desert outside Tehran where a huge military manoeuvre was about to take place. I was settled in the clinic, a military tent, with an assistant called Goudarz from Lorestan who barely spoke Persian. For 10 days, I saw no one other than Goudarz. I had no news from the outside world, no books to read and absolutely nothing to do. I was bored stiff by the end of the third day, reduced to counting the minutes and hours, willing time to pass. Slowly I got used to it and began to take notice of the world around me. I had never had a chance to get to know the world of nature; now I spent my time walking in the desert or lying on the ground, looking up at the stars, trying to make out the constellations. I tried to observe the smallest living creatures and soon I realized that, despite the lifeless appearance of the desert, it was teeming with life.

This solitude gave me an opportunity to distil my life's experiences, make sense of all my thoughts. I had seen a lot, much more than I was supposed to have seen by the age of 25. I had too many scars on my soul, which I had spent most of my time trying to ignore. Now was my chance to stop escaping and began to embrace who I really was. We made tea and drank it together, my assistant and I, and we improvised different types of food while we counted the number of scorpions that constantly crawled past our tent.

Before the launch of the manoeuvres, the scorpions didn't bother us. My assistant used to catch them, kill them and dry their poisonous tails under the burning desert sun. Then he would crush them and turn them into a powder, which he smoked with great pleasure. He said scorpions' tails had a more powerful hallucinogenic effect than hashish and far greater sedative powers than opium. He strongly recommended I try some. Despite my curiosity and keenness to try something new in those days when nothing changed and nothing happened, I refused. I was happy with my cigarettes and determined not to get addicted to the pleasures of drugs. By the time they finished their military service, half the conscripts ended up with some sort of drug addiction that would accompany them for life.

However, no sooner had the manoeuvres begun than the scorpions grew aggressive; my solitude and longing for adventure was overwhelmed by the number of soldiers I had to treat for scorpion bites. I was out of corticosteroids in a day. Had the scorpions been of a lethal variety, we would have been left with a lot of dead bodies on our hands. Instead of thinking of their military duties, the soldiers were hunting scorpions! And the scorpions decided to resist rather than surrender their euphoria-inducing tails without a fight.

On the last day of the manoeuvres, Ayatollah Khamenei came to the camp and visited the clinic. He greeted the men kindly and praised their courage in the course of these manoeuvres. I tried hard not to smile as I imagined his reaction when he came to know that these 'brave' soldiers were suffering not from war injuries but from scorpion bites!

I was introduced to the Supreme Leader as a 'brilliant doctor' working hard to help the injured soldiers. He greeted me and held out his cheek. In the anxiety of being kissed by the Supreme Leader, I put my hand on his right shoulder. Suddenly, an electric shock ran through my body and I was thrown back. It took me a few seconds before I realized what had happened. Then I saw the face of his bodyguard who was wagging his finger at me, motioning 'No, no, no'.

That was my one and only encounter with Ayatollah Khamenei and it ended in my being almost electrocuted. I didn't know then what kind of device his bodyguard had used on me; later, I discovered it had been a powerful taser.

A quite different meeting from my mystical encounter with his predecessor, Imam Khomeini.

'Hi, I'm Dr Arash Hejazi. I've been assigned to this clinic.'

The short, young doctor held out his hand and said, 'Welcome, Dr Hejazi. I'm Dr Jafar Muhammadi. I'm not a conscript, unfortunately, but a cadre doctor of the Revolutionary Guard, sentenced to spend the rest of my life in this rat-hole.'

After a few days spent scrutinizing one another surreptitiously, a certain degree of trust was arrived at on both sides. We had two desks in the same room. My job was to examine and treat the patients, his to read the newspapers, magazines and books he brought in each day.

I tried to observe the behaviour of the Revolutionary Guard since I'd never been so close to such a powerful organization. The guards were all fervently religious. Shaving was prohibited, although long beards were frowned on as well. Everyone's beards were trimmed to 3–5 millimetres, unless they were commanders. Military ranking had just been introduced to the Revolutionary Guard in an attempt to make it more like a modern army. Until then, over the past 17 years, there had been no insignia or military ranks; they had all been 'brothers'. Nor was there any military etiquette: inferiors didn't salute superiors but kissed one another and shook hands. Uniforms were simple and void of any insignia.

But now, since the formal military rankings had been introduced, the air of simplicity had vanished. These guards, trained to defeat the enemies of Iran and to uphold the Islamic Republic, were reduced to fighting over military ranks, posts which inevitably had financial implications.

There was another problem: educational levels. In the Iranian army, the level of formal education was the primary determinant of rank. Most of the 'commanders' in the Guard, however, had minimal education or none; others were barely literate. Under the new system, they lost their ranks. This was unbearable. As 'commanders', they had led troops to victory; now they had to accept the superiority of a new recruit fresh from university. Such as Dr Muhammadi.

He had been admitted to medical school with a bursary from the Revolutionary Guard. Anyone whose background was impeccable according to the Guard's criteria could apply for a bursary. Those who were accepted had to sign a contract to serve the Guard for 30 years. That was why Dr Muhammadi was committed to spending the rest of his life here. Although he had no service history, he was now a Major, a rank much higher than the 'commander' of the Health Department who was a Sergeant.

It was the length of the beard, therefore, that indicated the 'real rank' of a person. Brother Hassani, commander of the Health Department had a long beard but Dr Muhammadi and I were not allowed to let our beards grow longer than 6 mm. No one dared to ask Brother Hassani to trim his beard: he had 'authority'.

Dr Muhammadi was not like the others; he adored Iranian cinema, especially films by Mohsen Makhmalbaf and Abbas Kiarostami, two directors frowned upon by the regime, and he insisted I teach him about Western literature. We talked for hours. I told him everything I knew about Western literature and culture, since its beginnings in the golden era of the Greeks right up to modern times. I also made sure that he understood that there was no such thing as 'Western Literature', that every country in the 'West' had its own particular literature. Every day, I gave him one of my books, which he read rapidly and then waited for me to explain. I lent him works by Camus, Sartre, Kundera, Hesse, Boll, Lessing, Auster, Vonnegut, Dostoyevsky, Sholokhov . . . and he devoured it all. He had grown up in a fundamentalist religious family and all he'd learnt was Islamic lore. His love for contemporary Iranian cinema had lured him into a world he could never have imagined. By the time we went our different ways, he had become a humanist who believed that religion was a private matter and that the state had no right to use it as a pretext to control the society. An extraordinary attitude for a Revolutionary Guard, until I realized he was not alone. A large number of the Guards, especially those who'd had some higher education, were also of the same opinion.

In return for my cultural tutorials, he told me about the undercurrents of Iranian politics. There was a serious conflict going on and the ruling class was now divided: the traditional right, including those who had supported the Revolution financially; the petit-bourgeois of the Bazaar; the hardline right created after the war, including those members of the Basij now critical of Rafsanjani's attempt to modernize the country; the technocratic left, represented by Rafsanjani and the Kargozaraan Party; and the reformists.

The reform movement had no single leader and was made up of different people from different classes: it included men who had lost their legs in the war, founders of the Revolutionary Guard as well as those who had occupied the US Embassy. They were closely related to the Kargozaraan Party, the first group to show any inclination towards reform.

'The Kargozaraan won the parliamentary election last year,' whispered Dr Muhammadi, looking around for eavesdroppers. 'But we, the Revolutionary Guard, performed a semi-coup on the day of the election and made sure they weren't elected.'

'No way! That's not possible!'

'Believe me, Arash. I was there. The polls showed that the Kargozaran were leading. The night before the election, the country was put on full alert. Election morning, the Guard took over the ballot centres and made sure its candidates won. The election was rigged.'

'I can't believe the Supreme Leader would allow it.'

'The order came directly from him.'

In June 2009, when everyone accused the regime of rigging the results of the presidential election, no one was aware that this wasn't the first time such a thing had happened.

'But this is not going to happen in the presidential election next year', concluded Dr Muhammadi.

According to him, Rafsanjani, the President, had made sure there wouldn't be any manipulation and that the reformists were getting together to choose a candidate.

'Mir-Hussein Mousavi was their first choice. He was popular because of his impeccable management of the country during the war. But he refused, claiming that he preferred to teach. But', he winked, 'everyone knows the real reason'.

They did indeed. When he was Prime Minister, Khamenei had been President. In a complicated dispute, Khomeini had supported Mousavi rather than Khamenei. But then Khomeini died and Khamenei became Supreme Leader. Everyone knew that he would never let Mousavi run for President.

'So, the next option is Khatami.'

Anyone involved in Iranian culture in any way knew Khatami as the open-minded Minister of Culture who had resigned in protest at the institutionalizing of censorship. I was puzzled: Why should anyone vote for Khatami? No one, especially in rural areas and small towns, had heard of him. Why should they care about Khatami being against censorship? I had to wait and see but I was excited. It was the first time since the Revolution that I actually cared about a candidate and I had already made up my mind whom to vote for.

Another revolution was happening simultaneously: the communications revolution. We had heard of something called the Internet but we had no idea what it was and what it could be used for. What was introduced in the pre-Internet stage was the BBS—Bulletin Board System. The idea was simple but effective. One server connected a huge number of users who logged into the system via their modems and then communicated with one another. For me it was like being in Wonderland. I'd seen this in science-fiction films but had never imagined it possible. I joined the Mavara BBS and soon made a hundred friends whom I had never seen but felt I'd known for ages. We formed several forums and I was chosen to manage the Book Forum. We had online seminars and conferences, file-sharing libraries, political discussions, poetry nights, all of them surprisingly popular. In only a few months, tens of thousands of the inhabitants of Tehran were connected through the BBS. They also played a crucial role in unifying support for Khatami among the educated class of Tehran. In just a few months, Khatami had become incredibly popular. People who wanted to show that they were educationally a cut above would do so by making clear their support for Khatami.

We in the Revolutionary Guard infantry were denied this pleasure. No one dared mention his name. Instead, we were ordered to support Nategh Nouri, Speaker of the Majlis, also running for President. In one of his morning speeches the commander of the corps said, 'It is our duty to guard the Revolution, and the Revolution has never been so much under threat as it is now. You are soldiers of the Hidden Imam and you are supposed to follow Him. I am telling you that the Hidden Imam does not want this hypocrite Khatami to be elected as president.' He didn't say when and to whom the Hidden Imam had made his wishes clear, and whether he could still be considered 'hidden' if he was so openly supporting a specific candidate.

Despite the alleged disapproval of the Hidden Imam, the popularity of Khatami reached the farthest villages. He won the election in June 1997 with 70 per cent of the vote: 20,000,000 people had voted for him. The sun shone brighter, hope and happiness returned to the country. People laughed in the streets and congratulated one another. Even in the Revolutionary Guard more than 70 per cent had voted for Khatami, though of course they all told their commanders they had voted for Nategh Nouri.

My brother-in-law said, 'I am privileged to live in a country where a philosopher is president,' referring to Khatami's degree in philosophy.

I wasn't so sure. Yes, Khatami had advocated the need for reform and the need for more individual and political freedom. I was happy, I couldn't deny that, especially now that I was entering the publishing business and Khatami had clearly promised to stand up against arbitrary censorship. People were celebrating in the streets and I heard from Dr Muhammadi that the Revolutionary Guard had done everything possible to prevent his being elected. He claimed that the chief commander of the Guard had asked the Supreme Leader to make public his support for Nategh Nouri, and that Ayatollah Khamenei had even seriously considered it. However, a few days before the election, Rafsanjani had asked for an urgent meeting with the Leader and told him to abandon any thought of taking sides in these election.

'He said that, according to the polls, Khatami was going to win by more than 70 per cent. Even if Agha took sides, the 70 per cent would not fall below 50 and this would discredit the Leader.'

The 1997 election was not perverted. Twelve years later, Khamenei ignored this valuable advice and openly sided with Ahmadinejad. The election turned out to be a huge fraud and the Green Movement denounced the Supreme Leader once and for all.

Nevertheless, I wasn't sure if things were going to go the people's way. Khatami wasn't a person who would fight for his ideals. He was definitely a good man who believed in what he said. But what he said was too good to be true. I had lived among the Revolutionary Guard for two years. I knew what they were capable of and I saw them propagating their hatred for him.

But I decided to seize the moment and enjoy the prospect of a better life as long as it lasted.

I spent a few months working at a private hospital after my military service and then decided to give up practicing medicine for good. I was paid a flat fee, plus commissions on each patient. It was a substantial income and I was making good money until I found out that even I, who always criticized the corrupt health care system, was being corrupted. The evil was too powerful for me. I had to get out before I gave in to the dark side. The temptation to create unnecessary expenses for patients and thus receive a higher commission was so strong that one night I went to my room, took off my white coat and left the hospital. Forever. Publishing would allow me more control over my thoughts and actions. At least, that's what I thought.

I had published Caravan's first book while still a soldier, a translation of *The Magician's Nephew* by C. S. Lewis. I had been fond of the *Chronicles of Narnia* in my childhood and was happy to be the publisher introducing the tales to Iranian children. I translated the book myself and didn't worry about the matter of rights. Iran has never signed the Berne or World Intellectual Property Organization conventions; anyone can translate and publish any book from outside Iran without paying royalties to the authors. Sometimes, several different translations of a work are published at the same time.

Once the 2,000 copies were ready, I found myself faced with a familiar obstacle: distribution. I went to several distributors but they wouldn't take on the title. Once again, I was left with the entire print run stacked in my room although this time I was determined not to go the same route: I would not be my own sales rep. If Caravan was going to become a respectable publishing house, I would have to act professionally. It was then that I decided to set up a distribution centre with two friends. At the same time, I began to explore the market. I read books on marketing, talked to people in the business, tried to make sure I had a plausible strategy.

There were other things I needed to learn: the censorship procedures devised by the government, at once strict yet secret from the rest of the world. For example, the resolution passed by the Supreme Council in 1988 was in direct contravention of Iran's international obligations and its constitution in which freedom to publish is advocated and censorship prohibited.

The resolution in question, 'The Objectives and Policies and Conditions for Publishing Books', outlined seven subjects that did not 'deserve to be published' because they may be 'misused for propagating intellectual carelessness and disturbing the rights of the public' and that the 'healthy and constructive atmosphere of book printing and publishing' should be 'guarded' and 'secured' by observing these limitations. The seven banned subjects were: books that 'promote profanity and renounce the fundamentals of religion'; 'propagate prostitution and moral corruption'; 'incite the public to rise up against the Islamic Republic of Iran'; 'propagate and promote the ideas of destructive and illegal groups and deviant sects'; 'advocating monarchy, dictatorship and imperialism'; 'creating tumults and conflicts between tribes or religious groups or inflicting damage on the unity of society and territorial integrity'; 'mocking and weakening national pride and the patriotic spirit, and creating loss of self-confidence and national values before the imperialistic regimes'. Anything 'propagating dependence on any of the global powers and contradicting the policy and insight based on guarding the independence of the country' was also prohibited.

A major problem with the resolution was its all-embracing impact. The ambiguity of its language and the frequent use of religious terms left it wide open to personal interpretation. Almost anything could be interpreted as violating one of the restrictions, especially when it came to 'profanity', 'moral corruption', 'uprising', 'destructive', 'deviant', 'tumult', 'mock', 'national pride', 'national values', terms for which no one could come up with a precise definition.

The other problem was that this resolution was (and still is) in opposition to Iran's international obligations to enforce freedom of speech, namely the International Covenant on Civil and Political Rights. Which was why the government had to come up with a way of implementing censorship without leaving evidence of it. The first step lay in replacing 'censorship' with 'scrutiny'. Publishers were told to submit final pre-press proofs of their forthcoming titles to the Book Department for the censors' 'scrutiny'. If they found no problems, they would issue a permission to publish. If not, they informed the publisher of the modifications required. This was on a sheet of paper with neither a letterhead nor a signature nor an official stamp. The publisher had to make the changes and resubmit the book. If it was decided that the book didn't 'deserve to be published' at all, the publisher would be notified verbally; no documentation was provided.

Even if you were lucky enough to receive prepublication permission, the government still had several other tools up its sleeve to control what you published.

According to a resolution promulgated by the Supreme Council of the Cultural Revolution, publishers are required to deliver between two and 10 copies of each book they publish to the Ministry of Culture and Islamic Guidance (Ershad) against an official receipt. This is known as 'Book Receipt' or BR, and is an official declaration of the publication of a book. The copies are then distributed to the Iran National Library, the library of the Islamic Consultative Assembly (parliament), the library of University of Tehran and a few others.

This document has also been taken as permission to distribute the books in question. But, even after the book is printed and bound, the BR is required before distribution is permitted. Therefore, the BR, apparently only a bureaucratic formality, forms yet another layer of censorship.

The Ministry didn't stop there. All publishers made a huge effort to get public libraries to buy their books. The Ministry of Culture and Islamic Guidance allocated an annual budget for the purchase of new titles by public and specialist libraries. It was also in charge of deciding exactly which books were worth reading. As a result, publishers close to the government received financial support and thus enjoyed a competitive edge over the independent publishers. Moreover, the Ministry ensured that books that had been authorized but were not looked on favourably did not find their way into the public libraries.

The layers thickened and grew murkier. Tehran International Book Fair is a major event for Iran's publishing industry, an important source of revenue for publishers and a significant attraction for millions of book buyers. The Ministry is in charge of the Fair, allocating stands to publishers and even determining which books that can be sold.

Even after obtaining all these permissions, a book is not safe. The Attorney General has the right to prosecute any books he finds 'disturbing'; those who have authorized the publication of such a book may themselves be prosecuted.

None of these layers were as powerful as censorship by fear, the most powerful tool in the hand of a tyrant. Publishers who have established a business and invested in it don't want to lose their licences by publishing dubious content; authors fear to let their imaginations fly lest they create a monster; the censors fear the loss of their jobs if they approve the publication of a controversial text; Ministry directors fear more open policies on the content of such books lest they are held responsible for errors . . .

The vicious circle has no end.

No one dares to push at its edges.

There I was, 26 years old, in the autumn of 1998, feeling stripped of my youth, stripped of my medical career, stripped of my money—I had lost my investment in the publishing house through a few fraudulent distributors and their bounced cheques—but I was still hopeful. Society had become much more open under Khatami's presidency: there had been an explosion of independent newspapers which openly discussed political matters. The film industry was flourishing, despite the restrictions—such as the law that actresses had to wear hijabs in the films, even in their bedrooms—and was attracting a huge audience to both its commercial and intellectual releases. The arbitrary and unleashed censorship on books and other media was done away with (although prepublication censorship was still at work). The economy was opening up as well as a result of Khatami's paradigm of 'Dialogue among Civilizations'. The idea had been well received in international societies and Iran's relationship with Western countries was improving day by day. Khatami had addressed the American people—previously the Great Satan—as a 'great nation'. There was nothing but hope to be seen on the horizon. I had dedicated myself full-time to publishing but it had got me nowhere so far.

It was the Internet, another great revolution, that changed my life forever.

In its early days the Internet was not available to everyone; it was considered a very dangerous tool. But we members of the BBS community managed to gain access. I remember one of my first discoveries on the Internet was Project Gutenberg, a vast database of books already in the public domain. For us, who had no access to the outside world and no way of buying books, it was spectacular! We could download a major portion of human wisdom! This was so exciting that we decided to download the entire Project Gutenberg and make it available to our BBS Book Forum.

But the major joy of the Internet wasn't information, it was communication. Until the Internet, we had no access to the outside world; now we could get in touch with anyone who had an email address anywhere in the world. The youth of today cannot imagine life without the Internet—without mobile phones and SMS and Facebook and Twitter—just as I cannot imagine life without radio and TV. We think we know how life was before TV but we haven't a clue. When Dad was a child, people spent their time playing in the streets and sitting under a special heating system powered by coal, listening to the stories of their grandparents. Nowadays the children don't have time. They are busy playing videogames, sending texts or emails, watching TV and surfing the Internet on their mobile devices.

For us, the Internet was a magic much more exciting than flying carpets and crystal balls.

Suddenly, I had an idea. As I have mentioned earlier, international copyright conventions are ignored in Iran. This can, at times, lead to a certain amount of confusion when it comes to translations. None are authorized and some are clearly a great deal better.

Then, I read *The Alchemist* by Paulo Coelho and was astonished by its resemblance to a story by Persian poet Jalaluddin Rumi in his book *Mathnavi*. *The Alchemist* was translated and published by a medium-sized Iranian publishing house and was relatively successful. But I thought the author deserved much more. He was Brazilian, and literature from Latin America was extremely popular in Iran, thanks largely to Jorge Louis Borges and Gabriel Garcia Marquez. He also touched on subjects close to Persian mystical lore and I felt that having their stories re-told by a Westerner might interest Iranians. Rumi's stories had been around for 800 years but they weren't reaching the younger generation any more. Now, Coelho had made these complex ideas accessible to everyone.

I searched for and located Coelho's website and sent him an email. I explained that I worked as an editor in a small publishing house and that I wanted to publish his latest book, *Veronika Decides to Die*. I also sent him a translation of my novel, *Grief of the Moon*.

He sent me the complete text of *Veronika Decides to Die* in Portuguese and told me that he was enthusiastic about having an official publisher in Iran. He introduced me to his agent, Monica Antunes, and told me that he was very interested in visiting Iran. He also said he had enjoyed reading my book.

We signed an agreement with Monica. All my colleagues said that this was stupid; I could easily translate and publish the work without paying a cent. But I was determined to respect Paulo's rights. He had trusted me by sending me his book and I had a good feeling about the relationship.

But the book was in Portuguese and we could find no translators. I decided to translate it myself. I knew a little French and a little Spanish, and one of my friends told me I could easily learn Portuguese. I spent eight hours a day teaching myself

Portuguese. I had no one to speak to but after three months I had a good grasp of the language, enough to begin to translate the work with the help of dictionaries and by checking my translation against the English and the French. When the translation was finished and we had edited and prepared the book, we sent it to the Ministry of Culture for prepublication scrutiny.

The book was published at the beginning of July 1999, with a note from Paulo Coelho introducing us as his sole official publisher in Iran. The book was released exactly at the same time that the political scene was changing again. The Iranian student protests of 9 July 1999 were on their way.

The two years of Khatami's presidency, from September 1997 to July 1999, witnessed a siginificant opening up of the political scene. Various independent newspapers kept alive the various political debates; new moderate parties were founded and the reformist movement that had begun by supporting Khatami was gaining power. The reformers believed it was time to revisit the Islamic Republic's strategy at home and abroad. Prominent leaders of the movement, most of whom had been Khomeini's closest friends and allies during the Revolution, claimed that having survived the war, international sanctions and internal threats, the Islamic Republic was now strong. They believed the world had accepted Iran as a legitimate power in the Middle East and that the government no longer needed to suppress every contrary opinion and idea to survive. At the same time, a more liberal political attitude would build up Iran's profile internationally and motivate all of society to participate in taking the country forward. And all of this, without betraying the fundamentals of the Islamic Republic of Iran and its constitution.

However, there was another political current very much alive: the hardliners, supported by the Revolutionary Guard. It had fallen silent for a while and everyone had assumed it had accepted the changes. Apparently it had not: the democratic environment created in the past two years hadn't appealed to it at all. Democracy meant that power was no longer polarized in the hand of the Supreme Leader and his army of followers. So, after a year of silence, it decided to show its hand.

There were incidents that accelerated the crackdown, the most important of them being the case of the Chain Murders.

The Chain Murders of Iran included about 80 murders and disappearances over a period of eight years. At first, no one realized that these mysterious deaths were related. Some were car accidents, some were stabbings, some were robbery-related shootings, some (staged) suicides and one a 'heart attack'. Some had even happened outside Iran and the victims were from varied backgrounds: writers, translators, poets, political activists and academics.

In 1998, three writers, a nationalist political activist and his wife were found dead within less than two months. Journalists associated with the reformist movement began to investigate the murders alongside the Revolutionary Guard and the Ministry of Intelligence. Khatami promised he would personally oversee the investigations and, finally, was forced to admit that the deaths had been masterminded from within the Ministry of Intelligence. It was revealed that over the past 10 years, the Ministry—or 'rogue elements' within the Ministry—had conducted several assassinations within Iran and abroad, including that of Shapour Bakhtiar, the last prime minister of Iran before the Revolution. Khatami discharged his Minister of Intelligence and arrested those involved. The entire responsibility was placed on the shoulders of Deputy Minister Saeed Emami who had been in the Ministry for many years. However, before a proper investigation could take place, Emami was found dead in his prison cell, allegedly having committed suicide by consuming

Vajebi, a powerful local brand of hair-remover. The rest of the arrested suspects disappeared without their identities ever being revealed.

This incident alarmed the hardliners who were responsible for the thousands of crimes, assassinations and illegal executions. The politically open atmosphere and the free press were not welcome any more. The press came under pressure and Khatami's administration was attacked via the judiciary (still in the Guard's control) and the full force of the Basij militia. A year later, Saeed Hajjarian, the director of one of the most important reformist newspapers, survived an assassination attempt but was left paralyzed for life.

As we were about to distribute *Veronika Decides to Die*, in which we had invested everything we had, the Judiciary ordered the shutdown of *Salaam*, a leading newspaper from the reformist front. This was the first of nearly a hundred other newspapers and periodicals that were to be banned in the years to come.

Our office was located quite close to the student dormitories of University of Tehran so we immediately realized that something was wrong in that first week of June 1999.

A number of students formed a group to protest peacefully against the closure of *Salaam*. We knew this was happening but we were sure that it would not be a problem. During Khatami's presidency, peaceful student demonstrations happened every once in a while, lasted for a few hours and then everyone went home. My partners and I decided to proceed with our marketing activities for Coelho's book. We had already signed a contract with two high-circulation reformist newspapers to publish our ads every day. We were the first publishers who had decided to advertise our books in the mainstream press and they had given us a significant discount to encourage other publishers to follow suit.

We had also printed a thousand posters. There was no money left to hire billboards so we decided to go out in the middle of the night and put them up ourselves in the areas designated for free posting. We began at 2 a.m. on 10 June 1998 and we had no idea of what had happened a mile away until our eyes began to burn from the teargas and we were seized by the police.

'What are you doing?'

I turned around and my blood froze in my veins at the sight of the patrol police.

'Putting up posters, Sir . . .'

'Get off that stool, now!'

I stepped down from the stool we had been carrying with us all night.

'Why in the middle of the night, if you are not doing something illegal?'

My partner was left speechless. I tried to remain calm.

'We didn't want to get caught in the daily traffic.'

'What is that poster? Give it to me. To which political group do you belong?'

My partner handed over a poster with trembling hands.

'*Veronika Decides to Die*? Is this a secret code for suicide attacks on the Revolution?'

'What?'

My colleague pulled me back and answered, 'No, Sir, by no means! It's an ad for a book we've just published. The book is authorized by the Ministry of Culture and has the permissions.'

'The Minister of Culture? You mean the same asshole who instigated this mess?'

'What mess, Sir?' I said, 'It's only a book, a nice novel on why suicide is a bad thing. And as you know, suicide is a cardinal sin in Islam. This book is preaching the same principle.'

I tried to speak in the language learnt during my years in the Revolutionary Guard.

The officer laughed and returned the poster.

'I don't mean this shit! Haven't you heard? The city is ablaze. Go home, boys. It's not a good time to promote your books. You might get killed. Tonight, Tehran is a slaughterhouse.'

Next day, we realized what had happened. My friends in the dormitory told me the whole story.

A few hundred plainclothes hardliners, the Ansar-e Hezbollah or Supporters of the Party of Allah, and the Basij had attacked the university dorm. They had broken the doors and windows, attacked the students and set fire to everything. They had thrown students from the third-floor balconies onto the pavement. Three students were killed and dozens were injured while the police stood by and watched.

Thus began the street protests that took over Tehran for the next few days. Students poured into the streets protesting the way they had been treated after their peaceful demonstration. The Basij and the plainclothes forces cracked down on them, killed a few more, arrested hundreds and beat thousands. My friends and I attended one or two of the protests. The streets were filled with armed plainclothes forces who beat us in front of the police. No one knew who these plainclothes people were, who could move around so easily and terrorize the people without being prosecuted. Then it was revealed that they belonged to the Revolutionary Guards' secret service.

People ran in different directions, the air was filled with teargas and terror governed the streets. But the students, led by the Islamic Society of Students, announced they would remain in the streets until justice was served.

Khatami appeared on National TV at the end of the week and implored the students to go home. He promised that he would investigate the raid on the student dorms and make sure that those responsible were punished. This statement calmed the students and the protests slowly came to an end.

However, over the next few months, not only was no one held responsible for the raid but hundreds of students were taken to court and sentenced to long-term detainment despite Khatami's objections. The Supreme Leader had decided to take control of the country into his hands again and strip the President of his powers.

But the reform movement proved stronger than the hardliners thought: in the parliamentary election of 2000, the reformists won the majority of the seats.

PART V

*Dialogue among civilizations,*
*but not among ourselves*

(2000–2005)

Paulo's book was a huge hit. We sold 10,000 copies in the first two months and demand for it spiralled. Distributors came to us, begging to take on the title and bookstores called us incessantly to order more copies. My publishing career had finally taken off. In the first year, we published 10 titles and our marketing campaigns, unprecedented in the history of Iranian publishing, attracted massive attention. Then I received an email from Paulo in which he mentioned his interest in visiting Iran.

Given the political context, we decided we couldn't invite him on our own. If he visited Iran, he would be the first non-Muslim Western author to do so since the 1979 Revolution. So I decided to consult both the Ministry of Culture and the International Centre of Dialogue among Civilizations, an organization founded by Khatami to promote dialogue between Iran and Western countries. I wrote letters to both, and they both responded by saying they would do everything they could to welcome this prominent Brazilian author—though they couldn't pay for the costs of the visit! I wrote to Paulo and we decided to share the costs: he would pay for his flight and hotel and we would pay for everything else.

Paulo requested his visa be sent to the Embassy of Iran in Warsaw. He was visiting Poland before travelling to Iran.

We began to plan: the places he had to visit, his conferences in Shiraz and Tehran, the book-signing session in one of Tehran's best bookstores and the press conference. We sen out press releases announcing his arrival at Mehrabad Airport on the evening of 25 May 2000. Moreover, during the Tehran International Book Fair, we began to register the names of participants for his conference in Tehran's former Opera House. In only a few days we had 5,000 names.

But then, a mere two weeks before he was due to fly to Tehran, Paulo called. 'Hi Arash, I'm just on my way back from the Embassy of Iran in Warsaw. I asked them for my visa but they said they had no idea what I was talking about.'

I said I'd check with the Ministry of Foreign Affairs. When I called them, they said they needed four more weeks to process the request. I said that was out of question, that everything was already planned, that the Ministry of Culture and the Centre for Dialogue among Civilizations were involved, that thousands of people were waiting for him. But their only answer was, 'Sorry, we need four more weeks.'

I called Paulo and explained everything. He remained silent for a few seconds, and then said: 'I am very upset, Arash. And this will not go unnoticed. I am a supporter of President Khatami, I believe he is doing really well. All I wanted to do was to visit Iran and see with my own eyes that this change and dialogue was real. I was planning to let the world know that they need to put aside their prejudices against Iran and accept it into the international community . . .'

'Perhaps we can reschedule the visit . . .'

'There will be no rescheduling, Arash. And I will let the world know how the government of Iran treated me.'

Then, after a pause, he continued. 'I will go back to the Embassy the day after tomorrow. If my visa is ready by then, I will happily come to Iran. Otherwise this visit will never happen and I will not remain silent.' And he hung up.

I threw myself into a chair, desperate to find a way out of this mess. When I had announced that Paulo Coelho was visiting Iran, the media had received the news with scepticism; they couldn't believe that a small publishing house was able to pull of an event of such magnitude. If the trip was cancelled, they would never believe I had been telling the truth. This would discredit Caravan and the prestige and popularity that it had built up over the past year. Our reputation as the first publisher to respect international copyright and acquire the rights of an international author, the first publisher to modernize book marketing and promotion in Iran, and the first publisher to invite an international writer, would be destroyed in a minute.

But I knew there was nothing I could do. I simply sat and stared at the wall in front of me. Exactly five minutes later, my assistant opened the door. 'I've just received a call from the Ministry of Foreign Affairs!'

'OK, put them through.'

'They hung up but they left a message for you.'

'And?'

'They said that Mr Coelho's visa is ready at the Embassy of Iran in Warsaw and he can collect it tomorrow.'

What?! I couldn't understand what had happened but I didn't need to. I called Paulo immediately and gave him the good news. He laughed and said, 'OK, then everything is all right and I am very excited. Thank the government of Iran for me.'

Then I began to give him guidelines about what he and his wife could and could not do in Iran. His wife would have to cover her hair and remember to never shake hands with men. Also, that they couldn't drink alcohol.

'I don't mind not drinking but I'm a smoker. I hope that's not going to be a problem.'

No, it wasn't a problem. Everyone smokes in Iran, I explained. Later, when we met, he told me that his harsh tone on the phone from Poland had been deliberate. He was sure our conversation was being overheard by the authorities and that short speech had convinced the Ministry to change its mind and issue the visa.

I was incredibly excited. I was at the airport's VIP lounge at 2 in the morning, waiting for Paulo's plane to land, knowing that there were nearly a thousand fans waiting outside to see him. Paulo had touched thousands of lives in Iran even before his arrival. His books were about believing in dreams and following the signs. With their new-found hopes for freedom, people in Iran embraced his ideas. His ideas weren't new or original but the simplicity of his stories had tugged at their heartstrings. Since I became his publisher, we have sold millions of copies of his books and I know they have changed the lives of hundreds of thousands of people in my country. It was Neda's generation that was most affected by his literature.

Later, I realized that his impact was universal and that the key factor of his success could be summarized in a single word: passion. All the individuals who created the domestic and international success of *The Alchemist* first fell in love with it and then decided to share their passion with others; a concept now forgotten but once one of the main founding principles in the publishing industry. This passion created the most powerful marketing communication tool—word of mouth—stronger and more effective than any advertising campaign.

*The Alchemist* is the story of a boy who dreams twice of a treasure hidden near the Pyramids. He leaves behind the world he knows and sets off on a quest to find this treasure. He reaches the Pyramids only to realize that the treasure is waiting for him at home, at the very place where he dreamed of the treasure in the first place.

It may sound simple but the concept of travelling the world only to find the treasure at home has very deep roots in all sorts of myths and legends. The plot first appears, almost simultaneously, as 'In Baghdad, Dreaming of Cairo: In Cairo, Dreaming of Baghdad' in Book VI of *Mathanawi* by Rumi, the thirteenth-century Iranian poet, and in *One Thousand and One Nights* where it becomes 'The man who became rich through a dream'. It also appears in the seventeenth-century English folktale *The Pedlar of Swaffham* and several others. Later, it finds its way into a novel called *Night under the Stone Bridge* (1952) by the Austrian writer Leo Perutz. Jorge Luis Borges, too, adapted it in his short story 'Historia de los dos que soñaron' (Tale of the two dreamers). That was in turn the source that inspired Coelho to write *The Alchemist*.

The recurring nature of the theme implies that the story appeals to people because its universal message addresses one of the most important sources of human anxiety, regardless of time, nationality, language or culture. Every human being has a dream. However, in order to adapt to a society demanding conformity, they often have to abandon their dreams and live with their regrets. The story asks people to trust their dreams, to be brave and to follow their individual paths. To do that, they don't have to be elite, intellectual, rich and flawless or even possess extraordinary strength. This is a path for ordinary people.

But Paulo's version was much more successful than its predecessors. When the book was published in Iran, there seemed to be no hope left for individuality; the excitement of the Revolution was over and people had lost hope that one day the world could live in 'peace and love', *The Alchemist* told everyone that they could separate their personal destinies from society's standards and that the conspiracy theory was an illusion. This new hope was what people needed at the time.

*The Alchemist* is full of archetypal symbols which appear in an apparently simple and straightforward style but which bear a deep and fundamental meaning that speaks to all: the alchemist; the wise old man; the female counterpart; the quest; the disguise; the thieves and warriors who try to postpone the mission; the four elements and several other symbols already established in the collective unconscious of the readers, especially in a culture like Iran's which is saturated with references to them. Iranians are familiar with these symbols from childhood through fairy tales, fables and myths and can instantly identify with them. Coelho used the known plot, the familiar characters and elements, the archetypal references and even the well-known style of fairy tales to revive an ancient but forgotten message: be brave; the real power lies within you, not outside.

The simplicity of style and language as well as the appeal of its story make it ideal for translation. It is the most translated book by a living author: it has been translated into 68 languages and sold more than 65 million copies in 150 countries.

Meanwhile, completely ignoring the views of the critics who claimed it to be a mere commercial product, I was waiting anxiously at the airport, sitting beside the Ambassador of Brazil and the delegates from the Ministry of Culture and the Centre of Dialogue among Civilizations. I had met the Ambassador a few days ago at the Brazilian Embassy, where he had invited me to discuss Paulo's trip. He had received orders from the Ministry of Foreign Affairs of Brazil to receive Paulo well. But he wasn't keen on Paulo's books and considered him very commercial.

'I will hold a reception at my house for him but I will not go to the airport. If I had not been instructed by the Ministry, I wouldn't do even this.'

'Paulo Coelho is a writer, and you are an ambassador, not a literary critic', I answered.

'But we don't want him to represent Brazil. We have many better authors.'

'Mr Ambassador, so far the world recognizes Brazil as the land of football and samba. Why don't you let Paulo Coelho represent your country for something more meaningful, like literature?'

He didn't say anything but he and his wife both showed up at the airport.

'I changed my mind,' he said, when I looked at him in surprise.

So there I was, waiting at the VIP lounge for the most important encounter of my life.

I was also anxious about the bodyguards. That afternoon, two armed agents from the Ministry of Intelligence and the Revolutionary Guard had arrived and introduced themselves as bodyguards for 'Mr PABILO KUBILO'. I was immediately bombarded with questions about Paulo's visit.

'Are you bodyguards or interrogators?' I asked.

'We need to report Mr Pabilo's every move. And we are going to keep an eye on you as well.'

I said that I had already given the reasons for Paulo's visit to the Ministry of Culture, the International Centre of Dialogue among Civilizations and the Ministry of Foreign Affairs.

'Yes, you have. But now we need to know the REAL reasons.'

This was an old strategy, one with which I was only too familiar. I explained again that I was his publisher, that he was very popular in Iran, that he was in love with our culture and that he was looking forward to visiting the land of Rumi and Saadi and the Muslim mystics. I told them that he was a religious person and that he had no ties with politics.

They pretended to accept my explanation, although I knew they were looking for signs of something sinister.

'Whatever. We don't speak English. You're supposed to translate every word that Pabilo utters. Is that clear?'

I said I was going to be too busy arranging everything. If the Ministry of Intelligence wanted to know what Pabilo said, they had better send a 'bodyguard' who understood English.

'That's the way it's going to be, Dr Hejazi. You don't want to say no to us.'

I said that I would interpret what he said if I wasn't busy doing a thousand other things.

I was pacing the corridor outside the VIP lounge when I saw a short man standing in front of me. I didn't recognize him at first: he was so different from his photos.

'Oh my god! You're so young! I've never had a publisher this young!' Then he hugged me and introduced his wife, 'This is Christina.'

Christina was wearing a headscarf that covered all her hair and most of her face, and a long coat that covered her down to her ankles. She had taken my warnings too seriously.

'Hi Christina, I'm Arash, very nice to meet you.'

She simply shook her head and said nothing. Later I realized she was scared to death as she stepped into the mysterious land of Iran. She was also under the impressions that women were not supposed to speak to men.

We went into the lounge. The representatives of the government and the Ambassador greeted and welcomed him. The Ambassador's wife laughed when she saw Christina wrapped in so much clothing and told her that she would give her a proper headscarf in the morning. The 'bodyguards' too, introduced themselves and greeted 'Mr Pabilo' in Persian and asked me to translate what they said.

We left the lounge and all of a sudden Paulo found himself among more than a thousand fans who burst into applause as soon as he entered the Arrivals area. The bodyguards stepped forward protectively. People held up their books, and Paulo asked the bodyguards to let him sign them. A dozen domestic and international reporters had arrived at the same time to cover the first Western author's visit to Iran.

Then we left for Hotel Homa, where we had booked a room for them. It was four in the morning when we left Paulo, Christina and the two bodyguards at the hotel but I had found a chance to have a private chat with Paulo, explaining that the two bodyguards were actually intelligence agents.

'I knew, Arash. Don't worry, I know how to handle them.'

We visited the Bazaar the next day, although the Centre of Dialogue had planned a lot of visits to museums. Paulo refused to go to any museums on the first day of his visit.

'I never go to museums. Whatever you want to show me, I can find online. What I can't find online is the actual life of the people. So I am going to the Bazaar tomorrow, and I am sure that Hamid and Khusro—the bodyguards—know a lot about the Bazaar and the life of people. They will show me around.'

So we went to the Bazaar. In the afternoon, when we returned to the hotel, about a hundred people were waiting for him. Instead of going to his room, Paulo sat in the lobby and chatted with them, drinking coffee incessantly, signing books, chatting, explaining, discussing scenes from his books, listening to tales from Iranian culture. Finally, he said he needed to go to his room and rest. Softly, he asked me to wait for a while.

After half an hour, he returned, laughing.

'The bodyguards are snoring. So I thought perhaps we could have a private chat.'

It was then that I met the real Paulo. He wanted to know about me, and he told me about himself. He believed I was too young to handle the situation and told me how to deal with the press, the government and the fans. He also said that he wanted to visit one of the Shia shrines if it were possible.

The next day was the fortieth day after Ashura, the anniversary of Imam Hussein's martyrdom. It was a day of mourning and Paulo wanted to watch the people. We went to the Shrine of Abdulazim, in South Tehran, after which the 'bodyguards' forced us to visit the graves of the martyrs of the war as well. My friend Farhad, from the Centre of Dialogue, was with us all the time. I was meeting him after 18 years. He was the one with whom I had founded the cooperative in our first year of junior high; we trusted one another.

'Listen, Arash', he said, 'we have a mystical ceremony at home tonight. Do you want to bring Paulo? I'm sure he'd want to be present at an authentic Sufi ceremony.'

I told Paulo about it, and he was very keen to attend. But it was dangerous. The government of Iran did not approve of alternative religion, especially mysticism. Farhad, however, said it wouldn't be a problem because the Centre of Dialogue was under the protection of President Khatami.

So we set off for Farhad's that night, accompanied by the bodyguards who thought we were going to attend a traditional mourning ceremony. People sat on the chairs or on the floor in the large living room. Everything seemed as usual: people were chatting, drinking tea, eating dates, introducing themselves. Paulo was talking to a professor of physics who was also one of the most important mystics in Iran, and I was chatting with

Maryam about the stress I was going through. The two body-guards sat beside one another, whispering.

Then the lights went off. One of the guests took out his *daf*—a Middle Eastern musical instrument mostly used during mystical dances—and began to sing and chant and call on the name of Ali and other famous Iranian mystics. Many of the guests stood up and joined in the dance. Within a few minutes they were all in an ecstatic state, shouting, dancing, whirling. I whispered to Paulo, 'Don't be afraid. It's normal.'

'Don't be stupid, Arash, I know.'

And then I noticed the two bodyguards leaving the house. I decided to follow them and see what they were up to.

'You left too? That's sacrilege, isn't it?'

I lit a cigarette and answered, 'I needed a smoke. I'm not really into mysticism.'

'Oh yeah?' Hamid said, while Khusro stepped to one side and spoke into his mobile phone.

'Your dear friend Farhad seems to be really into it, though.'

'Oh no, he's not.'

'He will pay for taking Pabilo to this heretic ceremony.'

'It's not illegal, is it?'

'You were supposed to tell us the plans.'

'I didn't know.'

'We'll see.'

During the next 10 days, while we were travelling around the country, Farhad and the Centre of Dialogue were in trouble. Apparently the agents had called the Security Department the same night and they had begun to investigate the case.

Mysticism in Iran is older than religion itself. It's part of the soul of the nation. Indo-Iranian mystery religions have given birth to several schools of thought and religions around the world. Worship of the mysterious Iranian god of light and the keeper of promises Mithra found its way to the Roman Empire and became the foundation of the Mysteries of Mithras, particularly popular among the Roman armies. Most of the Mithraic rites were absorbed and reapplied by Christianity. December 25, celebrated as the birthday of Jesus, was originally the birthday of Mithras and the beginning of the winter solstice; it is    celebrated widely in Iran as Yaldaa—the birth—marking the  victory of light over darkness before the nights shorten towards the end of the year.

There are other parallels between Christianity and Mithraism: shepherds attending the miraculous birth of a saviour; the idea of eternal life gained from the blood of a sacrificed saviour; communion; the Last Supper; Mithras' ascension to Heaven during the spring equinox and his unification with the sun god; Mithras' heavenly titles 'light of the world' and 'messenger of truth'; and baptism by the blood of the bull (lamb in Christianity); the Eucharist; and the idea of Mithras' eventual return to save the world.

Zoroastrianism was also a religion of mysteries in which the believers were regarded as warriors who had to take sides in the battle between Good and Evil. The idea of Satan, Apocalypse, the Last Judgement, Heaven and Hell have their origins in this mysterium. All these pre-Islamic Iranian mysteries were synthesized in third-century Manichaeism which then spread throughout the known world from China to the Pyrenees and survived for many centuries.

After the Muslims conquered Iran, the Iranians decided to camouflage their beliefs within Islam and they founded Shiism. Shiism was later divided into two paths: the orthodox religion or Sharia; and the mystic strand or Tariqa. The mystic strand was the continuation of Manichaeism and Mithraism and claimed that Ali was God's chosen representative in the same way that Mithra and Jesus were God's embodiment on Earth. It was even claimed that Ali was the reincarnation of the biblical Elijah or Ilia. It believed that mankind should communicate with God directly, instead of following the strict rules of the Sharia. Each person had a unique way of purifying himself or herself, and God wasn't a remote and vengeful being sitting on a throne but a harmonizing entity flowing through nature and connecting all beings. All were one. Love was the only thing that could keep this universal network going. And one had to get rid of his or her worldly prejudices in order to feel the presence of God. Sama, or the mystical dance, was a way of casting aside all assumptions and of experiencing God directly.

And it is as alive in today's Iran as it has been throughout history. And it is as frowned upon as it has been throughout history. Most of the Grand Muslim mystics, Sunni or Shia, died gruesome deaths and the stories of their lives form part of mythology. After the Revolution and under the pressure of the state-sanitized Sharia laws, people were turning to mysticism, more and more and the government did everything it could to prevent this. During Ahmadinejad's presidency, one of the prayer centres of the dervishes in Qom was attacked by the police and razed to the ground.

Paulo was fascinated with these rites and I made sure news of the trouble wouldn't reach him. I also needed to make sure that the journalists who accompanied him were not broadcasting any negative images about Iran. The 'bodyguards' had been quite explicit: if the Islamic Republic was hurt in any way because of this trip then it would be my responsibility. Farhad, on the other hand, was sacked a month later.

We went to Shiraz and visited the tomb of Hafiz, the great Persian poet, and to Persepolis. Paulo had two conferences in

Shiraz which thousands attended. Then we returned to Tehran for his meeting with the Minister of Culture and his public speech at the Opera House.

The Minister of Culture, Dr Mohajerani, received Paulo at home. He was as popular as Khatami, and everyone believed he had the best chance of being Khatami's successor. He had publicly declared that he was against censorship and that an Islamic government should welcome the expression of contradictory ideas without doling out fear and persecution. He had already begun to abolish prepublication censorship by making it a matter of choice for the publishers. If they were happy to accept responsibility for what they published, the Ministry wouldn't scrutinize the books.

Unfortunately, he didn't get the chance to do what he wanted. He was forced to resign a year later and he never forgave Khatami for abandoning him.

But that day he was a popular minister and I was excited to meet him.

He lived in a simple house, with a very small living room where we all sat after the initial greetings. Then Paulo and the Minister began a philosophical conversation on the concept of divine omnipresence.

'God is on Earth, and Earth is part of God,' said Paulo, 'Different races are only there to create endless possibilities for communication and the movement towards a final unification. They may have conflicts or fail to understand one another but they are one. In the Iranian story, *Conference of the Birds*, by the Sufi Attar, thousands of birds set off on a quest to find Simorgh, the king of birds. But when they reach the end of their journey, they realize that Simorgh is nothing but all of them together. They are one, and they are many. The same applies to different cultures.'

The conversation went on for an hour or more. At the end, Paulo said that he was going to fund a literary prize in Iran to introduce Persian contemporary literature to the world. The Minister said that he would do anything to help, and he would also protect the copyright of Paulo's books. They shook hands and said goodbye. They were going to meet later that night at the reception organized by the Centre of Dialogue to which several Iranian authors and poets had been invited.

The Centre had managed to convince Paulo to visit at least two museums. Paulo had accepted grudgingly, saying he wanted to be left alone; he wanted to meet the people and observe the ordinary life of the city. He didn't want to be followed all the time. This was not going to happen, of course. On the other hand, the bodyguards had forced us to move Paulo and Christina to the Laleh Hotel that belonged to the Security Department. That way, they would have more control over what he did, whom he met and what he said over the phone. Of course, Paulo was smart enough not to use the hotel phone; he used a mobile phone I had lent him.

While Paulo was travelling around the country and visiting the Iran that the government wanted him to see, there were several things happening on the political scene.

The absolute triumph of the reformists in the parliamentary election was the last warning to the hardliners. Having lost two major pillars of power, the government and the parliament, they decided to act before they were excluded from power completely. The judiciary began by clamping down on the newspapers. In the course of a week, 70 independent or reformist newspapers were shut down by the order of the judiciary. Some days earlier, a few Iranian authors, journalists and intellectuals had attended a conference in Berlin to discuss the new developments in Iranian politics and the reformist movement. The idiotic behaviour of the opposition in exile had turned everything upside down. A woman stripped in public in the middle of the conference to show that she detested reform and to prove that the Islamic Republic had to be overthrown. This led to the arrest of all the Iranian intellectuals and authors who had attended the conference as soon as they came home to Tehran. Some of them, such as the prominent author Mahmoud Dowlatabadi and the contemporary poet Sepanlou were released shortly after but the reformist journalist and author Akbar Ganji was held in prison and remained there for another five years.

Dowlatabadi and Sepanlou were both invited to the reception that night, a few hours after their release. As Paulo announced that he was launching a literary prize for Iranian writers, Dowlatabadi came up to me and said, 'Does he know what's going on in this country? Does he know we were interrogated before this party?'

No, he didn't. No one dared tell him what was going on and that it was only going to get worse.

Paulo's public conference was a huge success. Thousands gathered in the streets around the Opera House to get a chance to see their favourite author. The Opera House itself was packed. I couldn't believe my eyes; we, the five people who worked for Caravan Books, had managed to move several thousands. It made me feel a huge sense of responsibility. Paulo wasn't a rock star, he wasn't running for an election, he had never won a sports competition. He was, simply, a novelist, and there were thousands here to see him. Those who criticize him for being commercial have never been able to move such crowds nor affect lives in quite this way. I thought this was so only in Iran but when I accompanied Paulo on several signing sessions in various other countries, I realized he was able to touch people regardless of their backgrounds, race, nationality and religion. Isn't this an achievement? Isn't this the kind of globalization that is so sorely needed?

After a huge round of book-signing in the evening, when at least 10,000 fans blocked the streets for hours, and after a press conference and a Q&A, Paulo bade farewell to hundreds of his fans who had followed him to the airport. He left Iran promising he would be back in no time. That was 10 years ago and it hasn't happened yet.

After the plane had taken off, I was left drained of all the energy that had kept me going for the past 10 days. Maryam and I went home. I slept for 14 hours.

Next day, I was summoned by the Security Department to explain a few things. Why had I taken Paulo, a non-Muslim, to visit a Shia shrine? Why had I taken him to the night of the dervishes? Why had I not given a full report of whatever he had said during his visit? Why hadn't I translated for the bodyguards every single word he had uttered? Why couldn't I control the journalists who were accompanying him? Why had they been able to write about the Jewish inhabitants of Shiraz and the junkies on the streets? It went on . . .

I remained silent during the questions, then I showed them Paulo's interviews with the international media about his journey to Iran: he had only said good things about the country.

'But he has said that President Khatami is a brave man. What does he mean? Does he think that Khatami is brave enough to overthrow the Islamic Republic?'

No, I said. It meant that Khatami was brave to try to and battle the prejudices against the Islamic Republic.

'Very well, then. But the Ministry of Intelligence is not happy about his popularity in Iran, and it will make sure that the Iranians understand that their own culture is much better than this Brazilian's mumbo-jumbo.'

'Do whatever you think you should do.'

'And we are going to keep an eye on you. How is it that you began to publish only two years ago, and your books have already flooded all the bookstores? Are foreign intelligence agencies funding Caravan?'

'Of course not,' I said, and explained how we had earned every penny through nothing but our hard work. They could check our accounts whenever they wanted. We had nothing to hide.

They asked if I had succeeded in convincing Paulo to convert to Islam.

'I'm sure he was eager to,' I said, 'but the main obstacle is that he needs to be circumcised if he wants to convert. Can we exempt him from that part?'

I thought they wouldn't fail to notice the sarcasm but they took me at face value and began to discuss seriously. 'Unfortunately it's not possible', they finally concluded, 'he does have to be circumcised. But the procedure is totally painless nowadays. Please assure him that we can provide him with the best surgeons.'

'Sure', I said, 'I'll let him know.'

Paulo's visit to Iran sent ripples across the media, both in and outside Iran, and created the sort of publicity and prestige for Caravan that money could not have bought. We were on our way to becoming one of the most important publishing companies in the history of Iran.

Paulo had been fascinated by Iranian women. A few months later, when we met again in Barcelona, he told me, 'The Iranian women are genuinely beautiful. But what mesmerized me was their eyes. They have to cover their hair, their body, their legs and the only outlet for expressing their sexuality is their eyes. I've never seen so much passion in a woman's eyes anywhere else in the world.'

*26 December 2003*

1.56 a.m. Bam.

An enormous earthquake, registering 6.6 on the Richter scale, hit Bam, the 2,000-year-old city in south-eastern Iran. No one understood the scale of the destruction but the media were calling for help from doctors. Although I'd given up medicine I realized I needed to be there. I don't know what compelled me to pick up the phone and call the Red Crescent—the Islamic equivalent of the Red Cross—and volunteer but I did it without a second thought. The earthquake hit the city early in the morning on Friday 26 December 2003; I was on the only plane leaving for Bam at 8 that same evening.

Dust, rubble, a city in ruins. The middle of the night. The temperature: 10 degrees below zero. No water, no electricity, no roads. Sitting in the back of a van, listening. Someone seems to be moaning. The cold wind blowing in your face, piercing your skin with a thousand icy needles. Turning your eyes this way and that, staring into the darkness. Every once in a while, a fire in a corner: the palm trees aflame. Palm smoke is poisonous but the people here have no choice: they are freezing in the bleak

December air. The driver is asked to stop. My team and I move towards the fire, trying to see if we can help and if we can get a little warmth from the flames. Three people huddle around the glow. A woman lies on the ground. There are no blankets to cover her. Bleeding profusely, she has not even the strength to moan.

I sit beside her with my first-aid kit. Her femur is broken and she has lost at least a litre of blood. Her companions have tried to bandage the wound with a dirty rag. I have no light, no torches, nothing. I try to find a vein. I put in an IV. I take out a band-aid, write RED on it and stick it on her forehead. Everyone helps to move her into the van. Then we drive to the airport where a crisis headquarters has been set up. We have been told to do triage: to categorize patients into six colour-coded categories: WHITE, all right; GREEN, treatment on the spot, no need to transfer; YELLOW, transfer but low risk of death; RED high risk if the patient is not taken care of urgently; BLUE, no hope, this patient is going to die, don't bother; and 'BLACK', the patient is dead, ignore.

The chief of the Red Crescent apparently doesn't know that there is a seventh colour, too. The seventh colour that has no name. You are the seventh colour; you who have come to this city without roofs, where you don't have time to even comfort a dying patient. You are the seventh colour, as you are changed forever. You are the living dead. Mix the six colours and you have a seventh, the colour that defines you, you who are walking the deserts in the middle of the night, hoping to here a cry, a shout, something.

The sun rises gradually and throws thousands of golden lances over the city without roofs. You see a house without three of its walls, and without a roof. Only one wall is left standing and on it a clock, a clock that still shows the time, ticking . . .

As the sun rises so do the cries. As if the dark and the cold of the night had numbed the grief and the sorrow. The sun should have risen sooner so that the young man could cry over the enormous grave which now holds his wife and two toddlers. The grave that was once his 'home'.

People try pushing aside the rubble, to uncover the lifeless bodies of their loved ones or to hear a moan that would mean a life saved.

The van that took us to the city was gone. I begin walking the city, alley to alley, block to block. People are sitting on the ground, pale from fear and sorrow. I wish I had earplugs to block the unbearable sound of that silence. But I didn't, and couldn't. I had to be attentive to every movement, every sound. I was the seventh colour, waiting for a cry in the desert.

An old man calls out. 'Please help, my son is under these ruins.'

'Sorry, father. I am a doctor. I can't remove that huge mound. And I don't think your son is alive.'

'Please . . . I know he is . . .'

I begin to help him. It will take ages. It's a waste of time. But I work until a group with their dogs arrives and lends a hand.

I begin to walk again. Sometimes I can help, open an airway, fix a dislocated joint, label people with colours. Someone's there, his liver's torn apart, he's scarcely breathing but there's a spark of life.

'RED, doctor?' the nurse accompanying me asks.

'BLUE', I say. There is no pulse.

'I want to try. Let me put an IV line into him.'

'Do whatever you want.'

She brings the first-aid kit.

'Stop. It's BLACK now', I say.

282

Everyone in the girls' university dorm is dead. Dozens of students. My knees are giving way. No more moans. No one left to save.

Then I hear someone crying. I run towards the sound. It's coming from under some bricks. I push them aside frantically, the nurse helps, too. A head appears. It's a woman, she's alive. It's an hour before we can take her out. She's pregnant. Her husband and brother are buried under the rubble but she knows they are dead. This unborn child, too, belongs to the seventh colour, in that city without roofs, schools, water, electricity, telephone, streets, dorms, banks, supermarkets, pharmacies. The child is still alive, ablaze with the seven colours.

The earthquake in Bam claims 50,000 lives.

I'm been able to save only a dozen.

Khatami's two terms as President passed in a trice. By 2005, we were a well-established publishing house, releasing about 150 titles a year and a very popular literary magazine called *Book-fiesta*. We had founded Iran's first book club and one of the first independent literary prizes in Iran called Yaldaa. We had 20,000 official fans who avidly read everything we published.

My second novel, *The Princess of the Land of Eternity*, was published in 2003 and met with huge success. It was officially declared a bestseller in only a few months and nominated for two literary prizes. For reasons that are beyond me, one of the passages in the book became widely quoted.

> It is like the stare of a gazelle that has been fleeing from the hunter for many hours, and now lies on the ground, exhausted, with an arrow deep in her side. She lies down, warmed by her own blood. From where she is sprawled, she can see the brutal hunter approaching with a knife in his hand. Her gaze reflects neither hope nor despair. She has no desire. At this moment, a vague perception of life creeps into her veins, runs into her soul and spreads through her mind. How can I name

your feeling at that moment anything other than the
Gaze of the Gazelle . . .

Maryam had been promoted to managing director of a
large company in a conglomerate and was very successful. I was
both the managing director of Caravan Books and the editor-in-
chief of *Bookfiesta*. We sold more than 1,000,000 books a year.
We were an active member of the Union of Publishers and
Booksellers and had an undeniable influence on the industry.
All my dreams seemed to be coming true.

But, for the past three years, hopes for further reform had
been fading rapidly. Khatami had failed to fight for the rights
he had promised the people. The younger generation had lost
faith in the reformist movement. Khatami's Minister of Internal
Affairs, who had struggled so hard to support the formation
of independent parties and re-established city councils, had
been impeached and imprisoned for questioning the absolute
authority of the Supreme Leader. Minister of Culture Ata'ollah
Mohajerani had been forced to resign, and had fled the country
fearing persecution. Saeed Hajjarian, a prominent reformist figure and Khatami's senior consultant, had been paralyzed for life
after an assassination attempt by a hardliner; the assassin
was released from prison shortly after being sentenced to life
imprisonment. The Guardian Council had disqualified most of
the reformist candidates for parliament despite Khatami's
threats that he would resign. He didn't. Most of the newspapers
had been shut down. The Ministry of Culture had been overtaken by hardliners who had reinstated official censorship. Corruption had infiltrated all levels of the public administration and
people were beginning to believe that reform would go nowhere
as long as the Supreme Leader had absolute power and the
Guardian Council prevented independent figures from entering the political scene.

But something in society had changed: there was a new generation on the scene. Neda's generation, not yet born at the time of the Revolution, had only a vague idea of the years of war and oppression and all the atrocities of the regime. It had grown up experiencing a gradual opening up of society, with PCs, satellite TV, the Internet and mobile phones, and it was not as naive as we had been. This generation was not going to give up the comparative freedom that had been achieved during Khatami's presidency. It had not experienced the horrors of my generation: it had not lost friends to the firing squads and it had not witnessed how a strong man could crumble under torture in the interrogation rooms of the Islamic Republic. All it knew was that beyond the borders of Iran lay a world where people were free to do what they wanted and say what they wished. They could read and wear what they wanted and celebrate life. And this generation wanted that life, too.

Most important, it had arrived at the belief that freedom was the only thing in the world worth dying for. Women who, during Khatami's reign, had managed to re-establish their position in society as workers, writers, poets, artists, filmmakers, entrepreneurs, managers and politicians, were not going to give up their hard-won independence.

The student movement was there to stay, too. Although politically active students were persecuted, sometimes even expelled from university or imprisoned, they continued actively to challenge tyranny. What most surprised me was that the Islamic Association of University Students, responsible for spreading terror during my student years, was now the forerunner of the freedom movement. The regime was reaping its own rewards. It had sponsored anyone whom it had assessed as a loyalist, it had cleared the path for such people to enter higher education and it had supported them all the way. During my time as a student, I could feel their views changing. Those who were always looking to report 'misconduct' among their fellow students had become doctors and now wanted to be accepted by their colleagues. They had realized that there was diversity in the world, that everyone was entitled to believe in whatever they wanted: that difference led to a much more interesting society. This was exactly what had happened to Dr Muhammadi in the Revolutionary Guard.

Now the Islamic Association would be satisfied by nothing less than a secular government. An organization nurtured by the fundamentalist, religious government was no longer loyal to that government. Most important, the Islamic Association knew, inside out, the foundations and behind-the-scene interactions of the regime. The 2005 presidential election was drawing near and there was an unspoken consensus among the people to boycott it. They believed that Khatami was the best that could come out of this election and even he had not been able to fulfil his promises.

By then, I was a consultant to Tehran's Union of Publishers and Booksellers and we were trying hard to convince the Ministry of Culture to reduce its renewed grip on the control and censorship of books. I had covered most of Europe alongside Paulo and had many adventures—perhaps that will be another book—and made many friends in the publishing world. But Caravan was out of favour with the Ministry of Culture; it believed we were propagating 'deviant' Western culture among the young and, although it didn't try to shut us down, it tried to paralyze us by not authorizing many of our books.

In 2003, the Freedom to Publish committee of the Union sent an open letter signed by the President of the Union to President Khatami, reminding him of his promises and the illegality of prepublication censorship. We requested him to abolish the sophisticated system of censoring books prior to publication: 'censorship means prioritizing the opinion of a few over the taste and choices of a mature nation, and indifference to the right of freedom of speech as an inseparable right alongside other kinds of rights of a nation'. We also spoke of the 'indifference to the rights of authors and publishers and the choices of the readers', and the authorities' view of the nation as 'immature'. We concluded with the claim: 'The only way to put an end to the ambiguous, confused and unstable situation of books is to abolish censorship.'

Khatami never replied to our letter. However, two years later, we realized he had tried to pursue the case but his efforts had been neutralized. It seemed he had lost control over everything, and that was what disappointed people most. The president did not issue an order revoking prepublication censorship and no further actions were taken on the subject. It was as if an authority more powerful than the president had intervened and impeded any efforts towards the abolition of censorship.

Although Mohajerani had promised Paulo that he would support his contract with Caravan regarding the Persian rights to his books, the next minister decided to withdraw the protection: it was apparently against the law to prevent other publishers from publishing a foreign author's books without paying any royalties to them! So, despite the fact that we were his official publisher, 27 other publishers also brought out his books. People trusted our translations because they were recognized by the author. We also enjoyed the privilege of receiving his new manuscripts months in advance of their publication anywhere in the world. We held 80 per cent of the market share of his books. But there were parts of the market that were controlled by publishers and distributors who had oversaturated those segments with their own versions of Paulo's titles.

When I received the manuscript of Paulo's latest book *The Zahir* in 2005, an idea struck me: there was a way around this.

There's a clause in Iran's national copyright law which states that only works that are first published in Iran are protected by Iranian national copyright law. So, if we could publish the book in Iran before any other country, it would be protected. I shared the idea with Paulo and he agreed. The Iranian newspapers all had the same headline: 'Iran the first country to publish Paulo Coelho's latest book, *The Zahir*' and we sold thousands of copies immediately before the Tehran International Book Fair that year. We decided to make a big splash with the new book and stocked 4,000 copies of it at our stand at the Fair.

Tehran's Book Fair, described as the largest book fair in Central Asia and the Middle East, is the most important event for publishers in Iran. They meet their customers face to face, meet publishers from other countries, sell books and increase their cash flow. The inefficient distribution system makes the Fair an extremely important marketing and sales opportunity for publishers. It is also a major cultural festival for the public, especially young people, and every year it enjoys more than 3 million visitors. It is an opportunity for readers to access new titles from Iranian publishers as well as a selection of books from international publishers. No professional publisher can ignore the importance of the Fair, both for its prestige and as a major source of revenue.

We began a direct-mail campaign by way of advertising Paolo's book. We edited the footage of his interview on *The Zahir* and added Persian subtitles, and we were ready to break the sales record for any title in the history of the Fair.

Over the past years, our stand at the Fair had become extremely popular. We sold tens of thousands of books during those 10 days and the authorities were never happy about the crowds that gathered around our stand. They were young boys and girls, talking, meeting their favourite authors published by us, discussing literature, buying books. People travelled long distances, from the remotest parts of Iran, to come to the Fair. That's why one of the first things that Ahmadinejad did when he came to office was to move the Fair's location to the great

Musalla or prayer mosque of Tehran and destroy that atmosphere once and for all.

We sold 3,000 copies of *The Zahir* on the first day of the fair. People waited for hours in long queues to get a copy which had in the meantime received good reviews, despite Coelho's lack of popularity among the intellectuals. On the second day, when I got to the book fair at 9.30 in the morning, two bearded men, accompanied by an official from the Book Department were at our stand, waiting for me.

'Hello Dr. Hejazi, how are you?' said the official, Mr Kamali, who knew me very well.

'Hello Mr Kamali', I said, looking suspiciously at the two bearded men.

'This is Dr Hejazi, Responsible Manager of Caravan.'

They shook hands with me, unsmiling.

'How can I help, Mr Kamali?'

'How many copies of *The Zahir* have you got in the stand?'

I asked our sales manager. She said we had about a thousand.

'OK, Dr Hejazi, these brothers need to take all the copies you have. You will not be able to sell them any more.'

'What?' I shouted.

'I am sorry for the inconvenience. But they need to take the books now.'

'But why? The book has got prepublication and distribution permission. What has happened?'

'It is better you don't ask questions', one of the men said.

'Who are you anyway?' I asked, angrily.

'These brothers are from the Security Department.'

'What security protocol have we breached with this book?' I said, sarcastically.

'You'd better watch your mouth!' said one beard, 'This book has been declared harmful, poisonous and deviant.'

'Poisonous?'

'Yes, and before we raid your stand in front of all these people you'd better give us the books.'

'Are you going to pay for them?'

'Sure,' he said, laughing. 'With 100 per cent discount.'

'OK then, can you show me any written orders to confiscate these books?'

'We don't need to show you anything.'

'Can I have a receipt for the total number of the books you are confiscating?'

'There's no need for a receipt.'

'I can't let you take our books away without any evidence. I have to report to our board. How can I convince them that you just took a thousand copies of a book?'

'Ask them to call us if they have any questions.'

'Can I have your phone number?'

'No you can't.'

'Then, I'm sorry, I can't help you.'

Mr Kamali said, 'Dr Hejazi, be reasonable, please.'

'Reasonable? You are taking away our stock without any explanations and I'm the one being unreasonable?'

The beard took out his gun and put it on his lap.

'So? Are you going to shoot me in broad daylight, in front of all these people? It's armed robbery!' I said, smiling.

My colleague Muhammad tried to convince me to let them take the books. He said they were dangerous.

'OK, take them,' I said finally. 'But I'm telling you, I will let the world know what you did.'

The beards took all the copies and the one who had been doing the talking took me by the arm and pulled me aside. 'You will not talk about this to anyone, if you want you and your family to be safe. And you will come to the Security Department after the Fair to answer a few questions regarding this author and your loyalty to the Revolution.'

I was so enraged I ignored his warning. I called Paulo right away and told him everything that had happened.

'Arash, my concern is not the book but your safety. Why do they want you to report after the Fair?'

'I don't know, Paulo. They are taking control of the country. The presidential election is round the corner, and they want to keep everything under their control. They have already disqualified most of the reformist presidential candidates.'

'OK, the best way to keep you safe is visibility. I'll take care of it.'

'I'm not sure how they'll react if news gets out.'

'Don't worry. Once the news is out they can't touch you.'

That same night, news of *The Zahir* being banned and confiscated in Iran took over the international media: the BBC and AFP published detailed reports, and several outlets contacted me for an interview. I gave the interviews and I insisted that Paulo's popularity had frightened the hardliners in the regime.

Next day, I was taken away by the two beards as soon as I arrived at the Fair. They interrogated me for hours. Why had I talked to the deviant international media? Didn't I know the BBC was controlled by the Zionists? Hadn't they told me to shut up? Didn't I know that they could make me disappear? and so on.

I answered all the questions calmly. I said I was interested neither in politics nor in making news. But I was interested in my books and I wanted to be able to sell them. I hated making a financial loss.

They let me go after they were finished with me. I had been prepared for worse but, amazingly, Paulo had been right. They no longer bothered me; the next day, they returned all the copies they had confiscated.

There isn't much to say about the 2005 presidential election. While the majority of society who were disappointed with Khatami's presidency didn't vote, Mahmoud Ahmadinejad, Tehran's mayor about whom no one knew anything, won the election. Some said that the election was rigged. Some said he won by promising to bring fundamental changes to the government and promoting the interests of the poorer classes.

He won, and we who knew him, realized that the darkest days were yet to come.

PART VI

*I am the one,*
*ask the Hidden Imam*

(2005–2008)

One of the most important stories in Iranian mythology is of Zahak or Azhidahak.

Thousands of years ago, the earth was ruled by a wise king called Jamshid. He was appointed by Ahura Mazda, God of Goodness and Light, to make life better for the people. Jamshid expanded Iranian territory, invented chariots, created medicine, developed writing, architecture, social classes, different professions. He ruled for 700 years until he fell prey to the most fatal sin: Pride. He claimed that he was God and not his messenger. This cracked the shell that protected the people from Evil during his reign and Ahura Mazda stripped him of his divine grace.

It was then that Ahriman, God of Evil and Darkness, introduced his greatest creation: Zahak.

Zahak, a prince in Babylonia, was born a good man. But in his quest to win power over the world he succumbed to Ahriman and let him kiss his shoulders. Two kisses turned him into a powerful Dragon-king. Two serpents, satiated only with a daily diet of human brains, grew out of his shoulders.

Zahak then attacked Jamshid's realm of Iran which, at the time, covered most of the known world. The people, tired of

Jamshid's pride, didn't try to stop Zahak's invasion. He had promised them prosperity and abolition of the social classes and support for the poor. Jamshid's army was thus easily crushed and he was pursued to the end of the world where Zahak finally slew him and then took over his kingdom.

Zahak ruled over Iran for a thousand years. Every day, his agents killed two young men and fed their brains to the serpents. Then Zahak had a nightmare: a hero knocked him down with his mace and then took him to a high mountain. The dream readers said it was a sign of Zahak's downfall at the hands of Fereydun, a prince from Jamshid's bloodline.

Horrified, Zahak decided to consolidate his reign. He called an assembly of the patriarchs and forced them to sign a document testifying to his righteousness. Thus, no one could have any excuse for rebellion. But a blacksmith named Kaveh, who had lost 10 sons to the serpents of Zahak, spoke out against this charade and tore up the document. Then he left the court and raised his leather apron as his standard. People gathered around him and followed him to the Alborz Mountains. There they found the righteous King Fereydun and began their resistance. Fereydun defeated Zahak but Ahura Mazda did not allow him to execute the demon; instead, Fereydun was commanded to chain him in a cave, deep in the bowels of Mount Damavand.

According to the apocalyptic lore of Iran, Zahak will be released from his prison at the end of time and will destroy one-third of those living on earth. At that time, Garshaseb, the Iranian hero, supported by Kay Khusro, the legendary king, will emerge and kill the dragon once and for all with his legendary mace.

The Avestan texts hold that Zahak is the greatest lie that Ahriman created.

This story ran through my mind when Ahmadinejad won the election. He came to power by promising people that he would destroy the gap between rich and poor and bring glory back to Iran. Because of the corruption that had infiltrated all layers of the government, people were looking for someone who could bring good health back to the administration and who would support the poor. I believe the election wasn't rigged the first time Ahmadinejad came to power. He won fairly against Rafsanjani who had been in power for a long time and who had become associated with corruption.

But we knew that this was only the surface. Ahmadinejad was an ambitious and deluded man who would do anything to increase his power. The Supreme Leader and the Revolutionary Guard, who were losing control during Khatami's presidency, wanted to come up with a new face to regain their power. Ahmadinejad was just such a face, a manifestation of all the lies. The real Zahak was the Supreme Leader himself, a good man who sold his soul to Ahriman in his lust for power.

Lying is what defines Ahmadinejad. He thrives on lying and lying is his only weapon. The number of lies he has spouted during the past six years could fill a book. The world knows about his denial of the Holocaust, his claim that there are no homosexuals in Iran and that Iran is the freest and most democratic country in the world. But these are just a few. The Iranians needed only a few months to discover that their popular President was nothing but a liar. But it was too late.

The most dangerous aspect of Ahmadinejad's administration was his alleged relationship with the idea of the emergence of the Hidden Imam. There were rumours that he was part of a messianic Shia sect, led by the cleric Ayatollah Mesbah Yazdi.

According to Shia lore, the Hidden Imam had disappeared into a well in Basra in present-day Iraq, and it is from there that he will emerge when the time is right. Ahmadinejad, as a devoted disciple of Ayatollah Mesbah Yazdi, took these stories literally.

From the news leaked out of government circles, we learnt that Ahmadinejad was a puppet in the hands of this dangerous messianic sect that had gradually infiltrated all the centres of power in the regime, especially the Revolutionary Guard's Army. Ahmadinejad was apparently preparing for Armageddon. And he was planning to build a road from Basra to Tehran. When the Hidden Imam emerged, he could come directly to Tehran to establish his headquarters and wage war on all the world's infidels. Ahmadinejad was also rumoured to be consulting someone very often, someone who claimed to be in direct contact with the Hidden Imam. Someone who claimed that the Hidden Imam had asked him to seal the pact between Ahmadinejad and his cabinet, most of whom had backgrounds in the Revolutionary Guard's Army.

All of this may seem ridiculous to someone unfamiliar with Shia messianic lore. But the belief that the Hidden Imam will emerge is very much alive in Iran; and, as Islam is a highly political religion, the idea has overtaken the regime. If you review Ahmadinejad's behaviour over the past five years, signs of his belief in being the Chosen One preparing the ground for the Imam's reappearance become clear.

According to the lore, the world will be in a state of chaos just before the Hidden Imam appears; Christian rule will be dominant; a Sunni leader will emerge from the Middle East and will be engaged in a war with the Christians. There will be a dispute over who has won the war, the Christians or the Muslims, until a big battle ensues in which the Sunni ruler will be killed. The First and Second Gulf Wars between Saddam Hussein and the US and its allies were interpreted by this sect as the sign that Saddam Hussein was the Sunni ruler defeated by the Christians.

The red and the white death will arrive before the Hidden Imam's coming. The red death is the sword and the white death is the plague. There will be a great conflict in the land of Greater

Syria—present-day Syria, Lebanon, Palestine, Israel and Jordan—will result in its destruction. Death and fear will afflict the people of Baghdad and Iraq. A fire will appear in the sky and envelop them in a cloud of red. Adultery and fornication—and children born out of such alliances—will be rampant as will the consumption of alcohol; women will outnumber men; the Muslims will be riven with internal conflict; the nations will gather against the Muslims; acid rain will fall; the rich will get richer and the poor poorer; men will obey their wives and disobey their mothers; people will walk in the marketplace with their thighs exposed; great distances will be traversed in short spans of time; the people of Iraq will receive no food and no money because of the oppression of the Romans (the Westerners); people will leap from cloud to earth and back; female singers and musical instruments will become popular; people will dance late into the night; smog will appear over cities because of the sin of the people; earthquakes will increase; there will be attempts to make the deserts green; false messengers will appear; women will appear naked in spite of being dressed; India will be conquered by the Muslims; people will begin to compete to construct the tallest buildings; bearing false witness will become widespread; men will lie with men and women with women; trade will become so widespread that a woman will be forced to help her husband in business; women will enter the work force out of love for this world; family ties will be severed; there will be many women of child-bearing age who will no longer give birth; and men will begin to look like women and women like men.

An army bearing black signs, created by a man from Khorasan and led by his general Sho'aib Bin Saleh or Mansour (the victorious) will come to prepare the people for the Hidden Imam. This army, on their way to conquer Jerusalem, will kill many infidels. No power will be able to stop them and they will eventually reach and conquer Jerusalem where they will erect their flags. When the black flags of the Army of Khorasan appear on the dome of the Al-Aqsa mosque in Jerusalem, the Hidden Imam will show himself.

Rumour has it that each of these signs had been traced and interpreted by the sect. And the Coming was believed to be imminent.

Ali Khamenei, the current Supreme Leader, grew up in Khorasan, a province in north-east Iran. The idea of the Supreme Leader as the vicar of the Hidden Imam and the Rule of the Jurisprudent is compatible with the prophecy of the man who, immediately before the Coming, will rule the Muslims and conquer Israel and defeat the Jews. In this Shia apocalypse, the Jews are the main enemy who must be wiped out before the appearance of the Saviour.

Ahmadinejad publicly announced that Israel should be 'wiped off the map'; and if you count the number of times he has mentioned the word 'victory' in his speeches, you may be left with the feeling that he doesn't mind being called 'the Victorious'.

The Army of Khorasan will help the Hidden Imam when he emerges and together they will conquer the world. They will fight the Jews and kill them all. Ahmadinejad has said that the main reason for the US attack on Iraq was that it knew that a descendant of the Prophet Muhammad would emerge from Iraq to destroy all the oppressors in the world. According to Ahmadinejad, the US attacked Iraq to prevent the emergence of the Hidden Imam. He has also claimed that he was surrounded by a halo during his speech at the UN.

It was obvious since the beginning of Ahmadinejad's presidency that he was not looking at it as a political position but as a 'mission' assigned to him by God. Israel should be destroyed before the Hidden Imam can emerge. What the Western countries don't understand is that someone who lives under the delusion of being the Chosen One cannot be reasoned with. He will not give up his mission because he is convinced that he will be victorious.

There is yet another important element in this doctrine: *taqiyya*. This refers to a dispensation allowing Shia Muslims to conceal or disguise their beliefs, convictions, ideas, feelings, opinions or strategies at a time of imminent danger. In other words, lying is sanctioned. This doctrine has been widely used by Ahmadinejad's administration.

I was invited to participate in the Frankfurt Book Fair Fellow-ship programme at the beginning of the new government's term. The Fellowship Programme, which lasts three weeks, was one of the best times of my life. We were about 18 young editors and literary agents from around the world, travelling through Germany, visiting German publishers and making friends along the way. We spent the days visiting publishers, networking, discussing the future of books, exchanging ideas; the nights we frequented bars, talked, danced, ate, sang our local songs . . .

My friendship with Tirza, the Israeli editor, was a strange one. The first two days we didn't talk much. I had grown up fear-ing the Israelis; she too must have been apprehensive, knowing that I was from Iran, the arch-enemy of Israel. Then we began talking and found out that we had so much in common: we were both from the Middle East; we shared the same skin colour; we shared a history; we knew about the geopolitics of the region. But most important, we were both so inquisitive. So far I had only heard about the atrocities of the Israeli government; but what I had never thought about—although I always thought that I had—was that there were people living in Israel who were not even born when the state of Israel was formed. Tirza is one of the most amazing people I've met. She was very sympathetic to the Palestinians as long as they didn't bomb civilian areas in Israel.

The same was happening with Li from China and Grace from Taiwan. They kept their distance at the beginning but, by the end of the programme, they had become inseparable friends.

Then, the good times came to an abrupt end. First I received a call from my office in Tehran, saying that our permissions to publish 20 titles had been revoked, including *Le Desert* by J. M. G. Le Clézio, most of Coelho's books, *My Century* by Gunter Grass and several Iranian books. This was the first initiative of the new Minister of Culture: most of the books published during Khatami's presidency, especially those that were literary or dealt with the humanities, were declared 'deviant' and 'poisonous' by Ahmadinejad's administration. I could do nothing from Germany; so I asked them to wait until my return. Many of the books were already printed or reprinted and ready to be distributed. The Ministry's change of mind meant a huge financial pressure.

I was furious. I had expected as much and had implored everyone I knew to use their vote and to not let Ahmadinejad take control. I felt we were well and truly doomed now. And that was why, one night, when I was approached by a German reporter at a small bar in Munich, trying to have a shot of every drink from every country represented in our group, I spoke up.

I didn't know he was going to report our conversation. I thought we were just talking and, with an unreasonable amount of alcohol in my blood, I gave vent to my rage and spoke of everything: the censorship, the crackdown and the oppression. The next day, to my horror, I saw my name in an article in *Süddeutsche Zeitung*.

I received another call from my office. There had been queries regarding the 'interview', and I needed to explain as soon as I got back. The good times really were over. Reality had come calling with a crashing blow. No, although we all loved books and literature, although we had found more common ground than differences, although we had all been able to enjoy a few days of borderless peace and happiness, I bore no similarity to my friends from other countries. They had different concerns, adventures, excitements, businesses and hopes. They discussed literature: which author was going to win the Nobel Prize; which author they were going to bid for; how they were going to promote their books; what the future held for the publishing industry . . .

I had no one to discuss things with. I was alone, isolated. My concerns were different. Could we survive this government? Could we publish the books we had tried so hard to get to the point of publication? Was I in trouble because I had spoken about our condition? What was going to happen to all those students, journalists and intellectuals who were rotting in Iranian prisons?

We were from different worlds. I felt cut off from the group. But I hung on to my sense of humour and participated in the group activities; I danced and enjoyed myself . . . Eduardo, my Mexican colleague, once said to the others: 'You know what I like about this guy? His neck is on the line, yet he's laughing.'

I had to return to Iran earlier than I had planned.

I stepped into the censor's office. After several requests he had finally granted an appointment.

A polite man with the typical short beard. He shook hands with me and introduced himself: a philosopher. He explained that he didn't like his job as a 'scrutinizer' because sometimes people confused 'scrutiny' with 'censorship'. As 'scrutinizers' were not welcome in society, he preferred people not to know his name. He promised he would help us but that I had made a mess by speaking to the German journalist so openly. Although what I had said was correct. Hopefully, under the new government, everything would be resolved. Would I be ready to help them with the international media, now that I had managed to build up an international profile?

Of course not. I explained that I preferred not to get involved in any governmental matters. I wanted simply to remain an independent publisher and publish the books I wanted to.

Oh yes, he was impressed with how rapidly our publishing venture had grown over the past few years. Had we had any financial support from foreign countries?

No, for the thousandth time, we hadn't. We had made all the money ourselves. They could check our records if they so wanted.

No, no. He trusted me. Unfortunately we were in the spotlight and he couldn't approve most of our books; for example, *The Zahir.*

'What's wrong with *The Zahir*? It's a simple work of fiction. No sex scenes, no politics, no moral corruption.'

'Well, there is a Kazakh in the book who criticizes the Soviets for testing so many nuclear bombs in Kazakhstan that the ecosystem was ruined forever and agriculture was destroyed.'

'So what? What does that have to do with us?'

'Well, the author is trying to prove that nuclear activities are bad. And you know, we are going to develop our nuclear technology . . . of course, for peaceful purposes only.'

'If it's for peaceful purposes, why are we angry with the book's critique of nuclear testing?'

'There is but a fine line between these technologies. We don't want our public to turn against our nuclear programme. And this book on Buddhism. Buddhism is a pagan religion. We don't recognize it in the Islamic Republic. So why should we publish books on it?'

'We are not promoting Buddhism,' I said. 'But the fact that we don't recognize it as a religion doesn't mean that Buddhism doesn't exist. There are millions of Buddhists in the world and this book is trying to give a cultural background on it.'

'Yes, but there are hundreds of other books that could be published before we needed to have any information on Buddhism or other pagan traditions. For example, this book on Manichaeism. Why do we need that?'

'This book is an academic title in our religion and mythology list. The author is a prominent Iranian professor and he leads a course in Beheshti University on Manichaeism. This is his textbook.'

'Oh, so that explains it. Do you think that this course is really necessary, when we can teach courses on Islam?'

'It's not up to me to say. You had better talk to the Minister of Higher Education.'

'I'm going to let you publish Gunter Grass, though. Of course, you have to censor the part where he talks about the Shah.'

'I'm sorry but I cannot censor a book by a Nobel laureate.'

'Then you will let us know when you can, and we will re-issue the permission. And, please be careful with what you say from now on.'

That was it. I decided to hold back no longer. We didn't have anything to lose, anyway.

Over the next four years, the economy of Iran was ruined. The publishing industry was almost destroyed as thousands of books were banned or cut to shreds. The libraries began 'purging' 'poisonous' books. The government began expanding public, state-funded publishing companies to compete with the private ones. 4WD patrols began roaming the streets again, picking on women who did not observe the hijab strictly enough. All the bridges that Khatami had built with the world were broken; sanctions were imposed on Iran; inflation paralyzed the poor who had voted for Ahmadinejad; corruption got worse; newspapers were shut down; technologies to filter Internet content were introduced to censor international news or opposition websites; and bloggers were imprisoned.

In 2006, I was invited to the Göteberg Book Fair, both as a nominee for the Freedom to Publish prize given by the International Publishers Association, and to conduct a conference, 'Freedom to Publish in the Digital Age'. At the same time, I was appointed as managing editor of the Union of Publishers'

*Publishing Industry Journal.* I was determined to keep Caravan going, even though I knew the government wanted to tighten its stranglehold on us. I expanded some lists and put our fiction list on hold for a while. We decided to publish audiobooks as well, and I spent most of my time on our cultural magazine, *Bookfiesta* or *Jashn-e Ketab.*

The government banned most of our titles but we sent even more for permission. For every one book that managed to receive permission, we had to send 10. I worked from morning till the middle of the night to compensate for the time and money wasted on books that would never see the light of day. We couldn't reprint the successful books as most of their licenses had been revoked. Then the Ministry decided to relocate the Tehran Book Fair to the great mosque of Tehran and separate the Iranian publishers from the international ones. We began a campaign against this decision in the Union and asked the publishers not to attend the Fair. Hundreds of publishers followed our advice and the Ministry was finally forced to step back and keep all the publishers together. But they had their revenge by putting even more pressure on the publishers who were active in the Union.

In society, too, things were changing or, perhaps it is better to say, unchanging. Khatami's progressive steps were systematically reversed. The police declared they would shut down shops that sold inappropriately short coats to women. Politically active students in the universities were singled out and persecuted. The government began to expand economically, and, despite all its claims that it was trying to accelerate privatization of government property, it was the Revolutionary Guard that took over the industries and began to put pressure on the competition in the private sector. Parliament began to discuss imposing capital punishment on bloggers who undermined the authority of the Islamic Republic.

Fear governed the country again. People regretted not hav-ing supported the reform movement in the last years of Khatami's presidency.

Our son was born in October 2006 and he changed everything. As I looked at him for the first time, I was struck with terror. Was he going to grow up in the same destructive situation? Was he going to experience all the pain, sorrow, fear and restrictions that had polluted my childhood and adolescence?

We decided to name him Kay Khusro after my favourite character in Iranian mythology. He meant a lot to me and I was already writing a novel based on his story. The book was published a few days after Neda's murder, when I had already left Iran. I was not present to see its release although, deep within me, I experienced the emotions described in its pages.

In 2007, almost on the point of a nervous breakdown because of the government shutting down *Bookfiesta*—we had dared to publish an article on the story of Lilith and a short story by Primo Levi—I applied for an MA in publishing at Oxford Brookes University in the UK. I had fought hard, pushing against the restrictions and trying to survive. But the administration, it seemed, had simply drawn a line between 'trustworthy' and 'untrustworthy' publishers and was providing the former with every financial support while putting enormous pressure on the latter such as ourselves. I thought that a year away from Iran would perhaps help calm me a little; I could use the time to think about what to do. Maryam was exhausted after her many years of hard work and she, too, needed a break. I also thought that this course would give me the latest updates on the publishing industry and help me think about expanding Caravan internationally.

I was admitted to the course a few months later, and began sorting out my affairs for a year away from Iran. I also spent the last few months launching our audiobooks list.

Audiobooks had not been professionally and industrially produced in Iran until then; only a few poets had recorded their verse and a few children's books were available. But mainstream fiction had never been produced. I believed so much in their success and in the gap that we could feed that I wanted to make sure we published at least one significant audiobook before my departure.

We chose *The Alchemist*. I needed a genius to narrate, act, compose the music, play several instruments and sing. And to not charge us a stupendous fee. Only one name sprang to mind: Mohsen Namjoo, the icon of Iranian underground music. I discussed the project with him and he accepted.

An Iranian singer and musician, Namjoo was born in 1976 in a small town in north-east Iran where he learnt to sing and play traditional Iranian music and instruments. Later, when he became familiar with Western music, he made it his mission to bring together the apparently irreconcilable styles of Iranian traditional music with blues and rock. He began to write songs and music based on this idea but was rejected by the Ministry of Culture who believed his music to be too controversial and his lyrics too openly critical of the current situation in Iran. So he went underground although he continued to record his songs, waiting for the day he would be able to publish them. Hailing from a religious background, he even explored the ways in which one could use the Quran's verses as lyrics and he recorded those experiments.

Then his music leaked out into the world via the MP3 revolution. He said he hadn't intended to distribute his music unofficially; he had just loaned a CD to a few friends. One of them uploaded the music online, and the name of Mohsen Namjoo burst onto the Iranian music world. His songs became so popular that you could hardly find anyone who hadn't heard them. The year we began to record *The Alchemist* was also the year he released his first authorized album, *Toranj*. The lyrics were from Iranian classical poetry and the music—the hallmark of his success—comprised a combination of Western heavy metal with Iranian classical. His record was banned after its first 40,000 copies, then authorized, then banned again . . .

He did a brilliant job on *The Alchemist*. He composed 60 minutes of original music in an attempt to recreate the message of the book: the mystical union of all things. He read the book several times and then began writing his music almost in a state of ecstasy. He played all the instruments, from piano and guitar to Iranian setar. He also created 30 different vocals for different characters in the book.

We lived together in the studio for two months, after which he was overwhelmed by exhaustion and was hospitalized for two weeks. We had achieved the impossible. He left Iran for a music course in Vienna a few days after he was released from hospital, and we planned to launch the audiobook on his return. That never happened. None of us were there for the launch of the audiobook, although it was a huge success. The press dedicated pages to it, claiming it a revolution in the Iranian book industry. Caravan had marked another turning point in Iranian publishing history. It was going to be the last one, though.

A few months later, Namjoo was summoned to court and accused of 'insulting the Holy Quran': his experiments with setting its verses to music had leaked out. He didn't dare return to Iran for 'insulting the Quran' could result in a death sentence. The court sentenced him to five years in prison.

Ironically, I, too, was going to suffer a similar fate though for a different reason. But I'll talk about that later.

I arrived in the UK in September 2008 and Maryam and Kay joined me two months later. I was one of the oldest in class since most of the MA students were between 22 and 28. Living with these young students who had never experienced any of my horrors had a cathartic effect on me. We thought about nothing but our classes, and then about going out in the evening, sitting in a pub for a couple of hours, playing pool and teasing one another. Then we'd go to a nightclub or a bar where we'd dance and enjoy the evening. Our only concerns were about delivering our assignments on time and recovering from our hangovers. I had never had so much fun in my life. It was as if I were living the years stolen from my youth. And on many a night, when I returned to my room in the dorm, I would begin to cry as I thought about the youth in Iran who would never have a chance to enjoy their student life in this way, who would have to spend their lives in fear. While my classmates in the UK were having the best time of their lives, I had been persecuted for my long hair and for giving a speech on 'the healthy personality'!

When Maryam and Kay joined me, we rented a small house in Oxford and I spent my energies on my dissertation on censorship in Iran. I had decided to document everything. The government continued to deny it was practising censorship and Ahmadinejad had claimed on several international occasions that Iran was 'the freest country in the world'.

I was determined to go back after I completed my course although I wondered about whether I wanted Kay to grow up in Iran. I knew it would be hard for me to live away from my people. I was part of the culture and, despite all the problems, I felt it was my duty to be there. Living outside Iran would be fatal for me. Or at least I thought so at the time.

But when the presidential election campaign began, I was drawn out of my dreamlike wonderland and hurled back to reality. Everyone believed it was going to be a staged election. Everyone knew Ahmadinejad would run for a second term and the Guardian Council would disqualify any prominent rival reformist candidate. Everyone knew that the people wouldn't really have a choice, that the results were predetermined. Ahmadinejad was going to be the next president.

Everyone knew . . . until Khatami announced he was running for the presidency in February 2009.

This was it. This was a determining moment in the history of Iran.

# PART VII

*We are not dirt and dust,*
*we are the nation of Iran*

(2009–2010)

The people who had been disappointed with Khatami in his last two years as President and who had therefore refused to vote in the next election were now excited. Experiencing the four years of terror under Ahmadinejad had brought most people to their senses, especially the younger generation looking for quick results. One thing was clear: they had been better off with Khatami. The four years of Ahmadinejad's administration had taught them an important lesson: change should happen gradually.

When Khatami declared he would try for the presidency, I decided to do anything I could to support him. Mehdi Karroubi, another prominent reformist figure, had also announced his candidacy but I was sure that Khatami was the one we needed now. Apparently, millions of others had come to the same conclusion.

I followed the news obsessively, and regularly called home. However, a month later, Mir-Hussein Mousavi also announced his candidacy. Khatami pulled out immediately and chose to endorse Mousavi. Doubts were raised about this move. Mousavi had not been directly involved in politics for 20 years; the younger generation didn't know him and he was said to be more conservative than Khatami.

On the other hand, there was a lot of discussion about exactly *why* he had stayed away from politics over the last 20 years: because he had stood up to Khamenei when he was Prime Minister and Khamenei was President. There were rumours that Mousavi had decided to try for the presidency several times but the Supreme Leader had said that, while he was alive, Mousavi would not be allowed any executive posts.

It was also said that this time Mousavi had decided to run regardless of Khamenei's disapproval. The hardliners were certain he would be disqualified by the Guardian Council. But, after the unprecedented popularity he gained during the campaign, there was no way of disqualifying him without compromising the authenticity of the election in the eyes of the outside world.

The Green Wave began when, at an enormous gathering and in the presence of thousands of Khatami's supporters, Khatami handed over a green scarf to Mousavi, showing his absolute support. The green scarf symbolized the fact that they were both descendents of Prophet Muhammad, that they were both Sayyeds. This symbolic act officially launched the Green Wave, which became the Green Movement after the election and was soon, most unusually, adopted by all classes in society thus changing the religious implications of the gesture and giving it the wider connotations of prosperity and peace.

The Supreme Leader was perhaps happy that Khatami had pulled out because he had a high chance of unseating Ahmadinejad. He approved of Mousavi's candidacy based on the assumption that though he was a prominent reformist figure and his presence would help the election look more democratic, he had been out of politics for 20 years and the younger generation, most likely to determine the outcome of the election, was not familiar with him. Hence he didn't stand a chance against Ahmadinejad's populism.

What he didn't know was that Khatami's support would act as a trigger. He didn't know the extent to which the people were fed up with Ahmadinejad. He was not aware of the new revolution that the youth of Iran were going to introduce, not only to Iran but also to the world: the social media revolution.

In less than a month, millions of people around the country were wearing the green symbol: a green shawl, scarf, headscarf or ribbon. This worked like a badge of belonging and people realized they were not alone—indeed, there were many who wanted the same. The Wave that began in Tehran then flowed through all the cities and small towns, even to the villages and beyond the borders. For the first time since the Revolution, hundreds of thousands of Iranian emigrants and exiles became involved and joined the Wave.

Facebook, Twitter, YouTube, blogs ... The social media were taken over by the supporters of Mousavi. While Ahmadinejad enjoyed the unfair publicity provided by National TV which covered every move he made, every speech he gave, every campaign meeting he held and simply ignored the other three candidates, Mousavi was infiltrating cyberspace. He would give a speech at a meeting and a few minutes later it would appear on thousands of blogs and be shared by hundreds of thousands on Facebook and Twitter. Like a pebble dropped in a pool, sending out ripples to the four corners of the world. The polls began to reflect this: even those who had not voted during the past 30 years now decided to vote for Mousavi.

Mousavi changed his strategy when he realized he had already won the hearts of the hitherto silent part of society. He began to address Ahmadinejad's supporters, the poorer classes who still thought that Ahmadinejad was genuinely trying to provide a better life for them through social equality. Mousavi began to expose all Ahmadinejad's lies to the people, and soon proved that he, too, was a major contender. People knew that he had been most successful in abolishing poverty and bringing financial stability to the lower classes during the eight years of the war when he had been prime minister. He also uncovered the inconsistencies in the budget: US$1 billion were missing, unaccounted for. Ahmadinejad claimed that those who had checked the records had made a mistake; that nothing was missing. But the longer the scrutiny continued, the clearer it became that a lot of money was unaccounted for, and that the scope of the financial scandal was far greater than US$1 billion. Everyone in Iran knew where the money had gone: in support of Hamas and Hizbollah in Palestine and Lebanon, and in creating turmoil in Iraq and Afghanistan. The working class was outraged. While they had been struggling to support their families and provide them with basic necessities, the huge amount of money earned through the unprecedented increase in oil prices over the last fo  'ears was being pumped into Iran's nuclear ambitions an controversial groups such as Hamas and Hizbollah.

On the other hand, those who were committed to the Revolution knew that Mousavi had enjoyed the full support of Imam Khomeini, even during the conflict between him and Khamenei. An endless sea of supporters, from different classes, backgrounds, religious beliefs and ethnicities closed ranks behind Mousavi, committed to unseating Ahmadinejad.

The President knew this, and it was then that he decided to display his favourite tactics: populism and lies, on TV, in a desperate attempt to humiliate his opponents. For the first time in the history of Iran, live debates between presidential candidates were scheduled.

Back in Oxford, I was glued to my computer. Iranian National TV's website wasn't working but there were people who were recording and uploading the debates on YouTube within minutes of the live debate. Maryam and I said not a word as we watched Mousavi and Ahmadinejad challenging one another while Kay played with his building blocks.

Ahmadinejad claimed that Mousavi had spread lies about him, and attacked Khatami and Rafsanjani as the powers behind the scene. Mousavi produced facts and figures showing how Ahmadinejad had ruined the economy. He criticized the censorship, Iran's involvement in suspicious activities in the region, the lies and apocalyptic superstitions on which Ahmadinejad had based his administration ...

Ahmadinejad, taken by surprise, began to defend himself with a barrage of blatant lies. When Mousavi was, for example, asked about the 15 British Navy personnel captured and detained by Iran, Ahmadinejad said, 'Tony Blair sent an official apology for intruding into our waters. So I decided to release them.'

Everyone was aghast: this was an absolute lie. Tony Blair had sent no such apology but Ahmadinejad continued to insist that the letter was archived in the Ministry of Foreign Affairs. Mousavi simply smiled: it was too late. Now, even those who had no access to the Internet or satellite TV channels, and whose only source of information was National TV, knew that their President was nothing but a liar. Mousavi had won.

When I went back to Iran after the election, one of my friends said to me, 'You should have been here, you should have seen it with your own eyes. I cried so many times. The Green Wave brought a new energy and rejuvenated society. People grew kinder, they held up their green banners as a sign of unity. People were happy, they felt that it was finally their turn . . '

A few days before the election, the supporters of Mousavi held hands and formed a chain that extended 20 kilometres through Tehran. There was no doubt that Ahmadinejad stood no chance.

It was then that the Supreme Leader decided to intervene.

*Friday, 12 June 2009*

We woke up early in the morning. My mother-in-law, who had come from Iran to visit us and help Maryam while she was studying, Maryam, Kay and I. We took our passports and got on the coach from Oxford to London. We arrived at the Embassy of Iran in London at about 11 in the morning. Our plan was to vote quickly, then go to Hyde Park for a picnic since it was such a lovely, sunny day.

I wanted to be in Iran on election day itself but, since my mother-in-law and Maryam were not going to accompany me, we decided we would vote in London and I would fly to Tehran the following day. I had several things to do in Iran: I had to move house as the lease on ours had expired; I had to negotiate with our account manager at the bank for the loans that Caravan was going to need; I had to resolve a dispute between Caravan and one of our translators; and I had to attend a meeting to determine the titles we were going to publish over the next six months.

When we arrived in London, long before we could get to the Embassy, we felt that we were back in Iran. Everyone in

Kensington High Street seemed to be speaking Persian! I approached two girls and asked them in Persian, 'Where is the Embassy of Iran?'

'You want to vote?' the girl answered in heavily British-accented Persian which revealed she had grown up in the UK.

I nodded.

'Welcome to the club. All these people are here to vote, and the queue ends there,' she pointed.

We were nearly a mile away from the Embassy with thousands of Iranians crowding the street. We joined the queue; while we waited, we answered questions from the British passers-by who asked, astonished, what on earth was going on. When they realized we were all there to vote, their eyebrows rose in amazement. They had never seen such a commitment to an election.

I began walking along the queue, talking to people. Almost everyone was going to vote for Mousavi, even those who had never been to Iran, who were born and brought up in the UK. A group of about 20 communist dissidents had gathered in front of the Embassy, shouting that this was a charade and that people should boycott the election rather than participate in sanctifying the crimes of the Islamic Republic. People laughed at them and said it was time they put aside their differences and participated in the destiny of their country.

We left soon after casting our votes, confident that a significant success was on its way. I kept calling my friends in Tehran to ask how things were going. One of my friends who was working actively in Mousavi's campaign, said, 'There is no one in the country voting for Ahmadinejad. Mousavi has 70 per cent of the vote, even in the villages.'

So, having nothing better to do but wait, we picnicked, daydreaming about the bright future of our country now that the people had decided to take control.

When we got home at about 5 p.m., the first thing I did was turn on my computer and check the news.

The official news agency of Iran declared that Ahmadinejad had won the election with 63 per cent of the vote.

*Saturday, 13 June 2009*

We didn't sleep that night. We didn't utter a word. We just watched the news, every minute of it, hoping it was all a bad dream, a mistake. The Iranians began to express their astonishment on their blogs and across social media. No one could believe the news. There must be a mistake. Arguments and disputes broke out. How could they announce the results while the balloting continued? The ballots weren't computerized. The counters had to check every slip and record it by hand. It had taken days before earlier election results had been announced. Something was wrong. No doubt about it.

Mousavi, Karroubi and Khatami asked the people to remain calm. They said Mousavi had won without a doubt and that this was all a mistake. Ali Larijani, Speaker of the Majlis, had already called Mousavi and congratulated him.

The results were announced every hour, and Ahmadinejad's 63 per cent remained constant. Then information began to trickle out. Millions of ballot papers had been printed and were unaccounted for. The Revolutionary Guard had once again raided the ballot centres, thrown out Mousavi's and Karroubi's representatives and taken over the voting process.

The reformists kept asking the people to remain calm until further developments. But there were no developments, and in the morning a group of people began to protest in Tehran's Vanak Square, asking for a recount. They were crushed savagely by the Basij and the plainclothes police. Films of the first crackdown were posted on YouTube instantly and picked up by the international media. The night before, a few prominent reformists and strong supporters of either Mousavi or Karroubi had been arrested. No one knew why. One of them was a former Minister of Heavy Industries, the other was Khatami's Deputy Minister of Internal Affairs. Khatami's brother, a former MP, had also been arrested.

Without knowing what I was doing, I packed my suitcase to head towards Heathrow. Maryam tried to stop me, begging me to postpone my trip by a few days. Afraid of something happening to me, she even offered to come along.

But I was determined to go.

'Maryam, if I don't go now, I will die of anxiety. The country is going to turn upside down. I have to be there. My friends and colleagues need me there.'

I kissed Kay and headed out. I felt so empty. All the hopes had come crashing down, and the darkest times were on their way. If this fraud went unnoticed and if Ahmadinejad could retain his power, there was nothing to stop his wreaking vengeance on all those who had challenged him during the campaign.

At the airport I saw scenes from Iran on TV. The plainclothes guards and the police were attacking the unarmed people with their batons, pulling them to the ground, kicking them with rage . . . My heart was pounding. One or two Iranians watching with me decided to abandon their travel plans.

But I could not. I had to go back.

I don't know what it was that pushed me towards Iran that day. Perhaps it was a sense of responsibility for my employees. Many of my friends and employees were young. Most of them had been quite active during the campaigns and had participated openly in propagating the Green Wave. I already knew, having talked to them, that they were furious; they felt betrayed and cheated, and I was afraid they would go out and get themselves hurt. I also needed to talk to my friends, to discuss the situation and not to be left alone with my despair.

The most reasonable thing would have been to leave the airport, to go back to the haven of Oxford, to wait a few days and to go to Iran once things were 'safe'. But I couldn't. A voice within me called out incessantly, 'Go! Move! You're needed there!'

So I stepped into the plane on the evening of 13 June 2009, in order to take part in what destiny had determined for me.

*Sunday, 14 June 2009*

The Iranian passport-control officer looked at my passport.

'Are you a student?'

'Yes, Sir.'

He looked at the last page of my passport which bore the stamp showing I had voted two days ago. He smiled. 'I see you voted.'

'Yes, I did, in London.'

'And you know the results?' he asked sarcastically.

'Yes', I sighed.

'It's a big fraud, isn't it?'

I didn't answer. I had no idea if this was a genuine question or a test. He stamped my passport.

'Godspeed, student!' he said, and handed the passport back.

My parents were waiting for me at the airport. On our way home they filled me in on the news. The country was in turmoil. Despite Mousavi and Karroubi announcing that they wouldn't accept the results and accusing the administration of rigging the ballot, the Supreme Leader had congratulated Ahmadinejad and asked the other candidates to respect the results. The protesters thought this statement outrageous: Khamenei hadn't even left open the option of a recount. Several reformists and journalists had already been arrested. Mousavi had asked the people to show their objection to this fraud by shouting '*Allah-o Akbar*' from the rooftops at 10 every night, following the tradition initiated at the time of the Revolution. The police had begun to arrest anyone who carried a green symbol.

As soon as we got home and had had breakfast, I got into my car and drove to Caravan. I found my colleagues sitting listlessly, staring at one another, doing nothing. As soon as I entered, they seemed to emerge from their stupor and we began discussing the situation. I phoned some of my friends and asked for the latest news. One of them was Emad, an active participant in the protests.

'Emad, are you crazy? Go home to your pregnant wife! What would your unborn child do if something happened to you?'

'I can't, Arash. If I don't do anything now, the life of my unborn child will be destroyed. She deserves to live in a better country.'

He kept giving me updates about the situation. The government had blocked almost every website and blog. The satellite channels were unusable: the regime was sending out huge jamming waves. The phones were tapped, and the Internet speed slowed down to such an extent that we couldn't communicate with the outside world. The only way I could contact Maryam was via Skype.

Then, the social media revolution entered its next phase. Footage of the street violence was uploaded onto YouTube and Facebook. And Twitter began to provide immediate updates. Most of us couldn't even see the videos that were uploaded since YouTube and Facebook were blocked as well.

Another friend, very close to Mousavi—who'd better remain anonymous—told me that Mousavi had paid a visit to the Supreme Leader that afternoon but Khamenei had said that there hadn't been any cheating in the election. Mousavi had asked how they could know that before a recount. The Ayatollah had said there was no need; he was sure there had been no fraud.

Ahmadinejad celebrated his victory among his supporters in Vali-Asr Square the same day. It was there that he publicly declared that those who protested against the results of the election was 'insignificant, nothing but dirt and dust'.

That was a mistake.

That night, the police, the plainclothes men and the Basij attacked the dorm of University of Tehran, the same place they had struck exactly 10 years ago in July 1999. Five students, boys and girls, were killed on the spot.

That night, if you went out at 10, the roar of thousands of people shouting '*Allah-o Akbar*' from their rooftops would have made your heart race.

Or filled it with fear, depending which side you were on.

*Monday, 15 June 2009*

'It's a dead end,' my friend said. 'Mousavi, Khatami and Karroubi can't do anything against the regime. And now that the Supreme Leader has congratulated Ahmadinejad, there's no way the election is going to be annulled or a recount allowed. The only ones who can change the balance are the people in the streets.'

And that's what happened on Monday, 15 June. The people, without any leader, spontaneously decided to march from Enghelab Square to Azadi Square, where the great rally against the Shah had taken place on Ashura day in 1978. Ahmadinejad's remarkable feat of calling the protestors 'dirt and dust' had aroused widespread fury among the people. They had asked for a recount and in turn been insulted by the so-called President-elect. The murders in the university dorm fuelled that rage, and the energy that had built up over the past two months came rushing to the fore.

At the same time, the Revolutionary Guard spread the word that it was allowed to fire at the people. Mousavi, who had been under house arrest and could not communicate, released that day so that he could attend the rallies and ask the people to go home.

At four in the afternoon news that Mousavi had joined the demonstration spread through the city like wildfire. Millions left their homes and offices for Azadi Street. All my colleagues and employees set off in the same direction. I went out a little later and was soon a part of a sea of millions, walking through the huge boulevard.

How can I describe the rally, and the ones that followed over the next three days? It wasn't just the numbers. I was experiencing such a poignant déjà vu. This was the place where, 30 years ago, Dad had brought me on his shoulders. The difference, now, was that the crowd was larger and more diverse. Boys and girls walked together, carrying green symbols, forming the V sign with their fingers, holding placards with slogans like 'Where is my vote?', 'We are not dirt and dust, we are the nation of Iran!', 'The Epic of Dirt and Dust!', 'Liar! Liar! Where are the 63 per cent who voted for you?' Poetry, an inseparable part of any kind of Iranian demonstration, was as much part of the protests as the Green Wave, now called the Green Movement.

> The real dirt and dust is you,
> You are lower than dirt yourself,
> We are the passion,
> We are the light,
> We're the wounded ones in love,
> You are the oppressor,
> You are blind,
> You are the lightless halo,
> We are the fearless valiant,
> We are the owners of this land.

The outstanding thing was that everyone insisted on non-violence.

'We will not show violence. We are not like them.'

'We are all together, fear not.'

'Keep silent. Our silence echoes in the heavens.'

'Don't insult anyone.'

'We want out votes back.'

The administration had been trying hard to limit the Green Movement to the middle classes. But nothing could be further from the truth. Those rallies brought together people from all classes: clerics, labourers, shopkeepers, religious people with beards, former Basijis who had lost their legs during the war joining the crowd on their wheelchairs, women with chadors, women without chadors, 10-year-olds, 80-year-old men and women. Those who passed by in buses or cars showed us the V sign, encouraging us. The shops on the way gave out free water and juice. The police stood by and didn't dare do anything, either because the sheer numbers petrified them or because they had orders not to do so.

When we dispersed, we were sure that the Supreme Leader had witnessed the protests. That he had understood how upset the people were about the fraud. That he would now do something about it for certain.

But when we got home we heard that five of the protesters had been shot by the Basij after dark.

*Friday, 19 June 2009*

During the week I was attending most of the demonstrations and rallies, now called 'Rallies of Silence' after the main demonstration on 15 June. I also had to move house. Dad had rented a flat near their house for us and I had hired a few people to take care of the move under my supervision. I had delivered the keys to our former landlord and was driving towards my parents' for lunch. The radio was on.

That Friday was unprecedented in the history of Iran's Friday prayers. Friday, or *Jumah*, prayer is one of the cornerstones of Islam: a congregational prayer held at noon. The two sermons, one religious and one political before the actual prayers, have always played a crucial role in the government of the Islamic Republic. Tehran's Friday prayers are always held at the University of Tehran, led by one of the most important clerics who is appointed directly by the Supreme Leader.

That Friday Ayatollah Khamenei announced he would lead the prayers himself.

Everyone I knew was either listening to or watching the sermons. Everyone expected the Supreme Leader to call for a reconciliation and a recount. But, instead of trying to calm both sides, the Supreme Leader waged war on the nation:

> Over the past centuries, the West has destroyed our culture. But our nation wants to regain that spirituality ... The enemy wants to make us believe that we have been fooled ... Zionist, American and British radios are all trying to say that there was a competition between those who support and those who don't support the state ... The President was insulted and wrongly accused ... The legal mechanism in our country won't allow any cheating. I will not accept any illegal initiatives. If the political elite want to fix something at the cost of something else and break the law, they will be responsible for the bloodshed ... What people want and what they don't want should not be taken into the streets. Street-wrestling is not acceptable after the election ... I want both sides to put an end to this. If they don't, then the responsibility of the consequences will be on them.

The city had fallen silent. The flickering hope that the Leader would take a decision to investigate the fraud was snuffed out in an instant. I knew then that the next day, 20 June 2009, would be a day of fate. He had lit a spark in the already seething hearts of the people. The young would take to the streets.

And I knew that sermon had been a warning. 'If you protest, we will kill.'

*Saturday, 20 June 2009*

*I've seen that stare before . . .*

'DON'T BE AFRAID, NEDA! Don't be afraid!'

What I see in those brown eyes staring at me is far from fear or pain. I know that look, I've seen it somewhere. I press harder at the wound on her chest, below the neck, where the blood is gushing out like lava from an angry volcano.

*It's her aorta! Shit!*

As if disappointed at my inadequate response, her dark and lovely eyes turn towards the lens of Emad's new camera-phone. He's been bragging about it for days now, trying to convince me of its virtues.

'Stay, Neda!' cries the old man beside her, 'STAY WITH ME!'

She's not going to stay with anyone. She's leaving, that's for sure. I have an instinct for seeing death sucking out life and my ears are trained to hear the sound of Death's breathing. I have, quite literally, seen thousands of deaths.

*Her lungs too . . .*

Blood pours from her mouth and nose.

'Turn her head!' I shout to old man with the ponytail and the blue striped T-shirt.

'Open her mouth! Open the airways!' I command.

*Her father*, I guess, though later I find out he is her music teacher; he is teaching her how to sing, how to have a voice, despite the ban on women singing.

Her blood circulation is slowing down. Her body is slowly being drained of blood.

*My god, I've seen this look before but where?*

'Someone take her to a hospital!' I cry out, although I know that no one can save her.

The blood pours out of her nose and mouth and drowns an eye. I can see Emad's knees trembling while he records the calmness seeping into those eyes.

I remember it now . . . It's the gaze of the gazelle . . . My gazelle, the one waiting for the hunter to approach, in my book.

The heart gives up. There's no more blood left to pump. The gaze drowns in blood, in the three-decade old pain of a nation.

'My child!' the old man wails. 'My child! Motherfuckers!'

I lean back against the wall, soaked in Neda's blood. A Peugeot 206 arrives. People help the old man carry the lifeless body into the car which then races away to find a hospital in the faint hope that she may be saved.

I'm numb and Emad is very near collapse. My friend Hassan runs to me. 'What does she need?' he asks, his eyes filled with horror. 'What can I do to help?'

'Nothing,' I say quite calmly. 'She's dead.'

Hassan was one of my youngest employees, no older than 24, and it was because of him that I was there, standing beside Neda when she was shot.

When I went to the office that morning, I said that no one was allowed to go out that day. I even arranged a 'business' meeting with Emad at 5 p.m. to keep everyone busy.

All through the meeting we continued to follow the news. The Internet was horribly slow but we were among the few who had access to a broadband connection. There'd been a crackdown. I called one of my friends who I knew would be out there.

'I'm at Enghelab Square', he gasped. 'People were supposed to gather here to begin the rally but now the police are beating everyone . . . they're ruthless . . . don't come out . . .'

That was it. Emad and Hassan stood up.

'We're leaving. We can't sit here talking business while people are being slaughtered in the streets.'

'No one is allowed to go out today!' I shouted.

'Fire me if you want,' said Hassan. 'I'm going.'

I turned to Emad, desperate, 'You have a pregnant wife to take care of.'

'I'm going out, Arash,' he responded, smiling. 'Sorry!'

I went out, too, trying to protect Hassan and Emad. Hassan had no idea about the meaning of violence. He hadn't been there 20 years ago during the thousands of overnight executions. He didn't know what the devoted soldiers of the Hidden Imam were capable of. His long hair reminded me of myself 15 years ago, when I insisted on its length in order to prove that, despite all the controls, I had managed to keep my individuality intact. I had no power over the determination of a young man who wanted to protest, to claim his vote, his dreams, his essential rights—to do what our generation had failed to do. The least I could do was to try and be with him, protect him. I told them I would go with them on the condition that they wouldn't stray more than three feet from my side.

We didn't get far. The protests were on around the corner, at the end of the alley that joined our office to Kargar Street where more than 50 anti-riot policemen were trying to force back about 200 protestors with teargas.

But it wasn't working: neither the teargas nor the fear. The protestors lit a fire, trying to control the devastating effects of the teargas. Two young men stood over it, trying to soothe their reddened eyes with smoke.

*Baptism by fire*, I thought, *that's what it's come to.*

'Don't leave my side, you fool!' I shouted to Hassan.

That's when I saw Neda for the first time.

She was standing beside an old man with a ponytail, wearing the typical long black coat. She had tied her headscarf at the back of her head, either to battle the summer heat or to enjoy the brief opportunity that the protests had provided to free herself from the obligation of not exposing her neck. She was also wearing a visor to protect her eyes from the summer sun. The old man tried to keep her away from the crowd, although he was as successful as I in my struggle to keep Hassan by my side. They belonged to the same generation. I was trying not to be overwhelmed by fear at the same time as I was overcome with an unbearable premonition of something terrible waiting to happen.

'Let's go!' I shouted. 'It's enough!'

The girl stepped forward in the crowd and shouted, 'Down with the dictator! Ahmadinejad betrays us, the Leader supports him!'

The old man pulled her back.

An anti-riot policeman hurled a can of teargas. Clearly he wasn't sufficiently trained because the can, instead of landing amid the protestors, flew over them and through an open window of the building at the corner. An old woman appeared at the window. 'You idiots!' she shouted through the smoke billowing around her, 'Can't you even aim right? I'm suffocating!'

Everyone burst out laughing and a few young boys and girls rushed towards the house to bring her out and baptize her with the smoke rising from the small fire in the middle of the street.

'Welcome to the club, grandma!' a young girl said, laughing.

Suddenly, everything changed.

'They're coming!' someone shouted. 'Run!'

I pulled back Hassan and Emad. The anti-riot police and their red motorcycles, now in a line, began moving towards the crowd. People began to run in different directions. About 10 or 15 of them sped into the alley that led to our office. I pushed all my friends and shouted, 'Run, NOW!' We began to run, Neda and the old man with us. The anti-riot police didn't enter the alley; they preferred to keep control over the main street. This calmed us somewhat; we slowed down and stopped at the intersection. Neda turned to see if the old man was still with us. I looked around to see if Hassan and the others were all right.

'Go into the office NOW!' I shouted at Hassan, 'Or I will sack you on the spot!'

Then, suddenly, we heard a blast.

'What was that?' I asked Hassan. 'Was that a bullet?'

'I don't think so,' said Emad, trying to record everything on his camera phone. 'I've heard they are using plastic bullets to frighten people.'

'Go into the office, Hassan.' I repeated.

'But, Arash . . .'

'No buts! Now!'

'She's vomiting blood . . .'

I turned back and saw Neda bending over in astonishment, looking at the fountain of blood gushing out of her chest.

'She's not vomiting, she's been shot!' I shouted, rushing towards her.

'What does she need?' Hasan asks, his eyes filled with horror. 'What can I do to help?'

'Nothing,' I say quite calmly. 'She's dead.'

No matter how hard I try to stop it, I am now overwhelmed by fear. She was standing three feet away from me when she was shot. *It could have been me. It could have been Hassan.*' And then I try to push the thought aside, embarrassed. I try to replace it with *'It should have been me.'* That's when I hear someone shouting, 'I didn't want to kill her!'

The people have apparently caught a man. Emad tries to run his camera-phone again but the battery is dead. As if the scene it has just recorded has consumed all its energy.

He's a robust sort of man, the typical 'four-square' moustache. The crowd has ripped off his shirt and is now beating him. 'I didn't want to kill her,' he begs. I caught a glimpse of too many scars on his back.

A few men try to pull him out from under the feet of the angry mob. 'Wait,' they shout. 'We are not like them, don't hurt him.' Another one, holds up his man's wallet and ID cards, and shouts, 'See? He's from the Basij! This son of a bitch murdered that innocent girl!'

Reality sinks in soon enough. The crowd doesn't know what to do. There's no use handing him to the police since they themselves would be arrested for illegal demonstration. They can't hurt the man because they are 'not like them'. There's nothing left to do but to let him go and keep his ID card.

There's nothing left for us to do either. We walk back towards our office. I help Emad who is close to collapse.

He has never seen so much blood.

I helped Emad lie on the office floor, gave him a glass of water and nursed him until he came to his senses. Then we all sat around the table, trying to help one another out of shock, thinking about what to do with that bit of footage.

Emad was still trembling. Hassan was still, staring into space. Muhammad, my partner, who had joined us only after Neda had been shot, was pale. I was the only one who still had some control over himself. Neda's eyes wouldn't go away, the gaze, the question . . . *Why? How did it come to this?*

I pushed the thought away. There were only a few moments to decide. The speed of the Internet connection was slowing down by the minute and this could be my last chance to let the world witness the horror we had just experienced.

'Give me the video,' I asked Emad, making sure that Muhammad didn't know what we were talking about. It was for his own protection.

'I did nothing to help her!' Emad said, ignoring my request, 'I just stood there and filmed . . .'

I grabbed his arm, 'Listen, Emad. There's nothing you could have done. But you recorded it. Now it's our responsibility to let the world know!'

He looked at me in horror.

'But your face is clear. We have to blur it first.'

'There's no time, Emad. The Internet is shutting down exactly for this reason. They don't want the world to see what's going on. It's our responsibility. We owe this to that innocent girl. You don't want her blood to have been shed in vain.'

The hesitation in his eyes forced me to shout, 'GIVE ME THE VIDEO, DAMMIT!'

We connected the phone to my laptop. I knew I was putting myself in grave danger. Our vengeful government would not tolerate anyone who dared try to inform the world of its atrocities. But for how long could I stay silent? How much bloodshed would I witness before I finally decided to speak up?

I wrote an email, attached the video, and sent it off to a few friends, a classmate in Oxford Brookes and a professor who had been in touch with me ever since I had been in Iran. I also copied it to a friend of a friend who was currently in The Netherlands. He could upload the video onto YouTube.

Then I clicked *Send*.

I went to my parents' that night, soaked in blood. My mother fainted when she saw me. Before I could explain anything, the video was shown on CNN, BBC, Al Jazeera, VOA, France 24, almost every news channel in the world. And there I was, my face turned towards the camera, looking anxiously at Emad.

That was my way of looking up to Arash the Archer.

That video was my arrow. And I had put my life into it.

*Tuesday, 23 June 2009*

Two days later, when the video had already travelled across the world and its seven seas, I received an email from Paulo.

> Dear Arash
> I need to know where you stand if things that I am watching/reading are true. Then I can take a position too—depending on your advice, of course.
> Love
> Paulo

He had seen the video and he wanted to make sure that it was I who was trying to save Neda. I broke my silence for the first time and wrote back.

> Dearest Paulo,
> I am now in Tehran. The video of Neda's murder was taken by my friend and you can recognize me in the video. I was the doctor who tried to save her and failed. She died in my arms. I am writing with tears in my eyes. The government is massacring people who only want their basic rights. Please support us. The blood-shed is unbearable. Please don't remain silent against

this cruelty, this bloodshed. We have nothing more to lose. Please don't mention my name.

I'll contact you with more details soon.

I trusted him and I knew he would keep the secret. The smallest hint of it being me in the video would put my life in danger. Having grown up with this government, I knew that it would come after me; it would force me to appear on TV and say that Neda had not been shot by anyone affiliated with the government. I would also confess under torture that I was the one who uploaded the video; I would perhaps even reveal Emad's name. They had already tried to discredit the footage. The head of National TV had declared it a fake, while Fars News, an agency affiliated with the Revolutionary Guard, claimed that Neda was alive and in Greece. The ambassador of Iran in Mexico said she had been shot by the CIA, and other authorities said her death had been staged by the BBC correspondent in Iran.

I was suffocating from not being able to tell the truth. But I had to remain silent for now. There was a time for everything.

Then I received another email from Paulo.

Dear Arash
The post in Twitter and on my blog has begun to spread with incredible speed. Please send me news. Your name is never mentioned.
Love
Paulo
P.S. At this stage, I don't know whether it is safe for you to receive my emails. Please let me know.

What post in his blog? I looked it up and was aghast at what I read.

My best friend in Iran, a doctor who showed me its beautiful culture when I visited Teheran in 2000, who fought a war in the name of the Islamic Republic, who

always stood by real human values, is seen here trying
to resuscitate Neda—hit in her heart.

Oh my god! Paulo thought no one would recognize me with
that description. But everyone in Iran knew I was Paulo's best
friend in the country, that I was his editor and publisher, that I
was also a doctor and that it was I who had invited him to Iran
in 2000. A simple search on the Internet would reveal all the
information to the secret service. I understood what Paulo was
trying to do. He thought that acknowledging his relationship
with the person in the video would lend me a visibility that
would in turn help protect me. Just as it had when *The Zahir*
was banned. But this time was different. He has no idea how far
they were ready to go for power.

I was petrified and trying desperately to think of a way to
save myself. I didn't tell anyone about the blog post in order to
prevent panic and chaos. The Internet was shut down for the
rest of the day and I couldn't get back to Paulo. The next day I
received another email from him.

Dear Arash,

So far, no news from you. After I published the video
in my blog, it seems that it spread worldwide, including posts in *NY Times*, *Guardian*, *National Review*, etc.

Therefore, my main concern now is about you. You
NEED to answer this email, saying that you are all right
and the name of the person with whom we spent New
Year's Eve in 2001, just to be sure that it really is you
answering this email . . .

If you don't do that, I may leak your name to the press,
in order to protect you—visibility is the only protection at this point. I know this because I am a former
prisoner of conscience. If you do that, unless instructed
otherwise by you, I will stop the pressure for the

moment. My main concern now is you and your family.

Love

Paulo

P.S. There are several trusted friends in blind copy here.

Things were getting out of hand. The Ministry of Intelligence had already begun to enquire about the source of the video. It was a matter of time before I was identified. My main fear was: if they arrest me now, I'll never see Kay and Maryam. The pain of that thought made me call the travel agency and ask for the next flight out of Iran. Yes, there was a seat left on the BMI flight to the UK at 8 a.m. tomorrow. I booked it and then replied to Paulo's email.

Dearest Paulo,

Trying to leave the country tomorrow morning. If I don't arrive in London at 2 p.m. something has happened to me. Till then, wait. My wife and my son are in Oxford.

Please wait till tomorrow. If something happens to me, please take care of Maryam and Kay, they are there, alone, and have no one else in the world.

Much love, it was an honour having you as a friend.

Arash

I landed at Heathrow safely, although after an emergency stop in Georgia so that the crew could be changed. Because of the intense situation in Iran, the crew was not allowed to stay in Tehran overnight.

I was still at the airport when I called Paulo to assure him that I had left Iran safely, at which point he told me that he had promised the readers of his blog to reveal my identity as soon as he was sure I was safe. I was in such an emotional state that I said it was all right without giving it much thought. Then I picked up my small suitcase and took the bus to Oxford.

I had barely reached Oxford and met Maryam and Kay when my phone began to ring. Paulo had identified me on his blog and hundreds of reporters wanted to get hold of me.

'No way!' exclaimed Maryam, 'You've done more than enough already! This will put you in even greater danger!'

I turned off my phone. I had just arrived and was in no mood for more adventure. I just wanted to enjoy playing with Kay. I wanted to relax for a few hours. I had to make a decision with a clear mind. Paulo called me and we had a long discussion. He, too, believed that I was at the crossroads and any decision I made meant going beyond the point of no return.

'Arash, you were caught at the crossroads of history. Think! Either speak or remain silent. But the government of Iran claims that this video is fake. If you feel that your testimony will change anything, speak up.'

Yes, I had to make a decision. But not today.

The next day I decided to reply to the email from BBC reporter, Rachel Harvey, who had been trying to get hold of me for the past 24 hours. But first I shared my decision with Maryam.

'I hope you know what you're doing,' she said.

'I haven't got the slightest idea, Maryam.'

'So what's the rush?'

'I'll die if I don't speak out.'

'And you'll die if you do.'

'I'm not so sure about that. I thought everything through last night. If I don't speak up, the government of Iran will try to distort the truth. Soon they'll find someone and force him to confess that the girl was shot by an opposition member or something like that. She looked into my eyes before she died. I have a responsibility.'

'You've already shared her story. The world already knows.'

'I'm fed up with watching and staying silent. If our parents had said something when their friends were hanged perhaps Neda wouldn't have had to die. If I don't speak up now, this vicious cycle will never stop. Someday Kay will have to pay for my cowardice.'

'Haven't we suffered enough?'

'That's why I have to speak now, because of that suffering. She is dead. If I don't speak, they'll continue to shoot people on the streets. Maybe, just maybe, this can stop the violence. The government must know that there's always someone watching.'

I invited Rachel Harvey to interview me the same afternoon, 25 June. I gave another interview to Martin Fletcher of the *Times*. The BBC interview echoed around the world but the *Times* interview was overshadowed by the sudden death of Michael Jackson.

Two days later it happened. The chief of police in Tehran announced that I was being prosecuted for poisoning the Western media against the Islamic Republic of Iran. The intelligence agents raided my office in Tehran. They interrogated my father for several hours, threatened him, asked him to force me to shut up.

Done. I had crossed the point of no return. My son had lost his chance to grow up in his homeland. Was it worth it? Over the next few months, the Ministry of Culture cancelled Caravan's licence and banned all its books. My life's work was gone. We were left alone, in the UK, penniless. No job or security. And death threats. All the time.

Yet it was worth it. I have lost many things but an immense calm fills me within. The pain is gone. The very fact that the government of Iran was trying so hard to discredit my story proves the power of the blow. It could no longer pretend that it was a righteous government, supported by its people. No. In the eyes of the world, it was a government that shot unarmed civilians on the streets. It was over. It was the beginning of its end.

And I am alive. I will find my way. In the end.

Nearly 60 years ago, Sadeq Hedayat, the famous Iranian writer, wrote: 'There are sores which slowly erode the mind in solitude like a kind of canker.'

When I first saw Emad showing off his new phone, I asked him why people needed a camera in their phones. The technology was never as good as in a regular camera and the phone itself was disturbance enough.

'Life doesn't provide us with a lot of memorable moments,' he answered with a grin. 'I want to cherish all the happy moments in my life. I can't carry a camera all the time but the mobile phone is something we are doomed to.'

Alas, I'm not allowed to describe Emad nor give any details about him. It would betray his identity. So he is not going to be acknowledged for his achievement in recording those 47 seconds, an extraordinary and defining moment. Not a happy moment but one that was destined to seize the attention of millions and to haunt me for the rest of my life. Memory fades over time until one is left with only a blurred image. The impact of a tragedy lessens day by day and lets you heal. It will leave scars on your soul, of course, but time makes sure those scars fade, too. Until only a faint reminiscence is all that survives; the memory has left its mark but no longer enchains your soul.

The camera-phone is fine for recording crucial moments but not very helpful with the aftermath. Then again, camera-phones are performing miracles now. Foreign reporters are expelled from Iran, domestic reporters are either in prison or prisoners of their fears, leaving no one to record current events. Perhaps for the first time since their invention, these gadgets have taken on a new role, a new responsibility: they are bearing witness to the untold history of a nation.

As the last 47 seconds of life drifting away from young Neda was shown on every news channel in the world, millions of people shed tears for her innocent death. But I had to follow another destiny. I decided to bear witness to her death. I have had to watch that video hundreds of times. It's recorded, it's there. On 20 June 2009, at least 20 other people were shot—in their chests, eyes, foreheads, necks—but there was no camera to record their slaughter. The more I watch those 47 seconds, the more sure I am that their eyes, too, had the same final enquiring gaze.

*Epilogue, 15 October 2009*

Half the people on the Circle Line are reading the *Evening Standard*; a dozen are reading books and the rest are just staring into space. I try to spot someone looking at the others. No one. No one looks into the eyes of another. This stillness on the move is a constant feature of London when the working day comes to an end. People are exhausted. They're looking forward to going home, taking a shower, chatting with the family, watching TV.

An earthquake in Haiti. A hundred thousand deaths. An ad asks you to donate £2 to the cause: help hundreds of thousands left homeless in the streets of Port-au-Prince. That's how you can make your day worthwhile: help others, thousands of miles away. You don't need to think about the fact that 80 per cent of your donation goes into administrative costs and that the Haitians will be lucky if they receive the remaining 20. You don't need to look into the face of doom: it's too far away from this train on the Circle Line. You're a cavalier, donating £2 to humanitarian causes. You've got your problems, too, don't forget, although you're luckier than your friends who have been struggling to get a job for the past six months. You're working hard.

You wake up at 6 in the morning, try to catch the train on time. You make yourself felt at work so that your hard work and your skills are appreciated yet not too much: you don't want to be unpopular with your colleagues. How many days until the weekend? You begin to plan: go out, meet friends, catch a glimpse of the sun and the blue sky. Have a few pints at the pub, watch some TV, spend some time with the family, perhaps run for an hour. Make sure you don't look at other people. Although you have no trouble looking into the face of Steve Jobs as he holds his new invention across half a page of the *Evening Standard*, that famous sparkle of satisfaction in his eyes. A feeling you have longed for all your life but never even got close.

And there I am, in the crowd on the wagon, the only one looking at the rest. These are decent people, working hard to earn a living, securing the future for their children. They have their concerns, their pains, their joys. But how can I compare them to myself? I have been pulled out of my previous life and thrown onto this Circle Line on which I commute to work every day. I am Iranian. And I am not able to go back to my country because I witnessed the murder of a girl who became the symbol of Iranian suffering. My life that I had taken for granted has been taken away from me: I have lost my career, my country, my life's achievements. I have to learn to settle down in the UK, to acquire the British way of life, to understand British values. Or I will turn into one of those hundreds of thousands of exiles who never go back to their countries while, in fact, they never left it. As my friend Paulo used to say, in every life there comes a moment when one has to leave.

I want to leave now. I have to understand this way of life. I have to teach myself to enjoy the *Evening Standard*, *Metro*, *X Factor*, *Britain's Got Talent*, Rugby Union, Cricket, Tesco. And I have to learn how to satisfy my craving to change lives by donating £2 a month to a charity of my choice. I shall have to forget my love for international literature and let British crime stories or misery literature satisfy my yearning to read.

I am a writer, a publisher, a doctor. These are transferable skills. So what do I miss? What makes my heart so heavy that I can barely move on? You have to know what you are leaving behind before you can move on. It's like the farewell kiss of a passionate couple who know they will never see each other again. Nothing in the world can replace that kiss; it will fill the void of nostalgia forever.

I never had a chance to say goodbye. So I cling to my past forever. I left Iran in a hurry, terrified of an arrest at the airport. I was so overwhelmed with fear and I had so much adrenalin pumping through my veins that I didn't even stop to think that I might never see my country again. I didn't realize that that was my last drive through the streets of Tehran, my birthplace. That I might never see the Sierra Alborz again. Nor the the infinite scope of the Caspian Sea. Nor the everlasting blue of the Persian Gulf.

But I have heard that the mountains in Scotland look very much like the Alborz and I'm sure this ocean will inspire the same infinite joy as the Caspian Sea.

There's something else I miss. Perhaps it's the collective dream of a nation older than history itself.

In the UK, people complain about the unemployment rates, the corruption among politicians, the bad weather, the recession, Scotland Yard's inefficiency in failing to find the murderer of a young woman whose body has been found by a lake in Kensington Gardens, the increase in travel fares, taxes, etc. But they ignore the fact that they have freedom of speech and individual freedom, that there is a system that actually prosecutes corruption among politicians, that the unemployed can receive job-seekers' allowance and housing benefits, and that they can travel on their holidays to warm, beautiful places anywhere in the world. They ignore the fact that thousands of miles away there is a country, one of the richest in the world, that kills people when they ask for their votes to be counted, rapes them in the prisons and tortures them to death without accepting responsibility for any of its cruelties. A country that, despite possessing the world's fourth largest oil reservoir and the second largest natural gas reserves, has people struggling to put bread on their tables every night.

Leaving this country infected with political corruption, tyranny, oppression, poverty and injustice shouldn't be a bad thing; tasting freedom shouldn't be so painful. Then why am I incapable of enjoying this freedom? Why is my heart away from me, afloat on the waves of the Green?

The people I see on the Tube every day are trying hard to kill their knowledge of death's existence. They play at immortality, banishing death to a faraway land from where it can only manifest itself through fictional situations: an action film, a crime story, a bit of news. I guess that's why the 47-second video of Neda's death shocked the world in a matter of hours. She looked straight into its eyes before she died. I think most of the millions who watched her had never had such a close encounter with death. Neda was the testimony that everything can end here and now. The fact was overwhelming for a world that thought it had recovered from the horrors of the Second World War and the Cold War.

Maybe that's what I miss. I decide there and then to tell this story. This is the story that may help me heal. It is also my farewell to my beloved mystical land, the land of Arash the Archer, the Land of Kay Khusro, the Land of Neda. It will also be a reminder to all the people on the Tube: don't take what you have for granted. After reading my story they may embrace life with a little more enthusiasm and passion, living every moment as if it were the last.

Because this, too, shall pass.